More Lives than
a Ship's Cat

More Lives than a Ship's Cat

G.A. (Mick) Stoke MBE, DSC RN

The Most Highly Decorated Midshipman in the Second World War

Jeremy Stoke

Pen & Sword
MARITIME

First published in Great Britain in 2022 by
Pen & Sword Maritime
An imprint of
Pen & Sword Books Ltd
Yorkshire – Philadelphia

ISBN 978 1 39907 136 9

Typeset by Mac Style
Printed and bound in the UK by CPI Group (UK) Ltd,
Croydon, CR0 4YY.

Pen & Sword Books Limited incorporates the imprints of Atlas,
Archaeology, Aviation, Discovery, Family History, Fiction, History,
Maritime, Military, Military Classics, Politics, Select, Transport,
True Crime, Air World, Frontline Publishing, Leo Cooper, Remember
When, Seaforth Publishing, The Praetorian Press, Wharncliffe
Local History, Wharncliffe Transport, Wharncliffe True Crime
and White Owl.

For a complete list of Pen & Sword titles please contact

PEN & SWORD BOOKS LIMITED
47 Church Street, Barnsley, South Yorkshire, S70 2AS, England
E-mail: enquiries@pen-and-sword.co.uk
Website: www.pen-and-sword.co.uk

Or

PEN AND SWORD BOOKS
1950 Lawrence Rd, Havertown, PA 19083, USA
E-mail: Uspen-and-sword@casematepublishers.com
Website: www.penandswordbooks.com

This book is dedicated to my father, Paymaster Lieutenant G.A. (Mick) Stoke MBE, DSC RN and my mother, Doreen Stoke (née Le Poidevin), who together provided our family of three brothers with love and support in our early years, encouragement as young men to take all opportunities with both hands and enduring values that have stood us all in good stead throughout our lives.

Contents

Acknowledgements

The stimulus for this book came directly from my father writing so many regular letters and keeping a large number of Admiralty documents, reports and signals, as well as newspapers and periodicals. It is his story.

I would also like to acknowledge his parents, Stephen and Barbara Stoke, for keeping all his letters so meticulously, and my mother for keeping the letters and documents safe and dry for over seventy years, so they can all still be read.

Although there were Covid restrictions throughout the research for this book, I managed to visit the National Archives at Kew on eight occasions to review some fifty documents carefully (and cleanly!) provided by their dedicated staff. Regrettably, I had no direct verbal communication with the staff. I would like to thank the Churchill Archives in Cambridge for permission to publish excerpts from the memoirs of Vice-Admiral Sir Geoffrey Robson KBE, CB, DSO and bar, DSC RN and Admiral Sir Manley Power KCB, CB, DSO and bar RN.

I have undertaken all the research directly myself. However, I would like to thank in particular Paul Baillie, specialist military researcher, whose own record system identified the relevant ADM documents at the National Archives that included the recommendations for my father's gallantry awards (MBE and DSC); Peter Radford, who helped with the title for the book; and Henry Wilson, George Chamier and the Pen & Sword team for their support and professionalism in publishing his story.

Jeremy Stoke
Birmingham,
May 2021

Preface

My father, Gordon Alexander (Mick) Stoke, was born on 28 June 1921, nearly 100 years ago as I write. He was eighteen when the Second World War broke out and had just completed his education at a local High School in Essex, where he had achieved success both academically and as a fine sportsman in rugby, athletics and tennis.

Although there was no family naval tradition or connection, rather than go to university in the autumn of 1939, he chose to take the 'Special Entry' exam to join the officer ranks of the Royal Navy as a regular. Only 94 were accepted out of nearly 500 who took the exam. He was the last to be accepted into the Paymaster Branch (nineteenth out of nineteen!). In the first three months of 1940 he spent eight weeks at the Royal Naval College in Dartmouth, on a course that normally took eight months. He went from last in the entrance exam to achieving the highest grades of his intake into the Paymaster Branch, graduating with a First.

He served in the North Sea, the Mediterranean, the North African campaigns in Cyrenaica/Libya, the siege of Tobruk, some of the most desperate Malta convoys, Operation Torch (the retaking of North Africa), Operation Avalanche (the Salerno landings and the invasion of Italy), Russian convoys (torpedoed within the Arctic Circle), D-Day at Juno Beach and lastly the Pacific, liaising with the US Navy. All by the age of twenty-four!

He didn't talk much about the war, although we knew he had been decorated and served in quite a number of key theatres. He died some thirty years ago. After we had put a short notice in a national paper, the family was contacted by the Naval Obituary columnist (John Winton) of the *Daily Telegraph* for more details about our father. My mother pointed to some boxes of papers, and we provided him with the key dates and the ships my father had served in, plus some information on his decorations – he had been Mentioned in Despatches (MiD) and awarded the DSC (Distinguished Service Cross), both at the age of nineteen, as well as the MBE (Member of the British Empire) at the age of twenty-two. He also received the Atlantic Star, the Africa Star, the Italy Star, the Arctic Emblem, the Soviet 40th Anniversary Medal, the Arctic Star and the Pacific Star, as well as the 1939–1945 Star and Silver War Medal.

John Winton wrote quite a lengthy obituary in the *Daily Telegraph*, which started:

> G.A. (Mick) Stoke, who has died aged seventy, was once the most decorated Paymaster Midshipman in the Royal Navy …

and went on to describe his extensive and varied war service and his post-war career. We were obviously very proud of what he had achieved at such a young age, and after suffering the appalling experience of continual bombing and the constant threat of mines and torpedoes.

However, we were all busy with our lives and had young families of our own, so the rest of the boxes remained untouched. My mother (Doreen Le Poidevin) lived a fit and active life and passed away after a short illness just before her ninety-fourth birthday, six years ago. I am the youngest of three brothers and, as we cleared the family house, I took away the boxes of papers that had not been disturbed for many, many years, intending to open them up when I retired and had more time! I opened them in May 2020 to find 170 letters from my father to his parents written over that five-year period (1940–1945), his 'flimsies' (certificates of good conduct signed by the captain of each of his ships), service records he had retained and cuttings from newspapers and periodicals. My elder brother Chris also located 100 letters my father had written to our mother, starting after he met her briefly in October 1942, then as his fiancée after October 1943. They married in November 1944.

The following chapters are based on the weekly letters written to his parents and Doreen, and occasionally to Ivan, one of his old school teachers. Some are missing, presumed drowned! Luckily, nearly all are legible. Many are typed, as he had use of a typewriter most of the time.

As Geoffrey Broke, who also joined as a midshipman and served through the Second World War, wrote in his autobiography *Alarm Starboard*:

> Quite unexpectedly my mother produced most of my letters written home during the period covered (1938–1945). I also had a store of contemporary papers. Some of these sources are quoted verbatim as they give the atmosphere of the moment better than any subsequent reflection. This is a personal account but with enough background to set the scene.

There are some very informative resources online, and many books have been published about ship movements and naval activities on a day-by-day basis throughout the Second World War. These help to piece together the sometimes limited information in his letters that had to pass the 'official censor' – no specific information was allowed that would help the enemy if the letter should fall into the wrong hands. Since 1945 a number of autobiographies and eyewitness reports have appeared by officers or crew on the same ships, concerning the same events and operations and in which names and places have now been included. These provide additional and very relevant context to the events my father was experiencing and describing in his letters.

Looking through his service records and the captains he served under, it is clear that he was amazingly fortunate at such a young age to be mentored (and given responsibilities way beyond his years) by some remarkable leaders, who all rose to the highest ranks in the Navy during their careers.

This is, firstly, the story of one young man's war experiences as a midshipman, the lowest officer rank in the British Royal Navy; secondly, it tells of his luck in surviving multiple torpedo attacks on *Glasgow*, *Queen Elizabeth*, *Carlisle* and *Hardy*; thirdly, it tells how he survived very heavy and sustained bombing raids both on these ships and on land, particularly during the siege of Tobruk in 1941 and in the port of Bone, Algeria during the retaking of North Africa at the end of 1942 and early 1943.

Stoke Family History

Unlike most naval officers recruited before the Second World War, my father did not have a long family tradition in the Navy or any of the services. Nor did he go to a public school, as did most of his contemporaries at Dartmouth, although he had merchant shipping connections through his father and marine engineering heritage through his maternal grandfather.

He never knew his paternal grandfather (Morris), who had died when Mick's father (Stephen) was just two years old. Morris's family were clothing dealers and tailors in a Jewish ghetto in Warsaw, Poland, and after hiding in a cellar, Morris escaped with his fiancée (Martha) from a Russian-inspired progrom, and they arrived in East London as refugees and with no passports around 1890, having been assisted by an East London evangelical organization called the Mildmay Mission to the Jews.

Stephen's parents converted to Christianity and Morris became a missionary. After Stephen was born in July 1892, they moved to South Africa, where Morris died at a very early age in 1895. Martha returned to East London, and Stephen was again cared for by the Mildmay Mission, near Newington Green, whilst Martha went out to work to support herself and her son. She met her second husband, Samuel de Wolf (a Dutchman who had emigrated to London) at the Mildmay Mission, they married in 1899 in Central Hall, Philpot Street, and went to live on the Commercial Road, Mile End, East London.

Samuel de Wolf was also a tailor and dress designer, and he and Martha had seven more children (one died in infancy); but he, too, became a missionary, eventually emigrating to Tel Aviv in 1935, where he died in 1948. Martha never joined him, staying in London and helping in soup kitchens in the East End working with both the Mildmay Mission and the Barbican Mission. She passed away on 29 October 1940, just as my father left on *Glasgow* for the Mediterranean.

Stephen was brought up under the family's new name, de Wolf, from the age of nearly seven, and they moved to East Ham in 1903, where they joined the Presbyterian Church, which he attended every Sunday. In order to support the family, Stephen left school just as he turned fourteen in July 1906, working as an office boy for an accountant in Leadenhall Street in the City. By his own admission he read voraciously, and he went to night school. He then decided there was no future with the accountant and looked for another job, finding one as a junior in a shipping office. By then he had learnt shorthand and typing and started at the London office of the Hall Shipping Line on 20 January 1908 in the heart of the City's shipping district at ten shillings a week. Hall Lines was taken over by Sir John Ellerman, and Stephen worked with the Ellerman Shipping Lines until his retirement in the mid-1950s.

Stephen must have been highly regarded by his employers, as he recorded that his salary increased each year from an initial £25 p.a. to £45 in 1910 and £100 in 1914, with bonuses of £5 to £10 in gold sovereigns. In those days, £100 was a good wage; there was a restaurant in Fenchurch Street where you got a four-course meal with coffee for one shilling (5p).

When the First World War broke out, Stephen enlisted in the 25th London (Cyclist) Battalion on 30 November 1914. He hadn't the remotest idea how a war could be fought on bicycles, but as a keen cyclist he hoped for the best! He survived France and Belgium and towards the end of 1917 was evacuated from the Ypres Front with PUO (Pyrexia of Unknown Origin), commonly known as Trench Fever, to convalesce back in England.

Stephen had met Barbara Jamieson at the East Ham Presbyterian Church in 1912, just after her eighteenth birthday. Her father (Charles Jamieson) was a marine engineer and had come south from Scotland with his wife Isabella (née McGregor) in 1900, when he joined an old established firm of shipbuilders – R.H. Green in Blackwall – which then merged with another company. Charles Jamieson was conspicuously successful, becoming general manager of the merged company – R.H. Green & Silley Weir, based at the Royal Albert

Docks, East London. He was twice presented to the King during the war when he visited the docks and was awarded the MBE for his services.

Towards the end of the war, Charles Jamieson moved with his family to Falmouth, where he undertook the development of ship-repair, engineering and dry-docking facilities at the Falmouth Docks and Engineering Company. Stephen recorded:

> Charles Jamieson was a man of outstanding abilities, who achieved complete success and earned an outstanding reputation. He was an honourable man with a high standard of rectitude combined with a sense of moral obligation and social responsibility towards his staff and labour force, unusual in those days. He promoted the development of a housing estate to attract workers to Falmouth, stimulated the progress of technical education facilities and supported sports clubs and social activities.

Barbara left East Ham Grammar School, studied at Clark's College for a Civil Service Exam and came third out of thousands of candidates. She had many admirers but she preferred Stephen, who recalled: 'Conventions were strict in those days, but we would meet two evenings a week, and with permission from her parents we would go to the theatre, dances, concerts and church socials together.'

Stephen proposed to Barbara during the war, and with his impending marriage and the knowledge that Samuel de Wolf was not his father, he realized that he needed to establish his legal identity. Whilst convalescing he managed to obtain his original birth certificate, issued by the Superintendent Registrar for the District of Stepney (entry No 218 in the Book of Births No 36). This revealed his father's probably anglicized Polish surname as Stokefish. He decided to reduce the name to Stoke, and changed his name by deed poll. The couple married before the war ended, on 11 April 1918 at the East Ham Presbyterian Church. In Stephen's memoir he recalled Mick's mother, Barbara, in the following terms:

> To me your mother was a person of infinite charm with a capacity for radiating something of herself to others. She had a vivid, sparkling, generous personality, was true as steel, of unimpeachable integrity, unquestionable loyalty and unfailing devotion.

When the Armistice was signed on 11 November 1918, business organizations in specified categories could nominate men they wanted to be demobilized quickly. Stephen was one of them and he was back working at Ellermans by January 1919. He and Barbara moved further east towards the mouth of the River Thames, but still within commuting distance of the City, firstly to Seven Kings, then Manor Park and eventually out to Leigh-on-Sea, near Southend.

Westcliff High School was the nearest grammar school, and the young Mick Stoke attended it from 1933 to 1939. The school motto was *Fide et Fortitudine* – 'with trust, belief, faith, and confidence' (*Fide*); and 'with strength, resolve, bravery and courage' (*Fortitudine*). These were attributes Mick Stoke showed in spades to survive torpedoes, bombs and mines during his remarkable war career, becoming the most decorated Paymaster Midshipman in the Royal Navy.

Dramatis Personae

Family

G. A. (Mick) Stoke	The hero of the book!
Stephen Stoke	His father
Barbara Stoke	His mother (née Jamieson)
John Stoke	His younger brother
Charles Jamieson	Maternal grandfather
Grandma Jumbo	Maternal grandmother
Morris Stokefish	Paternal grandfather (Polish refugee)
Martha Stokefish	Paternal grandmother (Polish refugee)
John de Wolf	Stephen Stoke's stepbrother
Doreen Le Poidevin	Mick Stoke's wife
Eng. Capt. H.E. Le Poidevin	Doreen's father, from Guernsey
Winnie Le Poidevin	Doreen's mother (née Newbury)

School

Ivan Brown	History and house master

Naval

Captain H. Hickling	HMS *Glasgow*/Inshore Squadron
Captain A.L. Poland	SNOIS, Inshore Squadron/Tobruk
Captain C. Barry	HMS *Queen Elizabeth*
Captain D.M.L. Neame	HMS *Carlisle*
Commander P. Baker	NOIC, Bone
Captain N.V. Dickinson	NOIC, Bone
Commodore G.N. Oliver	SNOIS, N. Africa Inshore Squadron
Captain W.G.A. Robson	HMS *Hardy*
Captain M.L. Power	HMS *Kempenfelt*
Captain R.S.D. Armour	HMS *Rajah*
Commander A.W.D. Adams	HMS *Rajah*

Admiral A.B. Cunningham	C-in-C, Mediterranean Fleet
Admiral Sir Dudley Pound	First Sea Lord
Randolph Churchill	Son of Winston

War correspondents who knew Paymaster Stoke

Anthony Kimmins	Naval and national broadcaster
A.H. Rasmussen	BBC naval correspondent
A.D. Devine	US war correspondent/author
Larry Allen	US war correspondent

Naval Abbreviations and Slang

AA	Anti-Aircraft
AB	Able Seaman
ABV	Armed Boarding Vessel
Action Stations	Specific places where ship's crew went prior to battle
ADM	Admiralty documents at The National Archives
Affair	Naval operation
AFO	Admiralty Fleet Orders
Aldis	Signal Lamp
Alex	Alexandria, Egypt
ARP	Air Raid Protection
Asdic	Early form of sonar to detect submarines/U-boats
Broadside	All the ship's guns fired simultaneously
Bunting tosser	Signalman or Yeoman
Cable	Nautical distance of 200 yards
Carley float	A type of life raft
CB	Companion of the Most Honourable Order of the Bath
CBs	Confidential Books onboard ship
C-in-C	Commander-in-Chief
Clew up	Tidy up (originally sails)
Clocked one	Hit by bomb or torpedo
CO	Commanding Officer
COS	Chief of Staff
Colours	Ceremony when Royal Ensign is raised/lowered
Combing tracks	Standard torpedo avoidance – turn towards them
Corvettes	Small convoy escort vessels
CS	Cruiser Squadron
Cutter	Narrow rowing boat, 32ft long
CW	Commission and Warrant
Davy Jones	The bottom of the sea

D/B	Dive bomb
D/C	Depth charge
DCT	Director Control Tower
D/F	Direction Finding
DSC	Distinguished Service Cross (gallantry, junior officers)
DSO	Distinguished Service Order (gallantry, senior officers)
Director	Central weapons system on the ship
Divisions	Muster/assembly of the Crew
E-boat	German fast torpedo boat
ERA	Engine Room Artificer
FAA	Fleet Air Arm
Fairway	Entrance channel to harbour
Fathom	Six feet
FDC	Fighter Direction Centre
Flimsy	Certificate of good conduct signed by your Captain
FO	Flag Officer (Vice-Admiral and above)
FOIC	Flag Officer in Charge
Foc's'le	Forecastle: the working deck most forward in ship
Gash	Rubbish, garbage
Gunroom	Midshipmen/junior officers' mess
Gunwale	Upper edge of the side of the deck of the ship
He111	German fighter aircraft (Heinkel)
Heads	Ship's Toilets
HF/DF	High frequency direction finding
H/L	High Level (bombing)
HMAS	His Majesty's Australian Ship
HMS	His Majesty's Ship
JCS	Joint Chief of Staff
Ju.87	German (Junkers) dive-bombing aircraft – Stuka
Ju.88	German (Junkers) high-level bombing aircraft
Khamsin	Sandstorm in the Western Desert
K.R & A.I.	King's Regulations and Admiralty Instructions
Knot	Nautical measure of speed: 1 nautical mile per hour

MBE	Member of the Order of the British Empire (junior officers)
Me109	German fighter aircraft
MiD	Mention in Despatches
Mid/Middy	Midshipman
MTB	Motor Torpedo Boat
NAAFI	Navy, Army, Air Forces Institute
Nautical mile	2,000 yards (ten cables)
Near Miss	Within 50yds of the ship
NLO	Naval Liaison Officer
NOIC	Naval Officer in Charge
OBE	Officer of the Order of the British Empire (senior officers)
Oerlikon	Rapid fire 20mm calibre cannon
OOD	Officer of the Day
OOW	Officer of the Watch
Party	Naval battle or operation
PO	Petty Officer
Pompey	Portsmouth
Pom-Pom	Rapid-firing quadruple 2 pounder cannon (anti–aircraft)
Pongo	Army soldier
PRO	Public Records Office (now the TNA)
Pusser	In charge of payments/belonging to the Admiralty
Quarterdeck	Furthermost working deck aft (to the rear) of the ship
RA	Rear-Admiral
RAL	Rear-Admiral, Alexandria
RN	Royal Navy
RNR	Royal Naval Reserve
RNAMY	Royal Navy Aircraft Maintenance Yard
RNVR	Royal Naval Volunteer Reserve
Rounds	Inspection of the ship by the Captain
S.206	Confidential Report Form sent to the Admiralty
SM.79	Italian dive-bomber (Savoia-Marchetti)
SNO	Senior Naval Officer

SNOIS	Senior Naval Officer Inshore Squadron
Snottie/snotty	Midshipman
Snottie's nurse	Sub-Lieutenant in charge of Midshipman on ship
SOO	Staff Officer Operations
SS	Steamship (merchant vessel)
Stick	Cluster (of bombs)
Stuka	German (Junkers 87) dive-bombing aircraft
Tinfish	Torpedoes
TNA	The National Archives (formerly PRO – Public Records Office)
Torps	Torpedo Officer
TS	Transmitting Station
VHF	Very high frequency
Wardroom	Naval Officers' Mess
Watch	Usually four hours, except between 1600 and 2000
WIRs	Weekly Intelligence Reports
WRNS	Women's Royal Naval Service (Wrens)

Maps

Chapter 1

Royal Naval College, Dartmouth: Eight Weeks Training and Off to War

Westcliff High School (1933–1939)

Stoke's time at this grammar school had been mixed. His early school reports noted, 'He does not make full use of his undoubted ability', but within two years at age fifteen, 'decided progress has been made this term; his keenness, allied with continued hard work, should produce very good results.'

His physical fitness was always excellent and he was involved in most sports, finishing in the school's 1st rugby XV, the tennis team, cross country team, athletics team and as secretary of the sailing team.

He was a talented pianist, firstly in the school orchestra and then becoming the school's pianist for two years. He took an active part in a wide range of other school societies and clubs, notably the debating society, chess club, Spanish society and science club.

His final school report in the summer of 1939 noted, 'He has worked well and taken advantage of all his opportunities. He has always taken an active part in almost every school activity and his excellent qualities should ensure a very successful future career.'

In the summer of 1939 it was clear to most young people that war was inevitable. One of Stoke's contemporaries, Robert Clarkson, reflected in his autobiography:

My generation born in the twenties expected to be in uniform sooner or later. One of my chums gave up university to join the RAF. He said war was coming and he would rather be fully trained than half trained. Why not become a regular commissioned officer now, rather than be conscripted as canon-fodder later? I decided to apply to join the Navy in the Paymaster Branch. It sounded nearer to a trade than the profession of arms; although I had never met a Paymaster and had little idea what one did.

Joining the Royal Navy

There were two principal ways of joining the Royal Navy as an officer – at the age of thirteen to get into Dartmouth College ('Darts'), or at eighteen through the Special Entry Scheme aimed at public schoolboys ('Pubs').

For Special Entry there were three stages – medical, interview and examination. From the few written records of candidates at that time, it appears that the interview was the trickiest and most controversial part and provided quite the widest variation in marks. It was important as it provided 400 marks out of a possible maximum of 1,750 – the rest being obtained through examination on a number of set and chosen subjects.

Lieutenant E.W. Bush wrote a guide, *How to Become a Naval Officer (Special Entry)*, published between the First and Second World Wars. He advised candidates that consideration would be given to their school record, their conduct and abilities while at school and their general promise and officer-like qualities. Typical questions are listed, indicating the general preference of the Interview Boards, for example:

Which do you consider England's best Public School and why? Which schools did your school play at games? Are you in any of the teams? Have you any relations in the Navy?

The book continues with 'Remarks on the development of officer-like qualities':

The first thing to realize is that your principal function as an officer is to be a leader of men. Napoleon laid it down that the human element in war was three times as important as the material element. To be a really successful Naval Officer you require more than a knowledge of your job – you require a thorough knowledge of human nature. You must learn to understand the ratings, his point of view, how he lives and all about him. Make a point of getting to know them individually, and don't make mistakes over their names. The men cannot give of their best unless they feel that their leaders (officers) are in every way worthy of trust. Always be quite definite. Pass on orders firmly and cheerfully, whatever your private opinion.

The man who displays true courage in an emergency is the man who remains calm and is able to think in a logical manner. Perseverance is essential – what is known as 'guts'. Work hard and play your games hard – but don't be too serious minded.

If a candidate was successful, his parents were then required to make a private allowance to their boy of £50 per year and provide for uniform, chest, sextant and other items costing another £60. This was a considerable sum in those days. As Mike Farquharson-Roberts commented, 'Like the Ritz, Dartmouth was open to all … if you could afford it!' Stoke's parents were prepared to make sacrifices to provide the money.

Stoke applies for the Paymaster Branch

So, in September 1939, even though he had only been to a local grammar school and had no family naval connections, Stoke applied to the Royal Navy and passed the medical on 12 October. Candidates for all the Services sat the Civil Service Commission exams, which were held three times a year. His joining instructions included 'Candidates are requested to take their gas masks with them into the examination room'!

On 20 November, nearly 500 naval candidates sat the Special Entry exams. Only 94 were accepted for all four branches: 33 Executive, 22 Engineering, 19 Paymaster and 20 Royal Marines.

Stoke scraped through as the nineteenth and last of the 150 who applied for the Paymaster Branch. However, he got top mark of all 500 candidates in Modern History (87 per cent) and was 15th out 500 academically. Despite what looks like an outstanding school record in sports and extramural activities, he had a very low score in the Interview and Record section, just 180 out of 400. Perhaps the Admiralty Interview Board had not heard of Westcliff High School, near Southend!

Stoke and the others joining at the beginning of January 1940 were the 50th Special Entry cohort. It was a talented year. As Beattie noted, five of them were eventually promoted to the rank of Admiral. The previous cohort (the 49th Special Entry) included Prince Philip of Greece, later to become the Duke of Edinburgh.

The Paymaster Branch

Bush's guide to becoming a Naval Officer includes a description of what young Stoke might expect:

> The Paymaster (Accountant) Branch: Much of their time is spent cyphering and deciphering signals. They are instructed in Naval Law. Early training will be the study of pay, secretarial work, victualling, clothing and stores;

then assistant to the Accountant Officer of the ship in charge of a staff of writers or secretarial work in the office of a Commodore or Admiral, finally rising to the position of Captain's Secretary.

The Royal Naval College, Dartmouth – HMS *Britannia*

Suitable kit was duly purchased and Stoke arrived in mid-January 1940 to start an eight-week course that should normally have taken eight months. Paymaster cadets would then finish their training with six months in a cruiser or battleship before becoming a midshipman, the lowest rung as a regular officer in the Royal Navy.

It was only since early 1939 that Special Entry cadets had gone to Dartmouth – previously, it was Osborne on the Isle of Wight. They had to be squeezed into the site but generally kept separate from the existing 'Darts' who had joined at age thirteen. Stoke wrote his first letter home just a few days after arriving in Dartmouth.

23 January
We parade at 0650 for breakfast. Usually there is no time for much washing. We have now commenced strict routine with no mercy on either side. We are instructed in practical subjects – cutters, field training, signals etc. by a Chief Petty Officer, whilst Commanders downwards teach us theory.

We Pays have to cram into this next eight weeks, eight months work. We will have to work during all our leisure hours. Though the name may mean nothing to you, our chief lecturer is Lieutenant Watkins – Rugger Cap for England, at present as wing forward. Also, we have no leave on Saturday or Sunday if on Duty Watch. Although we break up on 2 April, I may not be back for Easter as, before being appointed to a ship, I have to undergo a gas course.

I find the mention of schooling difficult, as the others were all boarders. In my division we have Old Etonians, Whitgiftians, Edwardians, Merchant Taylors, Rugby, Charterhouse, Marlborough, Radleigh [*sic*] and Pangbourne. Nevertheless it could be worse. Daddy's fear that the fellows are snobbish is fortunately unfounded. The fellows are all decent – the only difficulty is that my school has never played theirs!

You may be interested in our general routine. An instructor rushes into the dormitory at 0615. Of course, it's pitch-dark, but having rolled up our hammocks, we parade at 0650. The leading cadets of each division dress, number and make their division form fours. Then we march up the hill to the College for breakfast. This consists of porridge and another course of scrambled or poached eggs, sausages and bacon with coffee or tea, bread, butter & marmalade. Butter is rationed but we get about half an ounce. After this we arrive at the barracks at 0745 for either rowing, gym, or rifle practice.

Divisions at 0900 – a short service – as short as the Parson is given time and hoisting of colours. We are inspected; then off to lectures. Lunch at 1200 is quite good – vegs and meat in fair abundance, with a sweet to follow. Then organized games or sailing – swimming in heated bath – till 1620 when lectures recommence.

Supper is usually one course – curry and vegs again. Tea at 1530 is optional. We are then free from 2000 till 2100 in which time we have to write up the notes we have been taking during the day in our journals. Rounds/lights out at 2130.

Saturday is make-and-mend day and we can go ashore. Reveille on Sunday is at 0715 because we don't turn in till 2330 on Saturdays. This is because the College cinema is open. On Sunday we have a ceremonial parade followed by Captain's inspection and a service.

I am in the Port Watch, on duty every fourth day – no leave and in general charge of cleanliness. Each division – there are four – Foc'sle, Fore-top, Main-top and Quarter Deck – each about twenty-five cadets – rules itself for parades. Each cadet takes it in turn and is responsible to the chief Junior Cadet. The latter is chosen in turn from all the cadets. He is responsible to the OOW (Officer of the Watch) for the day. Thus, every cadet is Leading Cadet and most are Chief Cadets in one term. The idea is to teach us to command and lead.

There is instruction on 0.22 rifle shooting, foils, fencing, boxing, rowing, rugger, athletics, swimming, squash, racquets, and tennis. Golf is played locally. You must be proficient at one. The weather here is awful. First it froze and now it has been raining continuously for three days. Yesterday I played rugger for the opponents who arrived short – the Frobishers won 9-5 in a good game.

I have got some details here which may interest you. I shall get 4/- a day after Easter & 5/- a day when I become a Middy in July. All Pays, except drunks etc, should get promoted to Pay Commanders and so cannot be retired till aged fifty and then at a pension of over £500 a year. It seems quite a good proposition.

Tonight, I am going to the weekly Gramophone Recital at the College, including a Brahms Symphony and some Wagner. Well I must close as the post goes at 4pm.

5 February

Saturday, I spent in Totnes, whilst Sunday afternoon was spent on DSB (Duty Steam Boat) – an irksome duty. So, unfortunately time was lacking. I notice Daddy's many questions and I think I can answer most of them.

In my dormitory there are twenty-three. We each have a chest of five or six drawers whilst our trunks are stowed in the baggage room. The whole idea is to duplicate the atmosphere of HMS *Frobisher* at sea; the pre-war Special Entry training ship, which has been removed to make it available for service.

Our Gunrooms vary in size and are equally distributed between the divisions. For our division we have two smaller rooms. In ours there is a piano of sorts, lockers, a large table and leather 'forms' round the room to sit on. We have central heating, so are quite comfortable. Some Gunrooms have wireless. Each dormitory has its own room attendant. He keeps the place clean & also sees to our boots etc. There are four bathrooms, separate in a building containing the drying room and showers. Laundry costs a fixed 2/6d per week and results in new clothes becoming rags and being returned dirtier than they went!

We have a canteen where you can buy food – bacon, sausages, apples, cakes etc. and a cadets' store which supplies clothing of all sorts, paper, ink etc. As you can see from the enclosed postcard, we are about ten minutes from Dartmouth – itself very small. Kingswear across the river is larger.

Daddy is correct that superfine is only worn on Sundays for Divisions. Daily orders are posted every afternoon giving the names of the Leading cadets and the Routine. We are paid weekly. We file past a table, salute the Pay Lieutenant and having received our cash, salute the Commander or his representative. Then we double away. If you salute badly, yell your number wrongly or need a haircut, you get pulled up.

Last Sunday night I heard Beethoven's 7th played by Weingartner & the Vienna Philharmonic. There are a few enthusiasts and we meet on Sunday evenings. The chaplain and some masters provide the records.

On Saturday it sleeted all day. It was awful for I played wing three for the 2nd XI against Totnes. Watkins played for us! Just to try himself out for he is playing this Saturday in the Empire v Army game. The first time I have played with an International. Needless to say, we won 6-0. But the weather! Well I must stop now as the whistle is blowing for parade.

11 February

We are in that delicate process of toughening! For example, on a shivery, wet morning it is thought good for us to row a heavy ship's cutter from 0745–0845 on the river against a fiendish current. However, we are still alive though I am still gargling due to tonsillitis.

Last night we were greatly honoured, for Captain Woodhouse of the *Ajax* – which has just arrived home – came and gave us a talk on the action in the River Plate. Naturally, he gave us many details which were new and OS (Official Secrets). He is a very good and modest speaker and we thoroughly enjoyed his lecture. We are also hearing many other secret things which the Germans would be only too glad to know. This will apply even more when we deal with cyphering – an important Pay duty.

You will be pleased to know I am having no difficulty living on my pay. I have my original £4/10 in the bank as well as 14/- pay in hand. So, you see I have the makings of a solvent future! The main reasons are that I neither smoke nor booze which certainly eats up cash.

There is a library here with naturally many naval books. In addition, it has the *Spectator* & many other periodicals. We get the *Times*, *Telegraph* etc. in the Gunroom. The books range from G.A. Henty to G.K.C's autobiography [G.K Chesterton], which I have just taken out in the vain hope of having time to scan. The Junior Chaplain is starting a choir & some of us lusty roarers have been invited to perform!

My Indian neighbour is a Zoroastrian/a Parsee. He has spoken English since the age of three. He says that, though he knows Hindustani and other Indian languages, he always thinks in English.

You will be pleased to know that on Sundays and if we ever have spare time we have sing-songs. I have bought a piano song book and perform, I hope, to satisfaction. When I go to sea I shall certainly take my music with me – I am continually being asked to play Beethoven, Bach etc.

18 February

Though I have not yet learned to hornpipe, there is a dance weekly at the college on Wednesday nights for the Darts, nurses etc.

We certainly have to use correct (naval) terms, especially when manning a cutter, gig or whaler. All orders are answered on the Parade Ground by 'Aye, Aye, Sir'. Normally at sea there are Wardroom, Gunroom and Warrant Officers' messes. Lieutenants and above are in the Wardroom, Middies in the Gunroom.

In the sermon this morning the parson continuously referred to the First and Second German Wars – rather apt, I think.

We have had horrible weather here. On Friday it snowed all day & since then it hasn't stopped raining. Illness here is rife – the hospital has overflowed. Last

Tuesday the doctor cut my bumps & so now I am all right. I am continuing to gargle though just as a precautionary measure.

Towards the end of term, we will be told which ships have vacancies. Dependent on seniority & Admiralty whim, one may get one's first choice granted. I shall choose a cruiser as, if I become a Snotty Captain's Secretary I get an extra 1/- a day.

We have had quite an exciting week here. I don't think I am letting out official secrets as it was reported in the papers, but on Thursday afternoon Winnie [Churchill] arrived with Simon, Lady Simon and Sir Dudley Pound [First Sea Lord]. They had just been to the *Exeter*. We marched past and then Winston Churchill made a short speech – nothing particularly mentioned. Still it was quite a thrill.

Yesterday, I was in Plymouth playing for the 2nd XV. We won 15–6 and I scored a try in the middle of the posts. This week we have had our first exams and you will be pleased to hear that I came first with 73 per cent. This was only in Accountancy subjects. In the Final Exams:

(1) 650 marks are given for Accountancy subjects – Victualling, Cyphering, Pay Office, Captain's Office & Stores.
(2) 100 for Seamanship, 25 for Gunnery, and 15 each for Signals, Torpedoes, Engineering and Squad Drill.
(3) 100 are given for Officer-like qualities.

Thus, the total is 950. Now for a first class pass you must obtain 80 per cent from all the subjects, 70 per cent for a 2nd Class and 50 per cent for a 3rd. Under 50 per cent means further training! Watkins says that as this is the shortest term, 1st Class will be hard to get. I may come down in the non–Accountant subjects like Field Training and if I get the same proportion out of 100 for Officer-like qualities as I got in the interview, I will also struggle. I have been asked by the Gunroom to see if I could get hold of the music to *The Mikado*. If you could find my copy I should be pleased if you could send it on.

* * *

Adrian Holloway was a Dart midshipman cadet in 1939–1940 and was also present when Winston Churchill addressed the cadets. He recorded in his autobiography:

Our House Officer would bring his radio to the gunroom so we could listen to Winston Churchill's broadcasts as First Sea Lord. I remember being thrilled and uplifted by these. For the first time one heard a politician who did not mince his words. He spoke of 'that guttersnipe Hitler' rather than the craven 'Herr Hitler' of the sycophants. One felt that here was a man of guts, a leader one could follow. He later inspected us at Divisions in a reefer jacket and cap that made him look like a chauffeur. He gave us a rousing speech and was loudly cheered.

*   *   *

10 March

I am sorry that you have had no letter since the 18 February but letters were *verboten* in hospital when I had German measles. It was so annoying to spend or rather waste a week, when the exams are only a fortnight off. Not only have I missed stuff that will not be repeated, but I have missed revision time. However, I am now hoping to secure a 2nd Class.

Added to this bad luck, I was unfortunate at Rugger yesterday. I came out of hospital at 1145 and was then asked to play for the 1st XV! I did and scored two tries out of a total win of 17-0. Unfortunately, I got a knee muscle bruised and today I have difficulty walking.

If you could spare an old suitcase and send it here I should be greatly obliged. For I have got extra clothing etc. to fit in. I thought that the big brown case with SS cut in it would be suitable. [SS were the initials of his father – Stephen Stoke – nothing to do with the Nazis!] We work up to the 30 March and Prize Giving is on the 2 April. I can't say I'll be sorry to leave here & become an Officer, instead of a hard-working cadet. 0615 in the dark is I can assure you not the best hour to commence a day's work.

22 March

On Monday morning Sir Charles Little is to present the prizes whilst the PDG (Paymaster Director General – a Rear-Admiral and the only one) is to honour us with a talk. The list of ship's vacancies came yesterday. There were six with two cadet vacancies – *Nelson*, *Rodney*, *Warspite* in the battleships, then the big cruisers of the County Class and the smaller Town Class. Bearing in mind the family, I decided to try for the Home Fleet. We have a fair idea where a lot of the ships are though I'm afraid I mustn't tell you. Also, I wanted to go with Weston – a fellow I am friendly with. We get on very well together, so we decided to pair up. Out of the pairs, there were only two in the Home Fleet – a cruiser *Glasgow* and *Resolution*. The latter is a battleship – old and clumsy, so we put down for the *Glasgow*. I believe she is stationed at Rosyth.

Yesterday was lost – but not to studying. After service, the padre took three of us out for the day in his car. We had a glorious time. We went along the coast in beautiful scenery to Slapton. We stopped at a hotel and had an excellent lunch – a tablecloth, napkins, well cooked food etc. Then the Padre beat us at snooker, darts and table tennis. We arrived back just before supper. It was a very welcome break. The padre – fairly young and RNVR – is very decent. Apparently, he is an ex-Dart but his eyesight prevented him from becoming anything except a Pay. So, he followed in his father's footsteps and became a parson.

The *Glasgow* was completed in September 1937. She has 9,100 tons displacement with a complement of 700 men. Her length is 591'. Her offensive armament consists of twelve 6-inch guns, eight 4-inch AA guns, one 3.7" howitzer, and sixteen smaller guns. She has six 21' torpedo tubes. It should be quite good being on a cruiser.

Last night the Gramophone Concert was Mozart's 39th Symphony and the 2nd movement of Elgar's Violin Concerto. The Sports were last Saturday and I managed to come 2nd in the 440 yards. Our division won the relay and all the rugger, soccer, hockey and cutter competitions.

*   *   *

At the end of eight weeks at the Royal Naval College, the 50th Special Entry cadets had learnt the basics and were familiar with some of the naval abbreviations and vocabulary. All of this had been written up in their midshipman's journal, which recorded their lives, work and activities at college and continued on their ships. Paymaster Midshipman Stoke's journal has never been located and was probably lost in the Western Desert. The cadets were now ready to take their written and practical exams.

Stoke passed out with a First, despite having been in the hospital the week before the exams with German measles and previously having his tonsils removed! He achieved top marks in academic subjects and was third overall, slightly let down again by his marks in 'Officer-like qualities'. He achieved 98 per cent in Victualling, 95 per cent in Pay Office and 92 per cent in Cyphering, and also won 1st Prize in Accountant Officer's Duties.

Chapter 2

Torpedoed in HMS *Glasgow*: First Experiences of War

Appointment to HMS *Glasgow*

On 18 April 1940, Stoke received a letter appointing him to *Glasgow* for additional training and to obtain his Ledger Certificate. A letter dated 26 April from the Captain's Secretary requested him to report to the Office of the Commander-in-Chief, Rosyth, Scotland for instructions, 'as our future movements are always very obscure.' So, on 1 May 1940, Stoke arrived in Rosyth on the Firth of Forth to embark on the next stage of his life in HMS *Glasgow*, with the Second World War just eight months old. *Glasgow* was a recently built Town Class Heavy Cruiser, which had good lines and happy crews. As one officer remarked, 'I have sailed on fourteen ships but the most beautiful was *Glasgow*.'

Icelandic Offensive, May 1940

Following the German invasion of Denmark and Norway and the withdrawal of King Haakon of Norway at the end of April, the position of the Faroe Islands and Iceland appeared uncertain. It was decided to make a pre-emptive move to land 'friendly' troops in Iceland. On 5 May 1940, Royal Marines arrived in Greenock and over the next two days their stores and ammunition were loaded.

The cruisers *Berwick* and *Glasgow* set sail on 8 May, seven days after the young Paymaster Cadet had joined, making their way at 22 knots for Iceland, to secure Reykjavik and Hvalfjord. The weather during the passage was rough and many of the Marines were seasick. At 0230 on 10 May they were thirty miles offshore from Reykjavik. In the early morning the two cruisers dropped anchor half a mile from the harbour entrance. The Marines were transferred ashore at 0400 in a violent snowstorm.

Their main objective was the German Consulate, in order to impound any secret documents. On arrival, they found the German Consul's wife and daughter trying to dispose of all the confidential books and secret papers in a bath of blazing paraffin. Within forty-five minutes the rest of the Germans on the island had been arrested, and at 0930 the Marines were able to report, 'All quiet, inhabitants friendly'. The young cadet had had his first successful experience of war, as *Glasgow* sailed back to Liverpool with thirty-two German prisoners on board.

The bizarre capture of the SS *Gabbiano*, June 1940

Captain Hickling assumed command of *Glasgow* on 6 June. With France still reeling from Hitler's onslaught, Benito Mussolini, the fascist Italian leader, was about to declare war on Britain. Aware of his intentions, the Admiralty issued orders on 10 June that all Italian shipping in home waters was to be seized. War with Italy was formally declared at midnight. Hickling, aware that the Italian vessel SS *Gabbiano* from Naples was berthed in the dry dock next to *Glasgow*, sent a boarding party to seize it. The master of the *Gabbiano* was unaware his country was even at war with Britain and nearly died of fright! No resistance was offered, and a somewhat puzzled Italian crew was taken ashore into captivity. Whilst in Liverpool, young Midshipman Stoke was happy to express his (over-confident) views on the state of the war in letters back home.

* * *

22 June
It is the fixed feeling of many officers that we are well on the way to victory. One midshipman told me that his father – who is head of the defence of our ports – feels more confident than ever. If we hold on till September our blockade of food – let alone raw materials – will reduce the Germans to a 1918 basis.

6 July
This week I spent a day with the other midshipmen on the *Prince of Wales*. She was launched last year and really is a lovely ship. It does seem a great pity that we have had to hit the French such a blow but there, it does at last show that it is not a mere war we are waging but a frenzied fight for life – not freedom or any 'ism but the right to live. I feel very confident of this issue. I don't know the <u>exact</u> date, but maybe 18 months will see us in Munich.

* * *

Collision with HMS *Imogen*, July 1940

Glasgow stayed in Liverpool before sailing for Scapa Flow in Orkney on 7 July. A week later, the Home Fleet was deployed in the North Sea looking for German warships. *Glasgow* sailed with the two other cruisers led by *Southampton* and accompanied by destroyers from the 7th and 8th Flotillas. The 7th was in command of Captain Philip Vian in *Cossack*, together with *Sikh*, *Fortune* and *Fury*. Vian was later promoted in early 1941 to Rear-Admiral in command of the 15th Cruiser Squadron under Admiral Cunningham, C-in-C Mediterranean.

The ships left Scapa on a beautiful summer's day but were soon enveloped in a thick fog, while overhead the roar of enemy bombers could be heard. Learning that the enemy squadron had returned to their base, the fleet was ordered back to harbour. On hitting a bank of fog, the commanding officer of the *Southampton* decided to abort the approach and signalled the squadron to turn back into clearer weather. They tried a second time but again aborted. Darkness was falling fast when the fleet altered course back into the fog for a third time. The cruisers were in line in the centre of the formation, with the destroyers on each quarter. The speed of the fleet was 22 knots in clear weather and 15 knots in fog.

As the fleet turned sharply for the third time, at 2353, *Imogen*, one of the destroyers in the 8th Flotilla, suddenly appeared out of the fog heading directly for *Glasgow*, which struck *Imogen* forward of her bridge, embedding herself in the engine room of the very much smaller destroyer. The two ships were locked in a deadly embrace, like malformed conjoined twins. Aboard *Glasgow*, Stoke and the other midshipmen tumbled out of their hammocks believing the ship had been torpedoed.

The *Glasgow* eventually freed herself. Although many were saved, seventeen were posted missing presumed dead from *Imogen* and one midshipman from *Glasgow*. He had been lowered into the water to help survivors and had started to climb the ladder when *Glasgow* had gone full astern. Due to the oil soaking the ladder and his own exhaustion he slipped off and was not seen again. The commanding officer of the *Southampton* was relieved of his command for ordering a dangerous manoeuvre. Captain Hickling was absolved of any blame, and the *Glasgow* returned to Liverpool for repairs.

*   *   *

Harland & Wolff
Liverpool
22 July
I am hopeful of fourteen days home leave starting around 1 August. The Commander has issued a notice saying that Officers are to make themselves useful when on leave by attaching themselves to military forces. So, expect me to come home with a 6″ gun to defend Puttenham Golf Course from sacrilegious landings of gliders or other aircraft!

Liverpool
26 August
I have definitely got my job in the Transmitting Station – in fact I am in control of the 6-inch armament. The spotting officer will tell me if the shot is over or short. It is then my job to find the target, hold it and hit it.

*   *   *

Following his training, Cadet Stoke obtained his ledger certificate and was appointed Paymaster Midshipman on 1 September 1940, the first rung in the Royal Navy as a regular officer. During September *Glasgow* was based in Scapa for more gunnery practice.

*   *   *

HMS Glasgow
1 October
The invasion threat seems ever present. I still think it's coming. When it comes it'll be a hard fight and boats, planes, subs and battleships will appear from their lairs and we will be off.

*   *   *

Arrival in the Mediterranean, November 1940

In October *Glasgow* was based in Immingham on the east coast, before sailing to Rosyth to have some additional equipment fitted and then on to Greenock, where she was then allocated to the Mediterranean Fleet. She sailed from the Clyde on 30 October with the battleship *Barham*, aircraft carrier *Ark Royal*, cruiser *Berwick* and four destroyers down through the Bay of Biscay. Paymaster Midshipman Stoke was getting much nearer the action!

At the end of October, Italy declared war on Greece. Admiral Cunningham noted in his diary:

> This was good because we could now use Suda Bay in Crete as an advanced refuelling base for naval operations in the central Mediterranean, but bad, as we will need to support Greece with a steady flow of convoys across the Med to the Aegean. The difficulty was there was no proper boom defence in Suda, nor was any to be forthcoming for several months.

A boom and net defence was absolutely vital to prevent submarine- and aircraft-launched torpedo attacks.

During October and November, the Mediterranean Fleet was very busy crossing the length and breadth of the Mediterranean, almost at will, as the Italian Navy preferred to remain in harbour rather than face the British on the open sea. Admiral Cunningham had planned a series of operations with major fleet movements and escorting convoys to hide his main purpose – Operation Judgement, the attack on the Italian battle fleet in their main harbour at Taranto on the toe of Italy. This was originally planned for 21 October – Trafalgar Day – but had been postponed to the next suitable moon, 11 November.

Glasgow arrived in Gibraltar on 1 November and then sailed on to Malta with other ships to drop off troops – this was Stoke's first taste of these two famous naval bases. Two days after her arrival in Valletta, *Glasgow* was sent out on Operation Coat as part of the 7th Cruiser Squadron with *Berwick*, *York* and *Gloucester* to support the aircraft carrier *Ark Royal* in the bombing of airfields at Cagliari; then to provide a defensive screen escorting the aircraft carrier *Illustrious* through the Mediterranean, ostensibly to Alexandria, but in fact for an air strike on the Italian battle fleet in the Bay of Taranto.

Illustrious was closely escorted through the night, with a cruiser stationed ahead, astern and on either side, and destroyers on her port and starboard bow and quarters, all one mile distant from the carrier, all ships darkened, all steaming at 30 knots. A fantastic sight for the young midshipmen! A high standard of watch-keeping and vigilance was required as the carrier made numerous changes of course, without signalling her intentions, due to wireless silence. Any mistakes, and ships would be approaching each other at a closing speed of 60 knots! Midshipman Stoke and others on *Glasgow* didn't relish a repeat of their experience with *Imogen*.

*   *   *

10 November
Inside a year we shall have invaded Italy I hope and be ready to attack Germany on two fronts: on the West by air and on the East by land. I am in excellent health and good spirits. It was good to hear Beethoven's 3rd Piano Concerto on the radio today from a German propaganda station!

*   *   *

Operation Judgement (the Battle of Taranto), 11 November 1940

With *Glasgow* and the other escort ships standing by, two waves of Swordfish aircraft flying from *Illustrious* attacked the Italian Fleet in Taranto harbour, catching them completely by surprise and inflicting considerable damage on Mussolini's warships. The Italians had indeed been confused by all the fleet and convoy movements.

Taranto was a successful and decisive operation. Three Italian battleships were put out of action, plus one cruiser and a number of destroyers, changing the balance of power in the Mediterranean at that time in the Allies' favour. The Italians promptly moved the ships that remained to Naples, further up the west coast. Totally demoralized by this action, the Italian navy's future actions were characterized by excessive caution. Copies of messages of congratulations sent to the C-in-C Mediterranean from the King, the Prime Minister and the First Sea Lord are held in the Stoke archives. Anthony Kimmins, one of the best known naval broadcasters, sent a live report back to the BBC. He was to cover many other famous operations over the next three years.

Glasgow returned to Alexandria and immediately put to sea with four other cruisers to deliver troops to Piraeus in Greece. All five cruisers ran twenty-one hours at an average speed of 30 knots! After disembarking the troops, the cruisers patrolled in the Aegean before arriving back at Alexandria.

Torpedoed and bombed

On 25 November, *Glasgow* and three other cruisers left Alexandria, joining *Illustrious* and four destroyers in attacks at Port Laki on the Greek island of Leros in the Aegean.

The cruisers were later detached to escort a fast convoy (Operation Collar) passing east through the channel between the south of Sicily and Tunisia, near the island of Pantelleria. Silhouetted against the light of the moon, the four cruisers presented a 'heaven-sent' target to the Italian submarines of

13th Torpedo Boat Division from Syracuse that lay in wait. Aboard *Glasgow* a heavy thud was heard. Three more quickly followed. She had been hit with four torpedoes. Luckily, they had all exploded prematurely, causing no damage! *Glasgow* and Midshipman Stoke had survived.

The following day, *Glasgow,* ordered to escort four corvettes arriving from England, was attacked in daylight by six German Junker Ju.87s. Swooping down, they released large bombs to bracket the ship with high explosives. Whilst the gun crews raced to Action Stations, orders were given for the helmsman to alter course and the engine room telegraph rang 'Full steam ahead'. A fusillade of shells was fired at the bombers, and one was soon hit and crashed in the sea. However, during the attacks, one of the bombs dropped so close to *Glasgow* that the sea heaved up, lifting the cruiser out of the water. It seemed *Glasgow* had been hit but she continued to fire her pom-poms and repelled the dive-bombers, whilst damage was checked. *Glasgow* had indeed survived again, arriving in Suda Bay, Crete with the four corvettes on 30 November.

Cunningham's diary notes:

> The monitor *Terror* had been brought from Malta and provided the mainstay of the Suda Bay defences with her 15″ guns. We had a fairly efficient boom which would prevent the entry of submarines: but our most pressing need was an adequate net defence against aircraft launched torpedoes. The improvised net defence was really quite useless and we very soon had proof of it.

Torpedoed again!

On Tuesday, 3 December in Suda Bay, the Royal Naval refuelling base in Crete, *Glasgow* was dive-bombed, this time by two Italian Savoia Marchetti 79s flying at just 50ft above the sea. She was hit by two torpedoes whilst at anchor. The first explosion blew a 22ft-square hole out of both sides of the forward part of the ship. The second blew a slightly smaller hole out of the stern, near the Wine and Spirits store! The crew quickly put out fires and stabilized the ship. Remarkably, *Glasgow* survived and stayed afloat! Having satisfied himself that *Glasgow* could get back under her own steam, Captain Hickling set sail later that evening. During the passage to Alexandria, the starboard inner propeller fell off.

The two Italian planes did not return to their base (having presumably been shot down by *Glasgow*'s gunners), so a reconnaissance plane was sent out to investigate. Finding the *Glasgow* not there, it reported she had sunk. This was then broadcast on Italian radio, which was picked up in Britain and left family and friends of the *Glasgow* crew fearful for their loved ones, until *Glasgow* managed to limp back to Alexandria on 5 December and advise she was still alive and afloat!

*   *   *

Back in Alexandria, no letters home could make mention of the torpedoes due to the censor. But a letter home by Stoke from Tobruk, three months later, escaped the censor.

24 March 1941

I can tell you now that the *Glasgow* stopped two torpedoes before Xmas. We had one tinfish forward and one aft. I was eating a piece of cake in the gunroom at the time – about 1545 and got thrown down and half choked by fumes and gas. We had quite a juicy fire or two and water pouring in, but good leadership and some hard work soon saw us through. I've never worked quite so hard before under such 'not so good conditions'. It was a great tribute to the designers & builders that she stood up to it so well and was soon again at sea. I've certainly had quite an exciting time this last six months.

6 December

My news is tremendous! I have been in Gibraltar, Malta and Alexandria. We were with the *Ark Royal* at the bombing of Cagliari, then with *Illustrious* at the bombing of Taranto and we have 'swept' away the Italian fleet, as the BBC puts it. I must say that I don't like it too much out here. The bad weather is even oppressive and the heat …! Still I am bearing up and the War will soon be over! The Ities have given us our first but not last major victory. Happy Xmas and New Year. Better times to come.

27 December (in Alexandria)

On Xmas day, we went to the Captain's cabin where he wished us Very Merry Xmas with some champagne. We then followed on his rounds to each Mess. If they like him they force him to drink or eat something, then sing 'For he's a jolly good fellow.' Then the Gunroom invite all the Chief Petty Officers and Petty Officers up to our Mess to drink at our expense which pleases them highly!

I have been ashore here in Alexandria and will say that the romance of the East seems to be lacking. It strikes me as filthy, dusty and full of pilferers and gypsies who think all Europeans are colossal ignorami.

*   *   *

The Allies had made rapid and successful progress, both at sea in the Mediterranean and in the land war in the Western Desert. The rapid progress the Army was making was severely stretching their supply lines, which needed more support and logistics from the sea along 200 miles of coast west of Alexandria, as the desert roads were almost nonexistent.

The *Glasgow* was going to take some weeks to repair, and so on 5 January 1941 Admiral Cunningham appointed Captain Hickling as Senior Naval Officer Inshore Squadron (SNOIS). He was allowed just one staff officer to join him and he chose a very young and inexperienced officer for that role – Paymaster Midshipman Stoke, then aged just nineteen and six months.

Chapter 3

A Young Naval Officer in the Western Desert?

Cunningham's diaries recall the start of this successful campaign:

On 4 December an important conference was held in Cairo for the coming offensive in the Western Desert. General Wavell stated that the forces would be led by Lieutenant General Sir Henry Maitland Wilson. A large and cheerful man, 'Jumbo' Wilson was greatly liked by the Navy. The front-line fighting was to be under the command of General Richard O'Connor. [The young Stoke was later to meet both generals in January with Captain H. Hickling.]

We formed an Inshore Squadron of the *Terror*, brought down from Suda Bay, with the three veteran gunboats *Ladybird*, *Aphis* and *Gnat*. They were reinforced from time to time by the Australian destroyers *Vampire*, *Vendetta*, *Voyager* and *Waterhen* under Captain Waller RNAS of HMAS *Stuart*. At the outset I placed the Inshore Squadron under the command of Rear-Admiral Rawlings.

Sidi Barrani fell, and Sollum was captured on 16 December. Bardia eventually fell on 5 January 1941. The Italians were routed and 25,000 were taken prisoner. Cunningham again:

The offensive had one result though hardly noticed at the time. It brought all three services closer together, and made them realize that success could only be obtained by continual co-ordination and co-operation; that each service depended upon the others; and that the campaign by sea, land and air was really one. However, the Luftwaffe was being substantially strengthened during January 1941 – estimated at 100 dive-bombers, 150 long range bombers and 50 reconnaissance aircraft. On the 5 January 1941, I appointed Captain Harold Hickling, previously of the torpedoed *Glasgow*, as Senior Naval Officer Inshore Squadron.

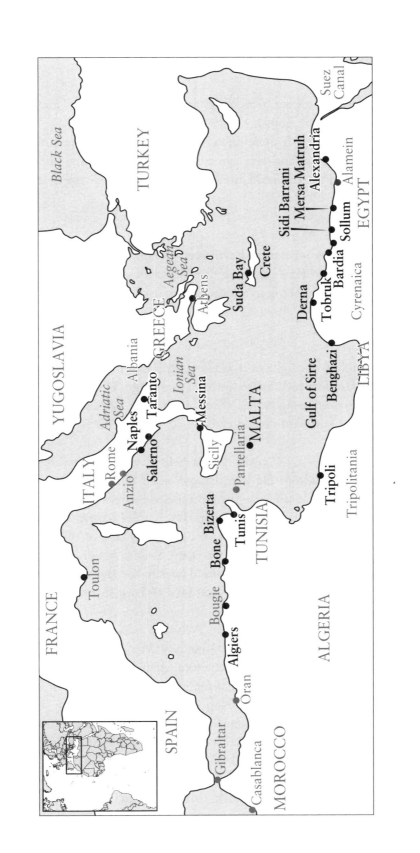

Hickling had just one other officer with him – the very young and inexperienced Paymaster Midshipman Stoke!

Arrangements for the Inshore Squadron's involvement in the initial capture of Tobruk from the Italians were agreed at a planning meeting on 16 January 1941 and approved by Admiral Cunningham in Alexandria the next day.

* * *

This is the first letter written by Paymaster Midshipman Stoke, ten days after arriving in an alien world – ashore in the Western Desert – aged nineteen and just three months from being a trainee cadet.

Western Desert
16 January
I am writing this by the light of an oil lamp in Sollum. It's on the coast on the Egyptian/Libyan border. Our troops have to date got beyond Tobruk though the town itself has not been taken. We are taking our time. I hope to be on one of the naval ships bombarding and enter the town with the first attack. But let me explain all this.

Captain Hickling – my *Glasgow* captain – has been appointed Senior Naval Officer Inshore Squadron. He is in charge of all Ports and Ships operating along the coast from Alexandria – the monitors, destroyers, gunboats, auxiliary craft, anti-submarine trawlers and so on. He is chief liaison officer between us, the Army and the RAF. He is in fact the naval boss of the operations in the Western Desert. And I am his secretary. Sollum is our base, though we go everywhere. We may go off into the desert to see the Generals in charge of the Army or to the RAF. We sometimes embark in one of the ships in his squadron.

So far, I have seen General [Jumbo] Wilson, O'Connor and others. I went to Bardia the day after it fell on the 5 January. We took about 45,000 PoWs there alone. When Tobruk is taken the total of prisoners and equipment will be colossal. Moreover, all the Greek armaments are the same as that captured. So, we can ship stuff to them. Naturally, it is tremendously interesting. Nevertheless, the sand in the desert is pretty bad. Give me the sea. Here we sleep, eat and live in sand. Yesterday, we had a terrible, ghastly sandstorm – a *khamsin*. The house was full of sand. It's the only house left standing in Sollum, after our naval bombardment, which has four walls and a roof. Before the 'I'ty' advance it had been owned by a Greek; then an Italian General, now us. I have made it quite comfortable with all sorts of wonderful plumbing, with pipes and rubber connections from a barrel on the roof. Today the sandstorm is so bad that visibility is about fifty yards. It is really quite annoying as water is limited. As for its taste – well, it almost makes me sick.

This paper and envelope by the way were captured in Bardia. We have passed through here about 37,000 prisoners and we all commented on them – small stature and lack of spirit. I have just heard the sad news about the *Southampton* being sunk, doing the same job as we were only six weeks ago – she is the first of her class to go under. I am very cut off from the news here.

*   *   *

The plan was to attack Tobruk on Monday, 20 January. In the event the attack was postponed for twenty-four hours because preparations were hampered by sandstorms and gale-force winds. The Inshore Squadron was particularly badly affected by the latter. Captain Hickling was flying to his shore HQ at Sollum when his aircraft was forced landed in the desert, obliging Hickling and his companions to walk the twenty-five miles back to Mersa Matruh.

The British attacked Tobruk on 21 January with the 6th Australian Division, fully supported by the Inshore Squadron. The Italians scuttled the steamer *Augusto Tomei*, trawler *Cesare* and their coastal defence ship *San Giorgio* in Tobruk harbour, setting the latter on fire to prevent her falling into British hands. Tobruk was captured and another 37,000 Italians surrendered.

Commander Carne RN was appointed Clearance Officer Tobruk, sweeping for mines, organizing salvage and undertaking immediate repairs to the piers. It was estimated this would take seven to ten days, and then the harbour was to be handed over to a permanent Royal Naval Base Party, commanded by Commander F.M. Smith RNR, with the title of Naval Officer in Charge (NOIC), Tobruk. Smith was to be responsible for maintaining the harbour boom defence and swept access channel, berthing and refuelling arrangements and establishment of a port war signal station, a wireless telegraph station and defence arrangements.

Commander Carne arrived in Tobruk aboard the minesweeping trawler *Moy* at first light on Friday, 24 January, accompanied by a small fleet of vessels assigned to clearing the harbour. These included the anti-submarine trawler *Southern Maid*, carrying the commander of the Inshore Squadron, Captain Hickling, and Paymaster Midshipman Stoke.

Fortunately, the Italians had not had enough time for too much sabotage, and the task of clearing the harbour that was expected to take two weeks was completed in six hours. Commander Carne declared Tobruk harbour safe for shipping at midday on 24 January. The first supply ship commenced unloading three days later. The monitor *Terror* arrived the following day to provide temporary air and sea anti-aircraft defence.

Major General O'Connor already had his troops organized to push on towards Derna, which the Italians withdrew from on 31 January. The Allies' supply lines were now sorely stretched, but as the Italians continued to withdraw westward, O'Connor had to follow. The Australians and British entered Benghazi on 9 February to accept the surrender of the Italian forces. The Italians had had far superior forces, but incorrectly thought the Allies were even stronger. The Allies took another 25,000 prisoners.

On 5 February, after just four weeks, Captain Hickling was sent back to take command of the repaired *Glasgow*. But in that short time, Paymaster Midshipman Stoke, aged nineteen, had made a significant impression on Hickling, who wrote on his departure Stoke's 'flimsy' and naval records (S.206):

Stoke is a hard-working, painstaking and competent officer who promises very well. As my Secretary and Staff Officer while Senior Naval Officer Inshore Squadron and in the Western Desert for the past four weeks, he has shown marked efficiency and common sense. He is most energetic, eager and enthusiastic. He is learning quickly and should develop into a very good officer. A very good physique, plays games well and his manner and manners are excellent.

Hickling was later promoted Rear-Admiral and in a letter in August 1947, on hearing Stoke was leaving the Navy, he wrote to his father:

I am delighted to get in touch with a father of a boy who served me so well in a job which would have daunted many an older and more experienced man. Your son and I had some exciting times when I commanded the Inshore Squadron and he comprised my entire staff. I knew your son as a Pay Mid in my ship – *Glasgow* – as I knew most of the junior officers. So when there was a choice of who should come with me to Tobruk, I decided on him and my choice was fully justified. He was my entire staff and simply splendid in every way. Were we steaming through minefields or being heavily bombed as at Tobruk, he never turned a hair, and single-handed he dealt most efficiently with all staff matters, signals, and cyphers. He further distinguished himself with my successor Poland. You can be very proud of him, as I am.

One of the first naval officers to arrive on 22 January at the Naval HQ in Tobruk, renamed Admiralty House, was Douglas V. Duff, an RNVR officer, alongside Brigadier Morshead, an Australian who would head up the Tobruk garrison. Shortly afterwards they were joined by Hickling, Stoke and Commander Smith, the NOIC at Tobruk for most of the siege. Duff's autobiography *May the Winds Blow* describes his excitement at bearing the title of 'King's Harbour Master and Chief Pilot of Tobruk' and also depicts the dramatic first days after the capture of Tobruk:

> First there was the job of getting ships into a mined harbour abounding with booby traps. These were plentiful ashore as well. Attractive fountain pens and watches exploded if you touched them. I lost my sub–lieutenant who found and decided to use a senior Italian officer's real flush loo. It was the last thing he did, as the whole place exploded as he pulled the chain.
>
> The Naval Staff were good and gallant men from our two most excellent chiefs, Captain Poland, recently from the *Liverpool*, and smothered with well-earned decorations, his Secretary, Paymaster Midshipman Stoke and Commander F.M. Smith RNR, the NOIC.
>
> Despite the constant stench of death, the almost continuous air-raids, the funerals I conducted every day when the chaplains were already too fully occupied, we were strangely happy in that shattered town. Inspired by Poland and Smith and backed by as fine a team of seamen and junior officers as ever served under the white Ensign, we pulled it off.
>
> We did not wash for weeks; we were filthy, for there was little fresh water. To ease the shortage, we shipped out as many PoWs on every ship that entered Tobruk for they out-numbered us ten to one. Then one day, Captain Poland asked me if I would like a command of my own and gave me the post of NOIC Derna, a port half-way between Tobruk and Benghazi.

Duff continued to keep in touch with Poland through Stoke, especially in late March and early April as Rommel made rapid advances.

The heavy and constant German bombing was immediately felt. Between the end of January and mid-February the minesweeper *Huntley* was sunk off Derna, the Egyptian steamer *Sollum* was sunk near Sidi Barrani and the hospital ship *Dorsetshire* was bombed twice, suffering damage from near misses. At the beginning of February, German planes started laying magnetic aerial mines in Tobruk harbour. One of the mines sank a motor schooner in the harbour, and the Assistant King's Harbour Master, Lieutenant Commander Cochrane, was lost.

Cunningham sent the following message on 9 February:

> The feat of the Army in clearing Egypt and occupying Cyrenaica in a period of eight weeks is an outstanding achievement to which the Inshore Squadron and shore parties along the coast have contributed no small measure – an unbreakable determination to allow no obstacle to stand in the way.

During February, aerial mines in Tobruk harbour set the Dutch tanker *Adinda* on fire (Captain Frank Smith was to be awarded a DSO for his gallantry in saving this ship), and the naval whaler *Southern Floe*, the naval trawler *Ouse* and the ex-Italian steamer *Rodi* and the steamer *Christa* were badly damaged.

Despite the bombing by the Luftwaffe, the Army had continued to move rapidly westward and had captured Benghazi by 6 February. Captain Poland and Stoke departed Tobruk on 12 February on board ABV *Chakla*, with three destroyers, a minesweeper and two corvettes arriving in Benghazi the following day. Poland reported his intention to Cunningham of taking all his ships to sea for the night on account of the heavy night raids. But as naval anti-aircraft cruiser cover could not be provided indefinitely, Cunningham instructed Poland to rely for the safety of the ships on good dispersion within the harbour. With the Navy now in place, orders were given for convoy AC1 to set sail for Benghazi.

General Wilson was keen to make Benghazi the main supply base, instead of Tobruk, since it was closer to his troops. However, Benghazi harbour was reported to be in a considerably worse position than first thought. Allied bombing earlier, during the capture of the port, had damaged the outer breakwater and left a number of sunken ships in the inner harbour. There were also heavy Luftwaffe air raids on Benghazi on both nights. Many mines were laid in the harbour. The situation in Benghazi was so important that Churchill was advised, 'The C-in-C Mediterranean reports that troops at Benghazi cannot be maintained by sea due to destruction of the port and heavy air attacks and mining.'

So Cunningham ordered AC1 to depart Benghazi without unloading, although Stoke and Poland remained based in the Hotel Grande Albergo Berenice on the seafront. Enemy air attacks now intensified, particularly on the harbour. Both corvettes were damaged by exploding mines during their sweeps. *Terror* remained, but with limited shore AA and non-existent fighter protection, the attacks reached their maximum on 22 February, when in a dawn raid two aerial mines and near-miss bombs caused extensive damage to *Terror. S*he was ordered to sail at dusk.

Cunningham sent another signal home: 'In view of the scale of air attacks, inadequate defences and damage to *Terror*, I have withdrawn HM Ships from Benghazi.'

Poland and his staff returned to Tobruk, where another naval ship was lost on 24 February. Commander Mervyn Thomas on destroyer *Dainty* was proceeding out of Tobruk harbour at 1845 on night patrol in company with destroyer *Hasty* 600 yards astern, when aircraft attacked the harbour. Both ships opened fire. A heavy bomb exploded in the captain's aft cabin on board *Dainty*, at once igniting the oil fuel tanks below. To avoid shrapnel from exploding shells, all hands were ordered onto the fo'c'sle. Within thirty minutes *Hasty*'s stern was alongside *Dainty*'s bow and a line was passed between the ships, but *Dainty*'s stern began to sink rapidly and the order was given to abandon ship.

Leading Seaman Samuel Stocker recalled: 'I swam towards *Hasty* and caught a line, but as I was being hauled up, my knuckles were scraped and I fell back into the water. I had fuel oil in my eyes and mouth and couldn't see clearly but somehow caught the line again and was hauled aboard like a drowned rat.'

Trawlers, motorboats and the captured Italian schooner *Maria Giovanni*, captained by an engaging Australian, Lieutenant Commander A.B. Palmer RNR, now sailing under the white ensign, arrived from inside Tobruk harbour to help rescue survivors. The next day brought no respite, as further bombing damaged the tanker *Tynefield* ; and a week later, *Knight of Malta* ran aground and was abandoned after more bombing attacks.

* * *

Stoke's letters between 16 January and 5 March are missing, presumed drowned!

Admiralty House, Tobruk
5 March 1941
Ring the bells – run up the bunting – I've received a letter today from you all – three letters! They are all dated 18 November 1940, which isn't bad! Please note my new address.

Hickling, my Captain in *Glasgow*, was appointed Senior Naval Officer Inshore Squadron and for some reason he took me as his Secretary and Staff Officer. So I have been ashore in the desert ever since 5 January. Captain

Hickling has since gone back to the *Glasgow* but I've remained in the same capacity to the new boss – Captain Poland.

Captain Hickling has brought me 'to the notice' of C-in-C Mediterranean officially and unofficially for my work with him. My 'flimsy' is enclosed, if you could keep it safe for me. Because it isn't [safe] here.

It is all most interesting since I have been in the front line of fighting on the sea and in the planning as well for the taking of Tobruk, Bardia and Benghazi. I've met and been introduced to Generals Wilson and O'Connor and the Air C-in-C. I've met Admiral Cunningham and hosts of other interesting personalities. On the whole, it's hard work and long hours – twenty-four hours a day with only four and a half hours sleep. I turn in at 0100 to 0130 and am up at 0630 irrespective of air raids.

Still, I am still kicking after two months. This notepaper came from Benghazi. I lived in the building on the top of the paper – The Hotel Grande Albergo Berenice. Our party – my captain, another officer and myself and four ratings – were the sole occupants of a hotel with 300 big bedrooms. It was continually the target for the Huns as it had been the I'ty HQ. My nearest escape was two big bombs ten yards away which didn't go off – or rather were delay action.

I enclose one letter that I forgot to get away before Tobruk fell! My first desert edition of the *Seven Pillars*! I am told the mail situation is awful so have been advised to recapitulate from late January.

I went into Tobruk with the first naval flight and indeed it was impressive. The guns, ammunition and stores captured were colossal. We at sea didn't have much resistance. Benghazi, however, has been exciting. Continual air activity with dive bombing. Temporarily we are again at Tobruk for we move all the time. Bombing is less intense. I am a sort of Jim Crow for the Services here – quite a responsible job.

I have received some back books from the Reprint Society – *The Seven Pillars*, *Round Dozen*, *All This and Heaven Too*, *The Duke*, and *Grapes of Wrath*. So, my bookshelf grows. But all my music and books are in store in Alex.

Mummy, I see your savings group has raised an impressive amount – £2,000 but it's probably gone up. Congratulations. I see Bulgaria has gone the same way as the rest. The Greeks seem all right, but can we hold the Germans when they come? Who knows? I am more than ever confident of ultimate victory but certain that the price will be too heavy. Money to me in my position has no value so people at home who declare they can't afford the theatre have no sympathy from me. In future so you can quickly see whether any of my letters have been lost, I will number them. This is 1.

* * *

Germans gaining ground/the Benghazi Handicap

The rapid advances of January and February were coming to a halt. Supply lines were stretched, and the Admiralty back in London had to respond to other political pressures. Tobruk was very soon to become the centre of attention from both the Luftwaffe and Rommel.

Cunningham's war diary summarizes the substantial change in Churchill's and the War Cabinet's focus during March 1941:

> The Libyan offensive was abandoned with great regret, as if we had pressed on we might have made ourselves masters of the North African coast. The extended army lines of communication made supply necessary by sea and the problem was greatly complicated by the strength of the recently arrived Luftwaffe units, who were able to bomb and mine at will our harbours, our supply ships and their naval escorts.

The Admiralty ordered Cunningham to organize Operation Lustre, which was the move to Greece of some 58,000 troops with their mechanical transport, equipment and stores. The operation started on 4 March but ceased on 24 April, just six weeks later, when the evacuation of Greece commenced.

*   *   *

Admiralty House, Tobruk
20 March
Many of my letters have gone astray and I have reason to believe No 2 of this series has been sunk – I know, since I saw the ship go down!

. Our news from here is encouraging. British Somaliland is in our hands and advances in Abyssinia, Libya held and the Italians repulsed in Greece. True I am heavily bombed here but so far so good. There are a lot of Australian troops around these parts, but I am not too impressed. Wonderful fighters, but not soldiers. What I mean is that if you give them gear to guard or be on sentry duty, they will be blind drunk in half an hour! What's more, in a battle they won't take any orders – it's just straight for the nearest enemy. However, they are fine fellows in their own way – generous, helpful and willing. Their engineers especially are first class with armoured vehicles.

I am on the go from 0600 to 0100 and ready during even those five hours sleep. Frequently I am disturbed in them. But it is interesting work and carries responsibility never accorded usually to such a growing lad.

Daddy will be interested that I have so far run into six Ellerman Line ships – *Palermo*, *Draco*, *City of Manchester*, *City of Florence* and one other.

Please forgive me if this letter seems disjointed. I am feeling a trifle tired, for I was up at 0600 because of air raids. I am in charge of Air Defence and Alarms here for the town – Military and Navy – a little extra job, besides a normal day's work. It entails being shaken and manning the phones etc. whenever a plane is heard, seen, reported or picked up in case it is enemy.

Tell me how the Savings Group goes. Are you picnicking in the car? Tell me the 101 things you are doing. Still, here's to Victory!

Admiralty House, Tobruk
24 March
Just another line to say all is well with me in the Western Desert. The sand still as nasty and the weather as good and glorious. Not too hot, rather like a June day at home. There is usually a wind to cool the fevered brow. The light certainly is rather strong, but I am very little out and about. The only drawbacks are the sandstorms. Visibility within an hour will be reduced from forty-five miles to ten feet. We then breathe, eat and live in sand. At Sollum it was far worse than here. At least here the water is drinkable. What will amaze you is the food I exist on. My only fruit is a large Jaffa orange per meal every day. They are so easy to peel, not messy and juicy. But I still don't eat rice pudding. Though the old saying has frequently come true: 'All right don't eat your rice pudding, but when you are hungry, really hungry you'll be glad of it.' When the water is too risky, we drink Chianti – a most mild, very pleasant wine. There is also a species of Vichy water which is rather acceptable. Actually, further west near Derna, where the land is cultivated to a certain extent, limited vegetables are still obtainable.

Why anyone would want to fight a war over this place astounds me.

*   *   *

Unfortunately, no mail had got through to Tobruk for many months, but Stoke was able to send a quick telegram back home:

26 March
Perfectly Fit. No Money Required. Have Written Continuously. Last Letter Received Dated November Fifteenth. Much Love. Stoke

*   *   *

The Battle of Matapan, near Crete, occurred at the end of March and was one of the few British naval successes at this time.

*   *   *

Admiralty House, Tobruk
30 March
Here we are again in happier circumstances. The Wops have had a colossal battering at sea [at Matapan]. At least one battleship sunk, three large cruisers, one flotilla leader and one destroyer definitely sunk and others damaged at no cost to ourselves. Glorious isn't the word for it. How I gnash my teeth to think that I'm in the Army now. Still, duty first and I trust that inadvertently I'm helping more in my present job than as an 'ullage' afloat. However, as Cyril Fletcher writes (you'll have to search Palgrave [dictionary] hard for that) the facto remains.

Ashore here, we're up against Jerry and his armoured columns. So, I've upped and cleaned my revolver. Parachutists won't spray me with impunity. We expect here a most violent assault. Here's to wishing the Hun a 'warm' but 'bleak' summer.

I had a most pleasant day this week up at Derna, 100 miles west of Tobruk where Duff is NOIC. It was called by the Wop 'the jewel in the Mediterranean'. It certainly is picturesque, but more than that it has flowers and greenery! You can't imagine what it's like to see flowers even for a Philistine like me. I got this envelope from the office of the Director of Colonisation for Libya in Derna. Yugoslavia seems to be putting up a good fight. This Lease Lend Bill seems to be a real thing. We can even repair HM ships there if we want. If things continue as they are now, we're passed the worst. Cheeribye, very much love and Good Luck!

*   *   *

In Derna, Stoke met up with Duff, who reported to Captain Poland and his staff. Later, in his autobiography, Duff wrote about his meetings and conversations with Stoke in March 1941:

> I made a private arrangement with young Stoke, the Paymaster Midshipman, to pass me the codeword 'Marathon' as an alarm signal should the Allies lines break and Rommel start overrunning with his Africa Korps … Rumours abounded … I got through on the telephone to

Naval HQ in Tobruk. I had the chance of a few words with that invaluable and very gallant youngster, Paymaster Midshipman Stoke, who told me a lot I wanted to know and passed me the codeword 'Marathon'. I admired the fashion in which the snottie passed me the information; he showed the greatest ingenuity in wrapping it up, so that even if someone had tapped the wire, they could have learnt nothing. Then I heard Poland's voice – he had that admirable gift, given to few, of inspiring confidence in every man who serves in his command, and I count it one of my greatest privileges and honours to have served under him.

In late March, Rommel arrived with the Afrika Korps in Tripoli and advanced eastwards rapidly against undermanned Allied forces, arriving in Benghazi on 3 April. Derna fell immediately, and the retreating Allied troops (mainly Australians) were surrounded in Tobruk by 10 April. The retreat was that fast it was nicknamed by the Australians 'The Benghazi–Tobruk Handicap'.

One of the last two ships to leave Derna, as the Germans rapidly advanced at the end of March, was the small schooner *Eskimo Nell*, which Duff navigated in bad weather, avoiding the Luftwaffe and arriving safely in Mersa Matruh, for which he was Mentioned in Despatches. The other was *Maria Giovanni*, under Lieutenant Commander Palmer, who recalled arriving in Tobruk, 'where we spent two or three very unpleasant days moving from berth to berth to dodge the incessant blitz on the harbour and dock installations'.

On 8 April, General Wavell, C-in-C British Army, flew into Tobruk to hold a conference with all the senior Army staff, including Captain Poland, SNOIS and Group Captain Brown, the RAF Commander. Within two days, the siege of Tobruk had started, not to be lifted for another 240 days.

Chapter 4

The Siege of Tobruk Begins, 10 April 1941

Rommel made the erroneous assumption that the ships unloading personnel and stores in Tobruk harbour were there to carry out a Dunkirk-style evacuation, so didn't immediately press home his advantage, and the Tobruk garrison held out for those first most important forty-eight hours. Rommel's men had travelled very far, very fast, just as the British had done twelve weeks earlier against the weak Italian army. But having found his renowned Panzer Division had been rebuffed over the previous forty-eight hours, he then ordered a now very tired Division to undertake a 'blitzkrieg' attack again on 13/14 April. Major General Morshead organized an excellent defence and repelled them once more.

It was later assessed that 14 April 1941 was the very first occasion on which a full scale 'blitzkrieg' assault of the type that had overwhelmed armies in Poland, Belgium, France and Holland had been stopped by troops capable of holding their nerve and their positions. A message of congratulations to all the troops was sent out, concluding:

Stern determination, prompt action and close co-operation by all arms ensured the enemy's defeat, and we now feel more certain than ever of our ability to hold Tobruk in the face of any attacks the enemy can stage. Well done Tobruk.

Morshead then bluntly told his commanders: 'There'll be no Dunkirk here. If we should have to get out, we will fight our way out. There is to be no surrender and no retreat.'

War Office documents record that enemy planes dropped leaflets over Tobruk with the following message:

The General Officer Commanding the German forces in Libya hereby requests that the British troops occupying Tobruk surrender their arms. Single soldiers waving white handkerchiefs will not be fired on. Strong German forces have already surrounded Tobruk and it is useless to try and escape. Our dive-bombers and Stukas are awaiting your ships which are lying in Tobruk harbor.

The official response from Tobruk HQ was to point out drily that the shortage of water meant there was a lack of white handkerchiefs within the perimeter!

The Luftwaffe retaliated with the first of continuous daily air raids. The attack began at dawn, involving between forty and seventy dive-bombers, and continued throughout the day. During the last raid of the day, hospital ship *Vita* was near-missed and disabled, an act which contravened the Geneva Convention.

Rommel's Afrika Korps were just ten miles away, and the British, Australian and other Dominion personnel in Tobruk were being shelled and bombed day and night. The naval HQ was in Admiralty House on the Tobruk quayside, where Poland, Stoke and Smith worked and slept. That and the harbour were two of the main targets of bombing raids on the port. It was reported that there were more than 450 bombing raids in eight weeks.

* * *

Stoke's next letter is written four days after the siege started, with Rommel's Panzer Divisions of the Afrika Korps still trying to smash their way through Tobruk's defences, rather than just laying siege to the British, Australian and Allied troops trapped inside, as they eventually settled down to do at the beginning of May.

Tobruk
15 April
I have deep regrets at missing a week in writing, but you may realize the position. Events have moved fast in Cyrenaica. I have been swamped with work, apart from the actual fighting. Of course, being so intimately connected with the campaign, as Captain's Secretary to the SNOIS, headquartered in Tobruk, I knew the plans for the withdrawal of Allied troops back from Benghazi, Derna and the rest of Cyrenaica. But we didn't expect the present system!!

Here, in Tobruk, we are besieged. We hold an area – a circle of radius ten miles from the centre of the town. I feel almost as if we are the war. The roar of heavy and continual bombardment is with us most of the time. There is constant attack on the perimeter by the enemy. As I write I have just heard we have repulsed his last effort. In addition, there are of course air raids. Our best so far was by fifty German dive-bombers for an hour. I spend the air raid in a sandbagged affair in an open trench, watching to see if mines are dropped. It certainly is fascinating to watch them dive and see the bombs leave the machine. So far, I've been very lucky.

Our nearest friends on land are 100 miles away. Still we are going to hold Tobruk until the last. All this means I am more than ever frantically busy. Not only do we administer our force as before, do routine patrols and convoys, we are now bombarding and landing troops for nuisance raids etc.

I am feeling quite happy even though rather tired. It's now over three months since I started this campaign and I have an awful amount of sleep to catch up. Still, I wouldn't have missed it for anything. I am now within shouting distance of Jerry and only wish him closer. Yesterday, he deliberately bombed the hospital ship *Vita*.

*   *   *

Soon after the siege began, Stoke wrote to Ivan Brown, his history teacher at school, with whom he kept in regular correspondence.

Tobruk
18 April
Dear Mr Brown,

I am afraid I am even later and more dilatory than usual in writing. I plead in my defence that out here in Tobruk, we have a small war on our hands and to me its success or failure is definitely personal!

I have actually been 'in the army' now since January. In this Western Desert campaign, the Navy have played a great part – bombarding, ferrying stores, minesweeping & working the ports. I have been Secretary and Staff Officer to the Captain in charge of the ports and the destroyers, minesweepers & escorts up the coast. He is also Chief Liaison between the Services.

So, I had an exciting time in the advances. I have mostly been ashore – at Benghazi, Derna, Tobruk, Bardia and Sollum. I have been necessarily at the front line and so have had great excitement. At the moment, I am in Tobruk, besieged by the Hun. We are dive-bombed, mostly by day, and high-level bombed at night. Sleep is rather scanty as we've a full day job of work let alone ARP day and night. I'm still kicking even though two large bombs smothered me in dirt with the hole they made ten yards from me on landing – fortunately delayed action!!

I am able to write this as there is a lull for the moment. In the air we've just shot down twelve Ju.87s. By land the artillery bombardment has temporarily ceased, as we've KO'd some of their advancing tanks. We hold Tobruk and ten miles around. On the perimeter, the Hun has guns going all day, shooting into the harbour. He is doing his best to break through but I know we shall hold him. I'm afraid, though, that I have become somewhat of a barbarian. Four months in the desert without books, music or even the daily rags makes me feel lost to this world. The only salvation is work.

On looking back on this letter, I realize how egoistical it must seem. And yet I am just as anxious to know how life in England is. How are air raids affecting the man in the street? Is he still supremely confident? For I have received no letters from home since 18 November and can't judge the spirit of England. I would be grateful if you could remember me to Mrs Brown and hope you both are well and as comfortable as is possible in the present difficult times.

Yours sincerely

G.A. Stoke

* * *

During April, more ships were lost to bombing or mines – steamer *Draco* on the 11th, hospital ship *Vita* damaged and anti-submarine whaler *Skudd IV* on the 13th, *Fiona* on the 18th near Sidi Barrani, the *Bankura* and *Urania* and the hospital ship *Vita* again on the 21st and 22nd. The corvette *Gloxinia* and anti-submarine whaler *Southern Sea* were damaged on the 23rd.

There were a small number of Hurricanes still stationed within the Tobruk perimeter, and although putting up a tremendous fight, they were heavily outnumbered in the air and attacked when they landed between sorties to refuel. The remaining few were completely withdrawn by 24 April. On the same day, London ordered Operation Demon, the evacuation of Greece, which continued for seven days, diverting more naval and air resource away from Cyrenaica and the Western Desert, leaving those in Tobruk stranded, exposed and having to fight for their lives.

* * *

Tobruk

20 April

Well here we are again still kicking! Things aren't so quiet in our village of Tobruk. I've just been counting that last week we had forty-one air raids. Still the damage was nil or rather we did lose a small dump of mosquito cream and the officers' latrines of one of our mess! The only serious casualty is Morpheus [the Greek God of Sleep]. The Hun loses planes steadily. A couple of days ago two dropped like gannets right before my eyes. In the midst of all the bombs raining down, I stood up and cheered the gunners of the ships concerned.

By now we are used to artillery bombardment and alarms when their tanks attack. We hear incidentally that Winston has sent a message exhorting Tobruk to hold to the last. Hardly necessary, as the Hun has already found out. There are continual excursions into no-man's-land, where prisoners and equipment are captured.

I don't know how the real wars are going. Greece seems still to be defensible, so we may hope. With America now really doing something active such as repairing our HM ships, who could doubt our success? (Letter interrupted by an air raid warning). I will try and write again but we have had six air raids since 0800 till 1300 today.

*   *   *

Everyone defending Tobruk was aware of the growing strength and intensity of air attacks, which were directed primarily at shipping in the harbour. In a raid on the harbour on 21 April by a force of twenty-four bombers escorted by twenty-one fighters, the quay was hit, two ships were sunk and two more were put out of action.

Then 24 April brought an intensification of enemy activity. At 0600 the harbour area was heavily raided, and raids continued throughout the day. At 1700 bombs almost destroyed Admiralty House, the Naval HQ. 'A good drop of slum clearance', commented Captain Smith.

Poland's diary notes for that day and the next morning:

Clocked a bad one at about 1700. My office gone but not much gear. One raid by Ju.87s dropped three bombs on the west wing of the building and completely demolished about 80ft of the end of it. The NOIC and I were in a slit trench outside the building.

A.M. Re-organizing and getting square. My jacket was hanging on the back of my chair in my office when we had the direct hit. The sleeves were blown off and out of the window and were picked up fifty yards away. There was no sign of the rest of the coat! A pocket book had been in the inner pocket of the coat. This was found a week later by an Australian soldier and handed back intact but with a small shrapnel hole through it.

There was a brief respite, when a *khamsin* blew up for twenty-four hours, obliterating visibility for everyone, including enemy aircraft. Cunningham, based all the time in Alexandria some 200 miles away but very aware of daily activity in Tobruk, noted in his diary that the naval staff in Tobruk 'lived and worked in the sand with little fresh water and no fresh food, side by side with the Army to whose successful resistance they largely contributed.'

On 26 April Cunningham felt so angry at the indiscriminate and deliberate bombing attacks on the hospital ships *Dorsetshire* and *Vita* that he sent a note to the Admiralty asking for permission to capture enemy hospital ships in retaliation.

On 27 April, as the *khamsin* abated and visibility improved there was a severe attack by twenty-four dive bombers on the heavy anti-aircraft guns near the harbour. Preceded by an attack by high-level Ju.88 bombers, fifty dive-bombers attacked the guns, at least twelve to each gun. Many planes were not seen, for they came directly out of the sun.

Troop-carrying ship *Chakla* was hit at 1630 on 29 April, during another of the many air raids by Stukas, and sank inside the harbour. About 1700, thirty more executed another raid, during which Paymaster Stoke led a party out in a small boat to help the survivors. In a letter six months later, he described how odd it was to see a newsreel in a cinema in Alexandria of the final moments of the *Chakla*, in which he had been so directly involved.

Morshead, in consequence of the sinking of the *Chakla*, sent a personal message to General Wavell urging that until adequate fighter protection and increased anti-aircraft artillery could be provided, personnel ships should arrive and depart at night, and only small vessels should be employed for the carriage of stores.

Cunningham agreed with this wholeheartedly and that policy was put in place. Palmer, commander of the schooner *Maria Giovanni*, recalls in his autobiography *Pedlar Palmer of Tobruk*:

The Stukas had a weird gadget that howls as they descend in their dive attack. This has a disturbing effect – the stomach muscles contract and you get scared – but the odd feature is that once the first bomber has made his run, even those being attacked recover and the subsequent aircraft get a good 'schallickin'. I have noticed this several times. The first onslaught is scary but immediately afterwards everyone is at their post and firing like crazy! By the way, if you ever hear a person say, 'I was not scared', I'll point out a liar to you.

The BBC *People's War* archive of memories from Tobruk includes one from a Bill Harvey:

> We were subjected to many daily bombing raids by flights of Stuka bombers. They timed their runs to coincide with the position of the sun so that they were on us before we could really see them. The target was normally the docks area and its installations. What with the banshee blood-curdling scream of diving aircraft, the anti-aircraft barrage and exploding bombs it was a nerve-racking experience. The biggest danger was from falling shrapnel from our own anti-aircraft barrage. Pieces of shrapnel were anything between one to three inches in size and all capable of inflicting considerable damage to any unfortunate individual caught in the open. We soon found the most effective cover was to dive under a lorry. At this stage it became evident that the navy and air–force were very conspicuous by their absence. It was evident that Jerry had the skies to themselves.

Captain Cortez, the Spanish master of a cargo steamer, just after his twenty-fifth trip on the 'Tobruk Run', described being attacked by three Me109s:

> We no can see them, but I get my big gun straight in sun because I know they are there. I am all the time working machine gun, swinging it in figure of eight to throw cone of bullets where they must be. Then I hear noise them diving, but still I no see. I tell my first officer, 'Wait. No fire yet.' He want to fire. I say, 'No. Noise get louder.'
>
> First one machine come one side of us and drop bombs; then another come other side. His bombs only fall twenty yards away. Then third machine come straight. I see him. I say, 'Fire!' Gun go. He almost over funnel when he turn, but pieces from his starboard wing drop off and fall on our deck. Beautiful! He go wobbling away, getting lower and lower.
>
> In the bows my man is working another machine gun when a piece of cannon-shell go through his thigh. 'Stick it', I say, but poor fellow he presently faint and fall beside his gun. He all right in hospital now. I stop his bleeding with bottle of peroxide hydrogen and put him sleep with bottle whisky.

April ended with more heavy air raids at Tobruk. Poland's diary noted numerous dive-bomb attacks during that day and a heavy raid by thirty-eight planes at 1915. Later that evening, Poland received a signal from Cunningham:

The difficulties of working the port of Tobruk and the danger of sailing ships to and from Tobruk without adequate fighter protection are fully realized by myself and the AOC-in-C. The Inshore Squadron and your men at Tobruk are doing magnificent work and I trust that the present bleak period will soon be ended.

However, three days later, Cunningham was so concerned that he wrote to Pound (First Sea Lord):

We are not having too good a time out here and it can all be put down to lack of air support. Two days ago the only fighters fit for action in the Western Desert were thirteen in number. Tobruk is without fighter defence and consequently my last little ship – the *Chakla* – after a career of much gallant usefulness was sunk three days ago. I am concerned in signs of strain among our officers and ratings.

Water was rationed from April till mid-June at four pints per man per day for all purposes. The limited diet began to take its toll, most markedly in the shape of ugly and painful desert sores.

Tobruk port averaged between one and three raids per night through April to June, mainly dropping mines into the harbour and Italian anti-personnel devices, nicknamed 'thermos bombs' due to their resemblance to a vacuum flask. These were dropped at a low level, thirty or forty at a time.

On 1 May the minesweeper *Milford Countess* was machine-gunned while picking up the crew of a downed aircraft.

* * *

Telegram
1 May
Mummy, very many happy returns of the day. Letter received today, the first since one dated 12 Oct 1940!! Hurray! Wonderful speech by Winnie. Tobruk holds out against the Luftwaffe even though I have a dent in my battle bowler from a 6″ splinter. Bombed and lost all gear on the 25 April.

* * *

In early May, Rommel was now restricted by some of the same supply issues the British forces had faced. Benghazi harbour was not operational, and Tobruk was clearly not available. It was over 1,000 miles from Tripoli to move stores, equipment and ammunition to Cyrenaica. He was therefore forced to wait for supplies and reinforcements, reducing his Panzer Divisions' ability to bombard the Tobruk perimeter and passing the responsibility of starving Tobruk of supplies solely to the Luftwaffe.

While the pressure on the perimeter diminished, the attacks on the port and the ships, whose cargoes sustained the garrison, was waged with growing intensity. The hospital ship *Karapara*, flying a huge Red Cross flag 40ft-square at its forepeak and bearing other Red Cross markings plainly visible, was circled by Messerschmitt aircraft as she approached Tobruk harbour. An hour and a half later, twelve bombers attacked her in waves of three. In view of this and the two earlier attacks on the hospital ship *Vita*, it was decided that all sick and wounded would have to be transported by naval destroyers – an already scarce resource.

Poland's diary notes for 7 May:

0530 bombs and dropping mines. 0640 H/L attack. 1115 D/B attack 9–12 machines. 1620 D/B raid by many machines on harbour. Minesweeper *Stoke* hit amidships – 21 lost. Minesweeper whaler *Svana* damaged. 1845 harbour being shelled again. 2235 more bombs and mines dropped. Two alarms during night.

*   *   *

Tobruk
8 May
Last week, the doctor put me to bed with overwork. He said that only three to four hours interrupted sleep was not enough for four months. I proved him correct by sleeping, apart from waking for meals, for three days and nights. I'm on the job again but feel a trifle weary and my diet now is only bully beef, biscuits and margarine.

But I'm determined the Boche won't break my spirit here. I think we have him taped. Winston sent a very heartening message to us yesterday. And yes, I am restless here. Not for excitement as there's unlimited here – but to rejoin the NAVY!!

Admiralty House stands just by the docks and quays, which of course are the targets. So far, we've stopped four bombs. I've lost all my gear as my office stopped three of them and near enough to blow me out of bed! During raids, I go to a little trench so that I can be handy for rescue work. I've taken a boat away twice to sinking ships in the midst of raids and I can tell you it isn't fun in an undefended boat in the middle of the target area. This morning I was first down to the quay that had a direct hit.

Our little semi-circle of radius seven miles, centre Admiralty House, is still stout-hearted and giving the Boche no quarter. We take no prisoners. They've bombed and put out of action two hospital ships and caused damage and casualties to the hospitals. The Australians have a very expressive word of abuse – conveying doubts about their parentage.

*　*　*

Smaller vessels carried in most of the food. The schooner *Maria Giovanni* was perhaps the most famous, making runs into Tobruk loaded to capacity with assorted victuals, alcohol and sometimes live sheep! Poland's diary again for 9–12 May:

Fri 9 May. Explosion shortly after midnight. Due to top ammo dump being hit by AA shell. 1115 air raid by five machines.

Sun 11 May: *Maria Giovanni* arrives between midnight and 0500. Five alarms – dropping mines and bombs.

Mon 12 May: *Giovanni* loading. 1145 H/L attack. 1505 D/B attack 45 machines and H/L first to west of harbour then on harbour. *Ladybird* got two hits, destroyed after part, set amidships on fire. Forepart above water, guns still firing but had to abandon. 2030 *Giovanni* sailed for Alex. Midnight two H/L attacks & thermos bombs.

Palmer's autobiography records on 12 May:

Maria Giovanni did not arrive until the early hours but was unloaded by 0600. The *Ladybird* was attacked in harbour by nearly fifty aircraft. She was hit twice and sank at her moorings, ablaze, with every gun in action to the last. The survivors were picked up by harbour craft, including Captain J.F. Blackburn RN. He had a reputation for imperturbable courage even in those blast-swept waters where brave men went daily about their occasions.

Commander McHattie of the *Chakla* wrote:

> We had received warning that 100 plus aircraft were heading for the harbour. *Ladybird* had been unable to use her normal tactics that day, which was to move to different parts of the harbour after each enemy reconnaissance, because she was firmly aground! During the raid most of the aircraft made a dead set at her and left her battered and burning. Almost immediately the attack started, her stern received a direct hit, which wrecked her after pom-pom and killed the crew. A second bomb burst in the boiler room, blowing out the sides of the ship. In spite of her damage and casualties, and the fact that an oil fire was raging from the foremast to the stern, her remaining guns continued to fire even when the vessel had settled on the bottom of the harbour. Not until the fire got too fierce that the magazine threatened to blow up and the guns put out of action, was the ship abandoned. There was a small harbour tug outboard of the *Maria Giovanni* which was used to help pick up the gallant survivors.

Ladybird, her guns still firing and her White Ensign flying as she grounded on the bottom, ended her career by shooting down a bomber as she sank. Lieutenant Commander Blackburn signalled Morshead before abandoning ship: 'One wicket down for Yorkshire. Nine more to go yet. Play up Australia. We will catch them on a sticky wicket.'

Morshead replied: 'Great innings by *Ladybird* and we are extremely sorry it has ended. We will beat them on any wicket.'

* * *

Tobruk

12 May

Don't please worry about me. Definitely my number seems to be the lucky one at the moment. I took a boat away with the remnants of a crew to rescue some chaps from the *Ladybird* and as we pulled way the Hun seemed to choose that moment for his peak. There were more bombs, bullets and shells. Still apart from being a trifle weary in body, though not in spirit, I am on the top line. I am actually the youngest serving lad here ashore in the Navy and probably also in the Army. And it's I who tell the troops not to panic or rush for the shelters but to follow me to the rescue! Last night, rather exhausted at about 0100 (i.e. this morning!) I made ready to turn in. Idle curiosity made me fiddle with the wireless – salvaged and Italian – I picked up a Hadyn piano concerto. It was heaven to hear life again.

* * *

Aged nineteen and still only a midshipman, after organizing one of the boats to rescue survivors from the *Ladybird*, Stoke wrote an official letter to NOIC Tobruk, copy to SNOIS, recommending three ratings for their courage and valour in helping him:

> I have the honour to report the meritorious conduct of the following three ratings: Leading Seaman McAlonan, Able Seamen Williams and Signalman Gordon C Hewitt. At approximately 1500 on 12 May 1941 HMS *Ladybird* lying in the west end of the harbour was seen to be struck by two bombs on her stern. Immediately the above named three ratings followed me down into the Fleming lifeboat. There was a lull and three soldiers joined our party. However, when the air attack was renewed with redoubled vigour the three soldiers fled back to their 'funk-hole'. Unmoved by this display, the ratings remained undeterred by the sound and effect of bombs and the barrage of shrapnel falling in the harbour and though many enemy planes could be seen overhead at low heights, machine gunning and firing cannon. In particular, I would bring to your notice Signalman Hewitt as he has been away during air attacks in my boat on every occasion since the 'blitz' started when ships have been sunk in the harbour
> Signed – Paymaster Midshipman G.A. Stoke RN

The *London Gazette* on 1 January 1942 records Signalman Gordon Clifford Hewitt 9C/JX 1442640 being Mentioned in Despatches, following Stoke's personal recommendation, supported by the NOIC and SNOIS.

* * *

Tobruk
20 May
How are you all? At the moment I can think of nothing more delightful than a pleasant family amble through the woods to the Art Gallery. I am not, as you know, by nature a country lover, but having seen this battle-scarred harbour

surrounded by sand as my sole view for many moons, a tree or so seems almost too impossible for worlds!

You know our routine is very settled! Raids from 0500–0630. Then 0730–0815 to disturb breakfast. A quiet spell to 0915, then continuous warnings and/or bombs till 1200. A lull till 1250, restarting just as we attempt to sit down to lunch. It is quiet between 1400 and 1530, then bombing continues till dusk at about 2000. We have dinner & another quiet spell till 2300, when we have half hourly raids every hour till 0300. Two hours sleep brings us to another day!

Of course, it has quietened down a bit lately. We have shaken the Boche up, and it will take many times more than that to irritate us! We can't be broken. Depend upon it. Tobruk will never surrender – the last ditch is ready to be manned, for evacuation would be impossible.

The weather today is delightful – just faint wisps of white cloud amidst a crystal blue sky. The water looks contented and only man is vile. Against this peace, suddenly up goes the Red Flag, on helmet and to the slit trench. The red warning has just gone but I'll ignore it till the guns open up and then I'll have to get my gun manned.

I am hoping to get some mail soon. I have only had one letter in the five months since the *Glasgow*. Of course, a lot gets sunk on its way to Tobruk from Alex. I am feeling well at the moment if a trifle weary. I heard the middle section of Tchaikovsky's piano concerto yesterday at midnight. It was grand to hear the concerto again.

Tobruk
22 May

Here we are, still kicking and bucking. I hope you are all well and happy and enjoying the spring. I saw a bird yesterday and somebody found a cactus plant. So, 'Nature still moves in a mysterious way, her wonders to perform' as Cowper so nearly said! Rest assured, all is well with us in Tobruk. True, some Germans did come inside the defences … but as prisoners! Well, what could go wrong whilst I am here. Well, bye–bye for the better.

*   *   *

Towards the end of May, petrol and other key resources were getting scarce, and Midshipman Stoke was extremely run down through poor diet, total lack of sleep and nervous exhaustion from the continuous coming raids.

*   *   *

Tobruk
26 May

In about three weeks, I will be joining the battleship *Queen Elizabeth*. I am being relieved to continue training and because I am rather tired and exhausted. I am confident food other than bully beef, a bath, clean clothes and a night's sleep will put me in the pink! Sixty Ju.87s have just roared past but my gun jammed! I have just received five letters – Nov to Jan and Daddy's Xmas present – but no others I regret.

*   *   *

Palmer also records this period at the end of May:

On 25 May the whaler *Southern Maid* and the sloop *Grimsby*, escorting the SS *Helka* with petrol and water for Tobruk, were twice attacked by dive-bombers. The first made by five Ju.88s. Bombs fell near the *Helka* and *Grimsby* but did no damage. The *Southern Maid* was then machine-gunned, but hit two of her attackers. The second attack came two hours later. The *Helka* was struck by two bombs, both of which burst in the water tank. The ship broke in two halves, each containing bulk petrol. The *Grimsby* shot down two planes and was herself hit twice and then sank, having transferred wounded and survivors to boats and rafts.

The *Southern Maid* was one of four armed-whalers manned by South Africans. Under the command of Lieutenant Commander Trew, they did valiant service throughout; their discipline, their morale and, above all, their marksmanship were unequalled in the Inshore Squadron.

Yet against the sombre background of all these sinkings and this sacrifice, there burnt, like a flame, the determination of the Inshore Squadron to play its part in holding Tobruk, while a ship remained afloat to carry petrol, food and ammunition to the defenders. The petrol and ammunition carriers knew that one direct hit meant almost certain death for the crew. They made the perilous trip not once, but again and again without respite because they were so few.

During May and June, while air attacks on Tobruk were at their height, the run was at night at high speed along an unlit coast, requiring the highest qualities of navigation and seamanship. Once inside Tobruk harbour, they had to berth alongside wharfs in complete darkness after negotiating a harbour strewn with wrecks. The naval based parties had then to secure ships and lighters, discharge the cargoes and get the ships away before dawn without any lights.

And on the evening of 30 May:

Maria Giovanni had sailed from Mersa Matruh and was attacked at 1700 north east of Tobruk by two Heinkel IIIs. The planes, thinking she was unarmed, came very low and their first salvo of bombs straddled the ship. But on the second run were met with return fire from our 13.2 Breda guns, with one plane crashing into the sea. The *Maria Giovanni* had precious cargo to protect – 200 tons of ammunition and 240 crates of beer!

The Australians still retained their sense of humour in the face of the incessant bombing. On their arrival in Tobruk harbour, General Morshead, in overall charge of the Australian troops, sent the following message: 'Splendid shooting and may you complete a brace next time. Many thanks for your consignment. Will you dine with me tonight?'

The German leaflet drops continued with a slightly different version of the original one dropped in early April:

After Crete disaster Anzac troops are now being ruthlessly sacrificed by England in Tobruch and Syria.

Turkey has concluded a pact of friendship with Germany. England will shortly be driven out of the Mediterranean. Offensive from Egypt to relieve you totally smashed.

YOU CANNOT ESCAPE

Our dive bombers are waiting to sink your transports. Think of your future and your people at home.

Come forward – Show white flags and you will be out of danger!

SURRENDER!

The Australians' answer was to hoist a white flag on top of one of the highest buildings with the inscription 'Come and Get It' in large letters, plus some appropriate Australian descriptions of the Germans and their parentage! They also sent back leaflets to the Germans on the other side of the perimeter defences suggesting different wording that might have been more successful:

> Aussies
> We have been trying to get you out of your rat holes for the past three months and are getting fed up. Every one of you we get costs us ten and it's getting a bit thick. Come and give yourselves up. The German beer is the best and we have millions of gallons here.

Poland's daily diary records that since the start of the siege there had been no days or night without bombing raids, and that the raids became more intensive in May and June. Cunningham also reiterated the unremitting nature of the bombing:

> May saw the hardest fighting of the war as far as the Mediterranean Fleet was concerned, between the weight of the German Air Force and the Fleet, without any fighter protection, picked off in succession by the concentration of torpedo and dive bombers.
>
> 2 June – To the Admiralty
> We must have the fighters, the bombers and reconnaissance or remain pinned in this corner of the Mediterranean
>
> 4 June – Middle East C-in-C's Committee
> The C-in-C Mediterranean drew attention to the difficulty supplying Tobruk. Ships were continually being sunk. Without fighter protection the slow ships now being used had little chance of accomplishing their journey in safety. The AOC-in-C explained the difficulty of providing air protection on these occasions. He was unable to agree to provide additional fighter protection to the navy, whilst supporting the army in the Western Desert.
>
> 7 June. *Vendetta* and *Voyager* arrived at and left Tobruk during the night 6th/7th returning to Mersa Matruh. In view of the recent losses and scale of air attacks the C-in-C ordered the suspension of all shipping other than destroyers until adequate fighter protection was available.

Paymaster Midshipman Stoke, still just nineteen, left Tobruk on the night of 6/7 June on one of the Australian destroyers, *Voyager* or *Vendetta*, that delivered stores during the early part of the night and sailed at 0130. He was to convalesce in Alexandria after five months in the Western Desert and Tobruk, lucky to have survived the atrocious conditions and incessant bombing, but having learnt as much in five months as he might have done in a lifetime. It was only some months later he was to find out that he had been Mentioned in Despatches and awarded the Distinguished Service Cross, becoming the most decorated Paymaster Midshipman in the Royal Navy.

Chapter 5

The Most Decorated
Midshipman in the Navy[*]

S toke's Mention in Despatches – 'For courage, skill and devotion to duty
in operations off the Libyan coast' – was listed in the *London Gazette*
No 35231, 29 July 1941. There is also an earlier reference in Admiralty
document CW19669/41 to Stoke's MiD, which also records the loss of HMS
Ladybird on 12 May 1941. It is clear from his own letters and the award to
Captain Frank Smith, NOIC, who shared the same office in Tobruk, that he
was involved in the rescue of a number of crew from the many ships that were
bombed and mined in Tobruk harbour during the period February to May 1941
– *Adinda*, *Tynefield*, *Chakla*, *Dainty*, *Rodi* as well as *Ladybird*.

His award of the Distinguished Service Cross (DSC) – 'For courage and
devotion to duty while serving in the Mediterranean' – was listed in the *London
Gazette* No 35357, 25 November 1941. This was for putting out a fire in an
ammunition dump during a very heavy air raid on Tobruk, whilst simultaneously
being under siege from Rommel's Afrika Korps, just ten miles away. Captain
Poland's recommendation for this decoration is dated 7 June 1941, the day after
Stoke had departed Tobruk, and was sent directly to Admiral Cunningham,
C-in-C Mediterranean in Alexandria. The document is preserved at The
National Archives (ADM 1/11498) and provides a fuller account:

> For courage, coolness and devotion to duty. Although nominally Secretary
> to myself, SNOIS, this young officer has carried out a variety of duties in
> which he has been a tower of strength and has shown exceptional ability
> and initiative under trying conditions. He has no regard for his personal
> safety and has always been to the fore in rescue work during air raids.
> When a small arms ammunition was set on fire, he immediately set about
> removing the burning boxes working in the middle of the dump, with
> ammunition bursting all round him, until the fire was brought under
> control.

---

[*] See also Appendix B, p.241.

On the reverse side of the recommendation, in Admiral Cunningham's own handwriting, is the single word 'Concur'.

Stoke was also mentioned in the *Journal of Commerce* (a London merchant shipping journal) in its regular column entitled 'A Modern Pepys's Diary':

I do oft-times glance down the lists of awards which appear in the Press. I be frequently cheered when I come across the name of one who be known to me. This be more often the case for awards made to men of the Merchant Navy, but this week my eye caught, amongst the naval honours, the name of Paymaster Midshipman G.A. Stoke RN, as having been awarded the Distinguished Service Cross for 'courage and devotion to duty while serving in the Mediterranean'. In July, he were awarded a mention in despatches 'for courage, skill and devotion to duty in operations off the Libyan coast' and my mind went back to a few months ago when I met this young lad in the company of his father, Master S. Stoke, the passenger manager of the Ellerman Lines. I were certainly impressed by him because he did appear to me to possess a knowledge and intelligence somewhat out of the ordinary, and there seemed to be no subject in our discourse with which he were not conversant and well informed.

A successful candidate in the Royal Naval Competitive Examination in November 1939, he were entered in the Royal Navy as a cadet at the beginning of last year and were sent to the Royal Naval College, Dartmouth for training. He left there having gained a prize, and were appointed to HMS *Glasgow*, in which ship he saw service in Northern Waters and in the Mediterranean. His ship took part in the attack on Taranto towards the end of 1940. Subsequently he were selected for special duties with the Senior Naval Officer commanding the Inshore Squadron responsible for naval operations off the Libyan coast throughout the first Cyrenaica campaign. His service during that campaign ashore and afloat took him from Sollum to Benghazi. With the turn of the tide, Tobruk remained a focus of naval activity and became his headquarters for some months. What a story he will have to tell when the war is over! This latest announcement did give me much pleasure and my old friend, Stoke, I be sure, must be a proud man this day.

The DSC is awarded to naval officers below the rank of Commander 'in recognition of an act or acts of exemplary gallantry during active operations against the enemy at sea'.

Stoke only found out about the award of the DSC in early 1942, and in a later letter written on 5 April 1942, in response to a question from his parents, he wrote:

> Your mention of an ammunition dump does ring a bell. It was quite a small matter. An ammunition dump of 8″ steel was fired by bombing and we put it out during the air raid. All I did was to stand on the dump and pass down boxes which were then put out by sand. Of course, there was a lot exploding and the bombs were falling around. But I must confess that I never regarded it as much of an affair.

In another much later letter in 1943, he refers to being blown up by a bomb beforehand, being hit by a large piece of shrapnel before he then went to save the ammunition dump.

Captain Poland DSO and bar, DSC (aged forty-six), later promoted Vice-Admiral CB, KBE wrote on Stoke's 'flimsy' on 6 June 1941:

> Paymaster Midshipman Stoke served to my entire satisfaction. A courageous young officer who has ability, zeal and good judgement. He has been an invaluable staff officer. Should do well in the services.

Poland also wrote on Stoke's S.206:

> As Secretary cum Staff Officer cum Signal Officer, this young officer has shown great ability, considerable initiative and has worked most zealously. He has been a tower of strength in every way and has, in addition, displayed considerable courage on many occasions. For his age he possesses an unusual amount of common sense and his judgement is very sound. Physically strong and fit or he would not have stood the strain and trying conditions under which he has worked for four months.

Captain Poland was awarded a bar to his DSO 'for sustained leadership, resource and devotion to duty, while under frequent, heavy and deliberate bombardment from artillery and from the air'.

There were many other courageous men in Tobruk. However, one who was ever-present was Commander Frank Mortem Smith DSO, RD, RNR, Naval Officer in Charge, who shared office and living space with Poland and Stoke. He was stationed in Tobruk from January 1941 through to June 1942 (apart from six weeks in Alexandria when he fell ill) and he, of all those gallant men in Tobruk, set the young Paymaster Midshipman Stoke the finest example.

Smith was awarded the DSO 'for bravery and devotion to duty at Tobruk', as reported in the *London Gazette* dated 19 August 1941, three weeks after Stoke's Mention in Despatches. The recommendation (TNA ADM 1/11371) states:

> On 8 February 1941, when the SS *Adinda*, carrying aviation spirit, caught fire after two mine explosions in Tobruk harbour, Commander Smith displayed great courage and initiative. In company with the Master and four of *Adinda*'s officers, he boarded the ship while the fore part was blazing fiercely, in order to close the hatch to the after part which was still open. At the time no one knew whether the after part would burst into flames.
>
> Again, on 25 February 1941, when the SS *Tynefield* was on fire after being struck by a bomb, Commander Smith boarded the ship despite the fact that an air raid and heavy gunfire were still in progress. By personal example, he organized the officers and crew into dealing with the situation. He arranged for the ship to be towed stern to wind by HMS *Aphis*, thus containing the fire in the fore end. He then organized a supply of water from the damaged main to play on the fire, thus saving 3,500 tons of fuel remaining on board.
>
> On these two occasions and also in other emergencies such as the bombing of HMS *Dainty* and the mining of SS *Rodi* Commander Smith has displayed a complete disregard of personal safety and shown himself full of initiative and resource. He has set a fine example on all occasions.

When Smith fell ill and was sent back to Alexandria to hospital for six weeks in July 1941, he was lucky to get there as his ship was sunk en route and he was cast overboard into a sea of oil. Fortunate to be picked up, he reached the hospital, where General Auchinleck personally ordered him to drink two bottles of Guinness a day at the Admiralty's expense! Admiral Cunningham specifically recalled Captain Smith in his autobiography:

> Whenever Tobruk is mentioned, my mind goes back to the NOIC, Captain Frank Mortem Smith, outstanding amongst gallant men. Except for a few weeks when he had to be withdrawn for illness, he was in Tobruk throughout the siege. Unperturbed and unafraid in the midst of the heaviest air attacks, he was always the first man to board any ship hit by a bomb, on fire, or in any other trouble. The first in any post of danger, he set an inspiring example to everyone. And at Tobruk, Smith was killed, the last man to leave after seeing the oil storage tanks well ablaze when the fortress fell into the hands of the enemy in June 1942. As a guide to

destroyers coming into Tobruk at night, the green starboard light was always shown in the sunken ship alongside of which they lay to unload. That lantern now rests on Smith's grave.

Pedlar Palmer, captain of the *Maria Giovanni*, summed up that period in 1941 in Tobruk: 'It was the atrocious logic of total warfare, carried to the limits of inhumanity.'

* * *

Recuperation in Alexandria (7–21 June 1941)

Stoke stayed in Alexandria with his half uncle, John de Wolf, his wife Phyllis and young son, also John. He wrote ten air-letters during those few days, catching up on the many letters from home which never reached Tobruk, answering their great number of questions and reflecting on the previous quite remarkable five months. He was still nineteen.

Alexandria

11 June

Well this will be such a long letter that it will have to go in a number of parts. I have just received Daddy's Xmas present and letter!! I like your comments in Daddy's letter that the Royal Navy must be having a busy time off Libya. Don't I know it!!

Your reference to concertos brings a tear to mine eye as my records have disappeared in my absence, with some clothing and a few books. Still, c'est la guerre! As for skill at the piano, how I've yearned for one these past six months.

I'm rather amused to see that you thought me safer ashore than afloat. Actually, the number of bombs near me has been well over 50,000 for the past two months alone! Tobruk had 450 air raids in my last seven weeks I was there! And I was not in the shelter for one of them. Alex had an air raid last night, which apparently kept the house up. For myself I slept through as I've grown rather blasé.

My story is quite interesting. I remained in Tobruk when it was surrounded, as Secretary and Staff Officer to the SNOIS. With little modesty, I say that he seemed to rely on me more than his official Staff Officer – rather a dull fellow. Well, what with secretarial work and staff work I got little sleep. In fact, I averaged only three to four hours sleep for five months. In these few hours, I frequently got disturbed. The air raids produced physical exercise as I made it my privilege to be in command of the first boat away to the many hit ships – also quite a nervous strain to appear unconcerned under cannon fire and machine gunning from Me110s – the Boche!

Still the result was that one day I went to sleep and stayed so for three days and nights. This rather upset the Doctor. He said I must return to civilization – bag and baggage. As for the latter, three bombs on my office and cabin had disposed of that! Fortunately, I had left gear behind in Alexandria. So eventually I was relieved by two brother Mids – surely great flattery to have two to replace one!

The Captain was good enough to say he was sorry to send me back – in fact he wouldn't have done so except for Doctor's orders. He said, too, he would endeavour to gain some sort of recognition for my services. So, my six months in the desert ended, when on the 7 June 1941 I arrived back in Alex – filthy, dirty and rather tired. I had not had a bath for three months, fresh food for two or paid for six.

I knew John's address, so gave him a ring and they have put me up. I was given fourteen days sick leave as I was in rather a mess with rotting feet, losing toenails and sores on my arms. Still I'm rapidly returning to normal now that I'm back with fresh food, more sleep and so on. I've been appointed to HMS *Queen Elizabeth* and join her on Sunday morning 22 June 1941.

John has put me up in his furnished flat that he took when they arrived with nothing from Malta. He has an excellent job and I think doing very well. Phyllis, his wife, tends to annoy me, whilst young John is badly spoilt. He's quite a nice kid but wants bringing up with a round turn – he needs to be told NO means NO and not YES if you ask a little longer. Still I'm very grateful for them putting me up. John is certainly most kind. He asks to be remembered to you. Sam [John de Wolf's father, and Stephen Stoke's stepfather – see Preface] is still in Tel Aviv and writes to John.

Financially I'm very well off. I wasn't paid out in the Desert and got an extra 2/- a day because of the conditions. Moreover, I put in a claim for all the gear I lost in Tobruk. It's only cost me a few pounds to re-equip myself here so that venture should show a profit! So, don't worry about my finances. I live within my income.

Roosevelt is really telling the Hun now what America thinks. Turkey, I think is facing both ways until we arrive at her border via Syria when she'll feel so much better. The RAF at home seem to have taken the offensive. It augurs well. An air offensive out here wouldn't be amiss.

Some of the Ellerman ships I'm afraid have been sunk – *Draco* in Tobruk and the *City of Roubaix* on her way to Greece. Still I expect you know more than I do. I wish Daddy a Happy Birthday. May the coming 12 months bring you joy and happiness, even as the War continues. Well I must finish now as I've run out of these Air letter cards.

Good luck and much love from Mick.

*   *   *

On Saturday, 22 June 1941, Paymaster Midshipman Stoke, still not twenty, packed his bag again, after just fourteen days sick leave, and was dropped at Ras-el-Tin, the naval base in Alexandria to join the battleship *Queen Elizabeth*, which was lying at anchor with the rest of the Mediterranean Battle Fleet, under the command of the C-in-C Mediterranean, Admiral Sir Andrew Browne Cunningham.

Chapter 6

HMS *Queen Elizabeth*:
Escape from Torpedoes, Again!

S toke joined the Paymaster Office of the very large (and old) battleship *Queen Elizabeth* on 22 June 1941. Commissioned in 1914, she was 643ft long, 90ft wide and originally drew 33ft, more recently increased to 42ft. She displaced a massive 33,000 tons, over three times that of his previous ship, *Glasgow*, and ten times more than most destroyers! She had a crew of nearly 2,000, three times that of *Glasgow*.

Here he would have much more time to write letters and chat about family news. It was a pleasant lull after Tobruk. The battleship spent most of her time moored in Alexandria harbour, so there was time for going ashore, catching up on the progress of the war elsewhere and playing some rugger. The letters show his keen interest in the various elements of the war at a strategic level: his dislike of the Germans, Italians and Japanese, and his increasing appreciation of the Russians, as well as his interest in rugger, music and reading.

However, although he was serving on what should have been the safest ship – the C-in-C Mediterranean's flagship – he was lucky to escape being torpedoed in late November and again in December.

It certainly wasn't all plain sailing, as immediately on his arrival on board on 23 June at 0315 German aircraft attacked Alexandria, and again at 0510. Battleships *Queen Elizabeth* and *Valiant* were missed but the other battleship, *Warspite*, was damaged by the near miss of a heavy bomb. The next day, thirty-one German aircraft attacked Alexandria, targeting *Warspite* a second time. The damage was too much to repair locally, so she steamed around Africa and through the Panama Canal to be repaired in Seattle. It was a significant loss to the fleet.

* * *

On 26 June, Paymaster Midshipman Stoke experienced his first day at sea in a battleship, as *Queen Elizabeth*, *Valiant* and seven destroyers departed Alexandria for gunnery exercises between Alexandria and Port Said.

28 June

Today is my natal day! I'm twenty! I am settling in to my new home and I think I shall be happy. Our fighter sweeps seem to be keeping 'im on the spot, and our bombing will crush the Boche.

5 July

I'm gradually getting used to this huge monster of steel but as my first letter written from this ship said, it is too impersonal. I'm perfectly fit and more than ever confident.

12 July

I hope the weather has improved and that you have been able to enjoy an English summer. For myself a little rain would be – well, Allah's paradise itself! However, it would tax even Churchill to make it rain out here. I've just been listening to another speech of his about 'that subject, abject province of Germany that used to be called Italy'. I felt the mood to be primitive but so welcome. No despair but determination to hit back.

19 July

In response to your question, I can give you authentic records as to my weight. I went into the desert fit and weighing just under 13 stone. Now I'm 11 stone odd. I see you heard I was missing from the old *Glasgow*. Out here, we are more than confident we are on top. Syria almost over and Abyssinia finishing, what have we to fear. The day of victory rolls nearer despite – no rude words – the Hun.

27 July

Here we are again in high spirits! It certainly has been a wonderful week. We've been to sea, and I always enjoy that. The convoy got through to Malta, and then Malta repelling such an impertinent attack. Moreover, Syria completely free, Abyssinia free and Tobruk being a nuisance, we have much to cheer! The news from the Home Front is encouraging. These Ruskies too have become more of an ally than a liability than I ever fondly dared to hope. Still, it doesn't take these successes to inspire one's hopes of ultimate victory. It is merely encouraging!

You will be pleased to hear I received my November mail today and a number of *Spectators* and *New Statesman*. Was I glad to devour them! My present mess I regret to say is too juvenile to have heard of such periodicals. Their average

age is two years at least below mine! I am getting quite an experienced veteran of war, now! I'm fairly busy at the moment. I think that I work so that I shan't get homesick.

3 August
This week we had a concert by some London Artistes led by Alice Delysia. It was a pleasant change, though nothing to enthuse over except the pianist, who commenced with the first page of Brahms' Piano Concerto in B Flat. However, he soon switched to more modern and so more acceptable music. There was the inevitable Lancastrian comedian. The conjuror – well Margate Sands! A couple of singer-dancers and a mixed comedy act. Alice Delysia, though rather well aged, has a terrific personality and completely held her own. Churchill, I see, has made his usual sparkling speech and shows he can hit his own MPs as well as the malignant Huns. Remember me to our various friends and say I am still on the top of the world.

10 August
I hope you are all happy and as cheerful as we are here. Time does seem to be flying. I can hardly credit that I've been away twelve months. For it has been an eventful period for us all – at home and overseas. I think we can be sure and more confident of complete success now than since the outbreak of war. I am going to buy some piano music as we have a piano in the Gunroom. You may remember a Pay Mid I was friendly with at training – Tammadge. I've met him again and he has come over to dinner to re-establish contact. He is interested in music and literature. Also, in the mess is a Mid with a very fine tenor voice. He has lots of music & we are going to put on a joint show. I am really astonished to find how much of the 'technique' I've lost, but, thank goodness, its coming back. The mess is indifferent to ALL music and so take no notice of us.

*   *   *

The *London Gazette* No 35231 of 29 July included Stoke's Mention in Despatches 'for courage, skill and devotion to duty in operations off the Libyan Coast', and the news was published a couple of weeks later on the local Admiralty Noticeboard in Alexandria.

*   *   *

17 August

You will bow down to me in future – I am now a very highly distinguished person. Actually, I think there have been very few Paymaster Midshipmen who have been Mentioned in Despatches. I shall be able to wear a laurel wreath on my Victory medals! But unfortunately, I have not been too well lately. My Western Desert efforts took their toll and I have just had a run of boils. Still, they're clearing up now.

In your last letter, you talk of me being in an old Battle Wagon – insult! *QE* is the latest to be modernized like *Warspite*. She carries 15″ guns and a devastating lesser armament with all modern devices. Of course, details and speed are secret!

In answer to your queries: I have to complete two years as a Mid i.e. till September 1942, and your query about my AA gun in Tobruk is easily answered. Outside my office and cabin was a slit trench I'd made. I used to go there with a light Breda machine gun – like a Bren – and fire off at the enemy aircraft coming over the harbour!

24 August

The news recently is quite reassuring. Out here, successes by our submarines, RAF and Fleet Air Arm seem to be mounting on an ever-increasing scale and Malta is standing firm, despite heavy air bombardment and surface attack … The cotton crop question is becoming really heated in Egypt. If we didn't buy the crop, starvation would be inevitable for most of the inhabitants. Egyptians are either very rich and selfish or really poor – there is no vestige of middle class, except for foreigners like Greeks and the French.

*   *   *

Larry Allen was an American war correspondent based in Alexandria and was to meet up with Paymaster Stoke on a couple of occasions when he was on board *Queen Elizabeth*. In his autobiography *Red Tobruk*, Captain Frank Gregory-Smith DSO, DSC RN, captain of *Eridge*, one of the many destroyers based out of Alexandria, describes the effect of having him onboard.

Overnight on 26 August we bombarded Rommel's forces at El Daba. Aerial photography showed we had been successful so we were asked to repeat it the following night. That evening, one of my officers reported that an American War Correspondent had joined the ship. 'Good, we could do with some publicity', I replied. 'But this is Larry Allen', he protested. 'He's a Jonah. Something happens to every ship in which he takes a passage. He was on *Galatea* and *Naiad* when they were sunk.'

Eridge bombarded successfully the second night and turned for Alexandria at 0445, when she was hit by a torpedo on port side aft. Explosions caused extensive flooding in the engine room with a loss of electric power. Significant structural damage including a twenty-foot hole. But we managed to return to Alexandria surviving multiple air attacks by Axis aircraft. Our reporter, Larry Allen, had watched the determined defence against the air attacks from the signal bridge. After the Stuka attack, he decided to walk round the ship to inspect the damage and to form an opinion of her company's morale. He was left in no doubt our determination to get back to Alex.

A few days later, Larry Allen wrote an article for *The Parade*, a local journal, published in Egypt:

Allied naval action is pushing the Mediterranean battleground right up to Mussolini's doorstep. Relentlessly, they seize every opportunity to beat up the chief naval bases of the boot-shaped Axis power. I like the British navy for many reasons – but there's a big one – that overworked phrase 'strategic withdrawal' does not exist. The Italians prefer to stay in port. But the British like action!

From Taranto – still regarded as one of the most daring and crippling blows ever struck at the enemy – to the action in December 1940 when Admiral Cunningham took his battle fleet into the mine-laden Adriatic and flung over 100 tons of high-explosive shells into the dockyards at Valona.

It's an inspiring thing to watch a ship go into action. No one needs tell another what his job is when an attack comes. Everyone knows – and his life as well as that of others, depends upon quick-thinking and fulfilment of that duty. The call to action aboard a warship is somehow like adding a powerful latent chemical to a temporarily latent mass. Men springing from their ordinary, calm ship routine duties into fighting machines.

On 26 September, the Mediterranean Fleet departed Alexandria with the three battleships *Queen Elizabeth*, *Barham* and *Valiant*, three light cruisers and eight destroyers to act as a diversion for Operation Halberd.

Larry Allen was on board *Queen Elizabeth* and filed this report to the Associated Press at sea the following day, through Paymaster Midshipman Stoke's office:

> Britain demonstrates anew her mastery of the Mediterranean sending her war fleet cruising in a wide area in an unsuccessful search for enemy shipping. The Fleet was unmolested by Axis bombers, although they sailed within easy range of enemy shore bases.
>
> From the Captain's bridge of this battleship, I watch warships plow majestically through the blue Mediterranean, their crews eager for action. But action was confined to test-firing of close-range armament since the enemy failed to appear on the sea or in the air.
>
> The movement of warships was the biggest I have seen since the evacuation of Crete. Destroyers and cruisers, spreading out like a fan, screened the squadron of battleships. Sailors, working in the bright sun, humming American tunes, sponged the long, grey barrels of fifteen-inch guns and tested their firing. Pom-poms were given a thorough workout aboard every ship. This was one of the dullest trips to sea with the British Mediterranean Fleet because of the lack of action. But it was news because it was the first time the Fleet was not attacked by enemy planes.

*   *   *

5 October

I have managed to play one game of rugger which rather ingloriously we lost 45–nil! Still, I'm taking over the ship's rugger and hope to buck them up. Of course, it's rather warm, but the game bucked me up no end.

Russia still seems to be keeping her end up though the Huns are throwing in a fair number of reserves. The situation in the Middle East seems to be intriguing. Iran is settled but German threats to Turkey are making her nervous. I often wonder how far we could go to help her, or whether her entry into the War would relieve pressure on Russia.

12 October

As I told you, I have taken over the ship's rugger and this week we only lost 5–3 and then only because of a very bad kick at goal from an easy position. I feel confident of good games in the future. I have today posted off a parcel – 2lbs of brown sugar, 3/4lb cheese, sultanas and raisins. Just a little for you to make a small cake.

* * *

In the afternoon of 12 October, battleships *Queen Elizabeth* and *Valiant* plus three light cruisers departed Alexandria with ten destroyers and proceeded westward on another routine sweep of the Eastern Mediterranean. Larry Allen was again on board the *Queen Elizabeth* and filed another report of this outing through Paymaster Stoke's office:

The Mediterranean Fleet, steaming top–speed with huge masses of spray and spume breaking over their bows, sent a hail of hot lead into two oncoming squadrons of Italian bombers, desperately trying to shove torpedoes into this flagship.

As the Marine bugler sounded 'All hands to Action Stations' just before noon today, a trio of Italian bombers swept out of the glaring sun and headed for destroyers screening this and other battleships of the Fleet.

I dashed up to the aft director tower, just as the four-point-fives of this flagship roared a crescendo of fire. This wall of flame and the whizzing shells were too much for the bombers. They turned out of range and sped westward. This was after another three enemy planes had attacked at dawn and three Italian torpedo bombers had suddenly dived upon the destroyer screen.

I was typing a dispatch in the Captain's cabin on the quarterdeck at 1400 when I saw three planes hovering about one hundred feet above the destroyers on the starboard side. From a port-hole I watched them, thinking they must be friendly aircraft since they were moving so close to the Fleet. I soon learned differently. The destroyers and other ships opened a heavy barrage. The Italian bombers veered directly over the destroyer screen, dropped a little lower, and fired three torpedoes aimed at this flagship. The battleship made a quick turn in course. One torpedo exploded harmlessly in the sea. Another streaked through the water just in front and the third raced past its stern.

This sudden flare of action, after many trips to sea without sighting enemy aircraft or ships, pleased every officer and the entire crew. In the aft director tower where I watched most of the firing, petty officers hummed American 'swing' while keeping close watch on the approach of enemy planes and the direction of firing of the ship's guns.

Throughout three days and star-studded, moonlit nights – the moon in this part of the Mediterranean is so bright that it looks like a giant searchlight on a Hollywood movie premiere – the Fleet ploughed steadily westward. But no sign of the Italian Fleet. The expressions on the faces of officers and sailors when they learned that the Italians could not be found was like that of a child losing an all-day lollipop!

The *Queen Elizabeth* then stayed in Alexandria for thirty-four days from 15 October to 19 November, allowing time for reading, writing Xmas letters home, going ashore, rugger and more music.

*   *   *

Xmas Letter
21 October
This is to wish you a most enjoyable and Happy Xmas. This I hope will reach you by hand from one of my friends who is coming back for his exams – that lucky man!! Five Mids are going from the *QE* and are taking some food for you.

I went to the cinema recently and had the rather peculiar sensation of seeing myself bombed! The newsreel showed the *Chakla* being bombed in Tobruk Harbour in May. She was about 4,500 tons and cross-panelled black and white for camouflage. She was one of the ships I rescued survivors from.

My thoughts are with you particularly on such reunion days. Let us hope we will soon be able to look out on a man's world instead of our vandals' world.

22 October
Dear Mr. Brown,
I feel very caged in now that I am in a battleship, doing a straightforward job, after a rather different responsibility in the Desert. I have wangled a 'Mention in Dispatches'. No words can express how much we all owe – I know I do – to WHS.

I have an exam in a year or so and taking one optional subject – Naval History. I think it should be interesting, but I do prefer to treat history as a whole, rather than an emphasis just on one aspect. However, I'm in the Navy now, so I might as well keep my opinions quiet, at least until I have enough stripes!

It certainly is startling the way Russia has been so united. It makes me, for one, reconsider my views on Russian Communism, though I do realize that only first-hand contact could tell how much is innate Russian pride, which would have emerged anyhow, or whether it is pride in their new achievements. Certainly, Germany is such a traditional enemy of Russia, that a fair measure of animosity is obvious.

26 October

I can't tell you more than this, but I can say, we are the Fleet Flagship and have the C-in-C on board. I haven't been gadding about much lately. In fact, I've been too utterly bored. As captain of the ship's rugger team, I'm hoping to have a match tomorrow against an army team called 'The Wolves', although we hope to do the biting!

11 November

It seems rather strange writing on Armistice Day. As I see it, Armistice Day was to re-dedicate ourselves to the cause of peace and to remember our heroes. To symbolize the beginning of the armed truce in a religious manner seems farcical.

Yesterday I managed to get to a club who call themselves the Informal Music Club. We are up to fifty strong and we have artists to play to us every other Sunday and records on Mondays. We had Brahms' 3rd Symphony and Ravel's *Daphne and Chloe*. The latter I can't comprehend at all. I hope to get to the Palestine Symphony Orchestra who are touring at the moment. One concert includes Beethoven's 7th.

On 13 November, the aircraft carrier *Ark Royal* was torpedoed thirty miles off Gibraltar. Another great loss to the Mediterranean Fleet, offsetting the destruction of an Italian convoy.

17 November

I feel very confident at the moment of the war in general. Certainly, this week has been most momentous. The surface and submarine actions culminating in four Wop destroyers and eleven supply ships joining Davy Jones' fleet was thrilling; and rather upholds the loss, fortunately not tragic, of the old *Ark Royal*. We hope here that soon we shall be able to deal a sharp blow at the enemy in Libya to make a real start towards concrete advance to victory. As for the Japs ... such slimy little ...! They should really get it where it hurts. I feel today most boisterous as I am confident we are now strong enough to implement Churchill's bluster but certainly no bluff. He reminds me of Palmerston often.

I am hoping to hear Dvorak's New World Symphony No 9 tonight on gramophone with a Mozart Clarinet Quintet. I don't know it but I presume it will be tuneful, though that's the last epithet one can apply to the modern use of clarinets!

* * *

On 20 November, the three battleships *Queen Elizabeth*, *Barham* and *Valiant*, and three light cruisers departed Alexandria with ten destroyers to support Operation Chieftan, the dummy convoy intended to divert attention from Operation Crusader – the breakout from Tobruk in the Eastern Med. The Fleet turned back after dark, arriving back at Alexandria the next day.

* * *

23 November

News is just coming in of the Libyan offensive. It may fizzle out. The enemy tank strength would appear to have been greater than we supposed. Still, it has smacked any Hun hopes of an offensive. Their supply ships must find it rather exciting crossing the Narrows now. I see we got another two again and our subs got two cruisers.

I'm following the Far East situation with keen interest. I have strong hopes of the opportunity presenting itself for hitting the Jap hard and not necessarily above the belt! The Russians seem to have had a good week and the German HQ must be putting wet towels on. Your letter of 24/9/41 says, 'the Med war begins to look like business.' How true that is, these two months later. Libya and the sea offensive are hitting the enemy hard. I am glad Mummy has carried on with her Savings Group – £4,000 is a tremendous sum, almost a Hurricane.

* * *

For close on five months the Mediterranean Fleet had been on a series of manoeuvres around the Eastern Mediterranean without any significant sightings of the Italian Fleet. However, the next four weeks, despite Stoke having two narrow escapes from torpedoes, were to provide a dramatic setback to Admiral Cunningham's ambitions.

Escape No 1 – The tragic loss of HMS *Barham*

Pressurized by Churchill to support Operation Crusader – the breakout from Tobruk – Admiral Cunningham took *Queen Elizabeth* to sea again on

24 November, accompanied by the other battleships *Barham* and *Valiant* and screened by eight destroyers along the Egyptian/Libyan coast off the Gulf of Sollum, waiting for the Eighth Army's requests to bombard any part of the coast.

At 1625 on the following day, the three battleships were steaming in echelon on the starboard leg of a zig-zag pattern, when a German submarine (*U-331*), commanded by Captain Tiesenhausen, managed to penetrate the destroyer screen at periscope depth, intent on sinking the *Queen Elizabeth*, as he knew it was the C-in-C's flagship. However, he then found himself too close to her to fire effectively, so he turned towards *Barham*, the next ship in line. She was hit by three torpedoes from point blank range, whilst *Queen Elizabeth* immediately executed an emergency turn to starboard and increased speed to 22 knots. Paymaster Midshipman Stoke was on deck watching in awe at the dreadful spectacle in front of him, in the knowledge that there were other midshipmen he knew on board who would not survive.

Barham's magazine exploded spectacularly, and the 33,000-ton battleship sank in full view of the Fleet and a newspaper cameraman in just four unbelievable minutes. *U-331*'s forward section broke surface for forty-five seconds, but before any of the destroyers could drop depth charges, it dived under *Valiant*, descending very quickly to a depth of more than 200 metres, and escaped.

Admiral Cunningham described what happened, from his position on *Queen Elizabeth*:

At about 1625 on 24 November, when the battle fleet was patrolling between Crete and Cyrenaica, I was sitting in the bridge cabin having tea. I suddenly heard and half-felt the door give three distinct rattles, and thought we had opened fire with our anti-aircraft guns. I went quickly up to the bridge, and then I saw *Barham*, immediately astern of us, stopped and listing heavily over to port. The thuds I had heard were from three torpedoes striking her. She had been torpedoed by a U-boat. The poor ship rolled nearly over on to her beam ends, and we saw the men massing on her upturned side. A minute or two later there came the dull rumble of a terrific explosion as one of her main magazines blew up. The ship became hidden in a great cloud of yellowish-black smoke, which went wreathing and eddying high into the sky. When it cleared, *Barham* had disappeared.

There was nothing but a bubbling, oily-looking patch on the calm surface of the sea, dotted with wreckage and the heads of swimmers. It was ghastly to look at, a horrible and awe-inspiring spectacle. The destroyers were quickly on the scene, some to hunt the U-boat, others to pick up survivors. But though the U-boat had broken surface after firing the three torpedoes and passed so close down the side of *Valiant* that the guns could not be sufficiently depressed to hit, contact was never made.

Eight hundred and six men lost their lives, as well as Captain Cooke and fifty-five officers. Many of the survivors sustained horrible injuries through sliding down the ship's bottom as she rolled over. The *Barham* had been at sea for six months and the barnacles had grown to an enormous size in the warm Mediterranean waters.

After picking up survivors, the rest of the Fleet returned immediately to Alexandria. One of those lost on board *Barham* was Midshipman William Hickling, the son of Captain Hickling, Stoke's captain in *Glasgow* and the Inshore Squadron in the Western Desert. Stoke wrote a letter of condolence to Hickling, which was later kindly acknowledged in Vice-Admiral Hickling's letter to Stoke's parents in 1947:

> Your lad was a pal of my boy William – they were in the Gunroom together – and he wrote me a very nice letter when our lad – a midshipman of nineteen – was killed in the *Barham*. I never replied to his letter though I appreciated it very much. There is nothing else to say when these tragedies happen.

* * *

Due to the highly sensitive news of the loss of a very important battleship so soon after *Warspite* and *Ark Royal*, there was an embargo on reporting it, so no mention of the sinking is made in any of Stoke's next letters. The only reference was in a letter from *Carlisle*, some four months later, after the news had been released publicly.

15 March
The Med Fleet was used for two purposes. As a decoy to attract the enemy's bombers away from the Western Desert and also to bombard. We were on decoy mission when the *Barham* was torpedoed about 100 yards astern of the *QE*. I saw her heel and blow up all within five minutes of being struck.

* * *

Whether or not this incident affected Cunningham more than usual, the fact remains that the *Queen Elizabeth* remained in Alexandria from 26 November until the end of December. Pearl Harbor was attacked by the Japanese on 6 December, bringing the USA into the war, and the siege of Tobruk was lifted on 8 December 1941.

* * *

9 December

This is scheduled to reach you on Xmas Day!! At the present time, I feel very confident about the war in general. Today the Huns announced the failure of their Moscow offensive. Libya is becoming another grave for Panzer Divisions. The Far East, it is true, does seem most bewildering. Attack, counter-attack, cut and run make it impossible to establish what is really happening, except we have a heaven-sent opportunity to rid this World of a lot of slugs and worms! (Not exactly a Xmas sentiment!) Happy Xmas!!

14 December

I am hoping to get a flight in a Walrus (the ship's plane) when it goes on an anti-submarine patrol. It will be an experience, especially if we have the misfortune to encounter a Me109! I think in that eventuality, I shall goose-step along the wing, shouting 'Heil Hitler'!

* * *

Escape No 2 – Not so lucky this time in Alexandria

On 15 December the beautiful new cruiser *Galatea* was also torpedoed and sunk by a U-boat within 29 miles of Alexandria, demonstrating how vulnerable the British Fleet was to underwater attack. On this occasion, out of a ship's company of 600, just thirteen officers and 129 ratings survived.

Admiral Cunningham, based on his flagship *Queen Elizabeth* in Alexandria, recalled in his diary:

On 19 December something very unpleasant happened in Alexandria. We had suspected for some time that the Italians planned an attack on our battleships. We had information that they possessed some sort of submersible explosive motor-boat which could travel on the surface or under the water, and was fitted with apparatus for lifting nets, which enabled it to pass under our normal defences. Besides the boom and the net defence at the harbour entrance, each battleship was surrounded by a floating net as a protection against torpedoes, human or otherwise.

Another midshipman, Adrian Holloway, was writing up his daily journal at the same time on board *Valiant*, moored next to Stoke on the *Queen Elizabeth*. He noted that the floating nets around each ship had only been put in place the previous day. After the war, he also had extensive correspondence with the Italian leader of the attack, Lieutenant Luigi Durand de la Penne, and one of his other colleagues, Commander Marceglia, so his account is likely to be rather more accurate:

The morning of the 18 December dawned bright and clear with no wind and the sea like the proverbial millpond. The C-in-C recognized the possible dangers and later sent out the following general signal: 'Attacks on Alexandria by air, boat or human torpedo may be expected when calm weather prevails. Lookouts and patrols should be warned accordingly.'

That evening the boom gate was operating like a zoo turnstile on a Bank Holiday and was open no less than three times that fateful night for a total of just over six hours. De la Penne approached the breakwater at 2300. He recalls that a large motorboat moved in front of him dropping small explosives into the water from time to time. This was in fact the *Queen Elizabeth*'s duty picket boat. Harbour lights were suddenly turned on and he realized ships were about to enter. He rode the bow wave of the first cruiser, then went underneath and came through the boom rounding the stern of the third cruiser undetected.

De la Penne was having difficulty with his submersible suit as it continually leaked and he got colder and colder in the water. Fifty yards from *Valiant* he came up against the anti-torpedo boom dropped round the ship only the previous day! He could not get through, but somehow, managed to go over, even with his Chariot [manned torpedo]. When only seven metres from *Valiant*, de la Penne submerged and with very cold hands unable to control the chariot, misjudged the distance and hit the hull, but nobody heard! Unable to fully grip with his cold hands, the chariot slipped out of his hands, falling seventeen metres to the bottom. He was unable to start it and had to drag it (effectively a 500lb explosive) towards the underneath of the hull across the bottom of the harbour mud.

After forty minutes, he managed to position his explosive chariot just five feet underneath *Valiant* and set the fuses.

At about 0315, very tired, cold and totally exhausted, de la Penne swam down the starboard side of *Valiant*, found his colleague Bianci who was sat on the bow buoy. De la Penne clambered up on to the buoy and within a few minutes they were both discovered by the forward sentry and taken on board. At 0332 the C-in-C made another signal advising it was suspected human torpedoes were inside the harbour. All ships were ordered to pass bottom lines and drop explosive charges, but as the explosive was on the sea bed, five feet below the hull and not attached, nothing was found!! The two Italians gave nothing away and were then confined below.

Cunningham again:

I was called in my cabin on board the *Queen Elizabeth* with the news that two Italians had been found clinging to the bow buoy of the *Valiant*. They had been taken on board and interrogated; had said nothing and been sent ashore under arrest. I at once ordered them to be brought back to the *Valiant* and confined in one of the forward compartments below the waterline.

As the time approached for the explosives to detonate, the prisoners got very restless and asked to see the Captain to explain what was about to happen. We found out later that luckily they had been unable to clamp the explosive charge to the *Valiant*'s bilge keels; but had dropped it on the bottom of the harbour, about fifteen feet below.

Holloway's journal records:

The two Italians were first taken ashore and then returned to a secure cell in the bottom of *Valiant*'s hull. At 0547 an explosion occurred under the stern of the Norwegian tanker *Sagona*. The bottom line was again passed under *Valiant* but nothing was found. In the *Queen Elizabeth* the bottom line fouled abreast the foremost gun turret and could not be cleared.

At 0550, de la Penne passed a message to the Captain that he had just ten minutes to clear his ship, but wouldn't tell him where the explosive was attached. Eventually, the ship's watertight doors and hatches were closed, but it wasn't until 0555 that the Captain announced, 'All hands on deck, immediately.'

At 0606 an explosion occurred on the port side of *Valiant* and she was heavily down by the bow but there were no casualties. De la Penne incarcerated below remarkably survived. As *Valiant* listed he could see the water through his porthole and thought he might drown. He could see no way of escape and in desperation tried the exit door to his steel compartment. Remarkably, it opened and there were no guards! He wandered upstairs, arriving on the fo'c's'le, to be met by a very surprised Commander Reid and other crew members.

But exactly as de la Penne arrived, there was another loud explosion aft of *Valiant*. This time it was the *Queen Elizabeth*, which immediately flooded A, B and X boiler rooms and cut off all light and power. Two submarines were ordered alongside to provide power. Although listing to starboard, this was corrected by counter-flooding. There were further small explosions near the *Sagona*, intended to set alight any oil that would have escaped from the tanker. The Italians had scored three out of three with spectacular success.

Cunningham again:

Just before 0600 when I was on the quarter-deck of the *Queen Elizabeth*, there was a violent explosion under the stern of the tanker *Sagona*, lying close to the *Queen Elizabeth* with the *Jervis* alongside. Both the tanker and *Jervis* were badly damaged. About twenty minutes later I saw another heavy explosion under the *Valiant*'s fore turret and four minutes after that, when I was right aft in the *Queen Elizabeth* by the ensign staff, I felt a dull thud and was tossed about five feet into the air by the whip of the ship. I saw a great cloud of black smoke shoot up the funnel and knew at once the ship was badly damaged. The *Valiant* was already down by the bows.

The *Queen Elizabeth* took a heavy list to starboard. Three of our boiler rooms were flooded, and we were unable to raise steam. We stabilized her by flooding the opposite compartment, but with thousands of tons of water in the ship the *Queen Elizabeth* was very low in the water. On investigation there was a forty feet square hole under the two foremost boiler rooms.

In spite of her disablement, I continued to occupy my quarters on board, in order to deceive the enemy that she was undamaged! I even ordered the ceremony of hoisting of the colours with a guard and band and myself on the quarter deck!

Both the *Queen Elizabeth* and *Valiant* had fortunately been moored in shallow water, and as their draught had been increased to 42ft, still had plenty of superstructure showing, so from a distance it looked as if they had survived. The full ceremonial rituals continued to be performed and smoke came out of their funnels. However, it is most unlikely the Italians and Germans were fooled, with so many 'neutrals' in Alexandria happy to pass on information to the enemy. Holloway recognized how close the whole event had come to becoming even more tragic a disaster than the *Barham*, just three weeks earlier:

> If the explosive had been attached to *Valiant*'s hull and the *Queen Elizabeth*'s nearer its ammunition magazines, 3,000 naval servicemen could have lost their lives and the oil from the *Sagona* set the whole of Alexandria harbour aflame, where the rest of the Mediterranean Fleet was moored.

Holloway inspected the underneath of the hull when *Valiant* was in dry dock a few days later. There was damage along almost 80ft of her keel. 'A' magazine was very close. Holloway realized they had been very, very lucky.

So, in late 1941, the Royal Navy had lost one battleship (*Barham*) and had four seriously damaged (*Queen Elizabeth*, *Valiant*, *Warspite* and *Nelson*); one aircraft carrier sunk (*Ark Royal*) and two seriously damaged (*Illustrious* and *Formidable*); seven cruisers sunk and seven seriously damaged; and thirty-three destroyers sunk or seriously damaged. Cunningham and his Mediterranean battle fleet were at their lowest ebb at the end of 1941. Despite the Army's initial success with the breakout from Tobruk, the first three months of 1942 in the Mediterranean were to prove an even greater challenge.

* * *

28 December

All being well this will be my last day in the *QE*. I have wired you, so you should now know I am going to the *Carlisle*. I'm not sorry to leave, as I should get a more varied time (if a little <u>too</u> exciting) and more friendliness.

The *Queen Elizabeth* is and has been for the last three months the Flagship of the C-in-C Mediterranean, Admiral Cunningham. We have seen our 'fun' and also the honour of visits by men like Sikorski [the Polish Prime Minister in exile], Auchinleck, Niyan of Mysore, American 'Observers', Oliver Lyttelton, the Minister of State etc.

Xmas here wasn't too bright, but I'm not surprised. Talk about homesick. Better not, else the ink will be too diluted!! Hoping you are all in perfect trim.

* * *

Stoke was immediately transferred in Alexandria to the AA light cruiser *Carlisle* the next day. In a letter a week later he reflected on his time in the *Queen Elizabeth*.

4 January 1942
The Captain of the *QE* said he was sorry to have me go. I'm afraid I did not bother to tell you much about the *QE* – I wasn't interested in her much. I was learning a Captain's Secretary's job – a stooge, not as I am now. Conditions in the mess were poor and the Gunroom was grossly overcrowded – we had thirty-seven in it – designed for twelve. Leisure wasn't plentiful but I did manage some rugger. Enclosing my 'flimsy' from the *QE*.

*   *   *

Captain C.B. Barry KBE, CB, DSO, then aged fifty and later promoted Rear-Admiral, Naval Secretary and Director of Dockyards, signed Stoke's S.206, the confidential report sent to the Admiralty:

> A particularly keen and able young officer. He has profited by his varied experiences and promises to be an outstanding officer. Charming manner, good mixer, will take on anything. Very good socially. Plays games well and hard.

He signed Stoke's 'flimsy', finishing with: 'Stoke served to my entire satisfaction. A particularly keen and able young Officer. Should do well.'

Midshipman Stoke's next assignments on some of the most dangerous convoys to Malta in early 1942 would test his resilience and courage to the full and beyond.

Chapter 7

Malta Convoys MF3, MF4 and MF5

A 'Sitting Duck'

HMS Carlisle
Alexandria
4 January 1942

Dear Mummy and Daddy,

This week is too full!! I've changed ships, had New Year and received two letters! I've joined *Carlisle*. She is a 4,000 tons cruiser – the lightest and smallest afloat, first commissioned in 1918. She is purely AA, having 8 x 4-inch guns, one four-barrelled pom-pom plus several other secret devices!! [She was the first ship to be fitted with Type 280 combined air warning and gunnery radar]. She's no protection practically, only moves at fastest speed of twenty-two knots, has a motion which has to be experienced to be believed. She even rolls at anchor in harbour!

The Commanding Officer is Captain D.M.L. Neame. There are twenty-one Ward Room officers and four Warrant Officers and just over 300 ratings. I am the Ship's Second Accountant Officer looking after the Naval Stores, Victualling and Pay Office. It will be an interesting job and certainly the mess is extraordinarily happy. The ship itself is not perfectly comfortable – in fact there are none less so. Nevertheless, I think I shall be happy, at least until the ship gets sunk!

At New Year, as I am the youngest officer on board, I carried out the traditional custom of ringing sixteen bells. Needless to say, the bell rope had been deliberately and thoroughly soused in jam. Then we went to the Captain's cabin and he treated us to some hot rum punch. This punch was good. It was a brown liquid with lemons at the bottom. He said it was innocuous, but on being pressed, did say it contained rum, brandy, whisky and curaçao with an equal amount of boiling water. He then ladled out the firewater into glasses. Talk about sizzle.

* * *

Admiral Cunningham recorded that he personally found the naval situation in the Eastern Mediterranean in the New Year of 1942 depressing in the extreme:

> There was no reduction in our commitments, while our resources to meet them were greatly diminished. Because of the heavy bombing of Malta our air reconnaissance was sparse and therefore, we were without the necessary intelligence. In January 1942, Malta had just one reconnaissance aircraft.

Cunningham accordingly sent the following message to the Admiralty on 10 January:

> The seriousness of the situation now developing must be accepted. In the face of the enemy's strength, our existing surface forces are powerless to intervene. Unless some naval and strong air reinforcements are shortly forthcoming, I can't see how Malta can be maintained. Nor can a seaborne attack on Malta be ruled out, particularly observing the increased scale of air attack to which they are now being exposed.

Cunningham had no battleships and only Vian's 15th Cruiser Squadron (CS15), consisting of just three cruisers, the anti-aircraft cruiser *Carlisle* and the sorely depleted destroyer and submarine flotillas. Opposing the British forces, the Italians had four battleships, three 8-inch gun cruisers, three light cruisers, thirty-one destroyers and ninety-one submarines.

Despite the shortage of air cover, the strength of the Italian Navy and the mounting danger from U-boats, Cunningham decided to send in another convoy to Malta of four more merchant ships, code-named Operation MF3, which departed on 16 January 1942.

Stoke wrote home on 11 January:

> I am well settled in to my ship now and expect to go to sea very shortly on a fairly exciting job – certainly a little too much so, I think.

Operation MF3, January 1942

This 'fairly exciting job' was to escort two convoys – MW8A (SS *Ajax* and SS *Thermopylae*) and MW8B (SS *Clan Ferguson* and SS *City of Calcutta*) through to Malta. Less than twenty-four hours from leaving, Cunningham's worst fears materialized. The destroyer *Gurkha* escorting MW8B was making 18 knots at

0738 when an echo was reported to starboard. *Gurkha*'s captain, Commander Charles Lentaigne recalled:

> A matter of seconds after the report of the echo, the torpedo hit on the starboard aft. I was thrown down on the deck of the bridge. Both engines were stopped owing to the failure of the forced lubrication pumps and the snapping of the starboard propeller shaft. There was also flooding, with the sea already breaking over the quarter-deck, and two fires burning. The first an oil fuel fire spreading on the surface of the water. The second fire fed by the ready use ammunition.

By 0820 *Gurkha* was showing signs of floundering, and preparations were made to abandon ship. Able Seaman Frank Hall was on the morning watch, facing aft against the bridge on B gun deck and savouring a cuppa, when the torpedo hit:

> *Gurkha* suddenly trembled. Flags running up the mast denoted a submarine attack. We ditched the ammunition from the lockers, but the bows began to rise out of the water. The sea was on fire. Finally, the skipper gave the order to abandon ship, so I jumped from B deck. I went down quite deep. It seemed to take an age to begin to struggle towards the surface and I remember thinking of my mother and how she would grieve the loss of her eldest son. I broke surface and swam towards the *Isaac Sweers*.

An hour later, four bombs were dropped close on *Carlisle*'s starboard beam but caused no damage either to her or to *Thermoplylae*. Later that evening, *Thermopylae* began to experience steering difficulties, and the next morning, during further enemy air raids, bombs dropped close on *Carlisle*'s stern quarter. *Thermopylae* continued to lag behind the convoy, and eventually *Carlisle* was detached to escort her, initially to Benghazi, later to Alexandria, with additional destroyer escorts *Havock* and *Arrow*.

The commanding officers of *Arrow* (A.M. McKillop) and *Havoc* (G.R.G. Watkins) described the chaos of the events of the following morning, 19 January:

> At 0932, three Ju.88 aircraft were sighted circling towards the sun. Then one went into a steep dive, releasing four bombs at about 1,000 feet and despite being engaged by our short and long–range weapons, at 0942

obtained one hit and three near misses on *Thermopylae*, which slowed down and went beam to wind. A fire broke out amidships.

Carlisle sent an emergency signal back to Alex W/T, 'Help. Boxer Two' and ordered *Havock* and *Arrow* to close *Thermopylae* to pick up those onboard, whilst she remained at Action Stations to provide AA cover against the enemy aircraft. Unfortunately, men were already seen jumping over the side of *Thermopylae*. At 1009 *Havock* was ordered to go alongside before many more jumped. This proved impossible as too many men were now jumping into the sea. *Havock* was forced to stop just to windward as she was crushing men as she drifted alongside. *Arrow* decided to approach the opposite lee-bow, drifting in parallel with *Thermopylae* and picking up several swimming men who had missed *Havock* when they jumped.

When the Master came onboard, he said that one of the bombs had penetrated the mess room and the engine room where much oil had caught fire. He had ammunition and forty two-ton bombs immediately adjoining the engine room and his pumps were out of action, so he ordered abandon ship. However, this was taken by some military and other ranks to mean immediately to jump into the sea. Several lives were thus lost, since nearly all those who remained onboard reached *Havock* dry. Having picked up all survivors, at 1130 *Arrow* fired two torpedoes which sank *Thermopylae*. Four were brought onboard dead and were buried at sea at 1210.

*   *   *

19 January
Today's letter is a day late, but we have only just secured alongside. We have just covered a convoy to Malta. Excitement was pretty tense and we were at Action Stations for five days running. Still, we're back. The weather this last trip has been foul – gun'nalls under <u>all</u> the time and water everywhere in the ship – she leaks something horrible! Still we are all happy together and so what does a little discomfort matter.

23 January
Just a very hurried note as I have just heard we are to sail again and we shall be out for more time covering convoys to and from Malta, thus being away on Sunday, my regular writing day. I'm hoping for a successful run and a dry return.

*   *   *

Operation MF4, January 1942

Carlisle sailed at 1619 on 24 January as escort to *Breconshire* with cruisers *Naiad*, *Dido* and *Euryalus* and a screen of eight destroyers. The plan was to hand *Breconshire* over to Force K (cruiser *Penelope* and five destroyers) from Malta and return to Alexandria with two empty merchant ships (*Glengyle* and *Rowallan Castle*) that would come with Force K from Malta.

There were persistent air attacks for five hours on 25 January, and many emergency turns to avoid torpedo bombs and mines spotted in the water, but *Carlisle* and the convoy arrived safely back in Alexandria on 28 January. The Governor of Malta was appreciative of the convoy and sent the following signal to Cunningham on 30 January 1942: 'We are most grateful for the valuable convoy which has arrived this week. It has greatly helped and encouraged us and I know how delicate an operation was involved.'

Woodman in his book *Malta Convoys* noted that the comparative ease with which this operation had been carried out was not to last. Admiral Cunningham recognized that to protect convoys to Malta it was necessary to hold on to the western aerodromes in Cyrenaica to provide a base for Allied fighters, but on 25 January Benghazi fell for the second time:

> It was particularly galling as the Navy had just got it operating again! We withdrew from Derna on 1 February and fell back again towards Tobruk. Any convoy to Malta now had to pass through the narrow 200-mile gap between Crete on the north and the bulge of Cyrenaica on the south, both in German hands. I pointed out to the Admiralty the damage done by the Army giving up land in Cyrenaica. We thus faced a period when convoys to Malta could only be carried out at very great hazard, as there was a long stretch over which no air cover could be provided. At the same time, we had no battle fleet to act as a deterrent to the Italian heavy ships.

* * *

1 February
Here we are still smelling of salt! We have just come in from running a convoy to Malta. It's not too good these days with the Hun back in Benghazi. Still, all ended well and the Hun has a few more to mourn.

* * *

From the limited information available in Admiralty press releases, the newspapers always saw the upside of most actions. The *Illustrated London News*, dated 14 February 1942, reported on this last convoy:

Mediterranean Convoy: Five-Hour Attack Is Beaten Off

Escorted by cruisers and destroyers, a large British convoy steaming in the Mediterranean was subjected to a long and fierce attack by waves of over one hundred German and Italian aircraft. These photos show some of the tense moments. Twisting and turning, and with anti–aircraft guns blazing the convoy continued on its way until the enemy aircraft were finally beaten off. Once again, the convoy got through.

Operation MF5 February 1942. *Carlisle* a 'sitting duck'

Operation MF5 was to escort convoys MW9A and MW9B to Malta and ME10 from Malta to Alexandria. The possibility of success was much lower than in previous operations, as the enemy had ejected the Army from Western Cyrenaica and therefore had control of the airfields, and largely neutralized the Malta fighters. Air superiority now rested with the Luftwaffe and Italian pilots based on airfields in Sicily, Cyrenaica, Greece and Crete. As Cunningham stated in a letter on 10 February to the First Sea Lord, Pound: 'I am now informed that the fighter situation in Malta has deteriorated to such an extent that it is doubtful if any effective fighter protection can be afforded to incoming convoys.'

Carlisle departed Alexandria at 1600 on 12 February, in company with destroyers *Lance, Heythrop, Avon Vale* and *Eridge* as escort to convoy MW9A consisting of *Clan Campbell* and *Clan Chattan*.

Attacks started early the next day. At 0937 a Ju.88 approached on a westerly bearing, dived and dropped a stick of three or four small bombs on the starboard side of *Clan Chattan* but caused no damage. During the forenoon numerous other hostile aircraft were detected and engaged.

At 1722 another four bombs dropped very close to *Clan Campbell*, who reported that she was leaking and that a bunker was flooding. The captain thought he might be able to make Tobruk. Ten minutes later, another Ju.88 dropped four bombs on *Carlisle* as she manoeuvred to avoid a mine, but they landed one cable length ahead.

Southwold with Convoy MW9B (consisting of just *Rowallan Castle*) joined up with MW9A at 1800. While the two convoys were joining up, there were about eight fighters in the vicinity which appeared on *Carlisle*'s RDF, but *Carlisle*'s officers could not tell if they were friendly or hostile! Whilst *Carlisle* was engaging a target on her port beam, a Ju.88 dived from cloud on to the *Clan Campbell*, which was about five cables off *Carlisle*'s starboard bow. Its bombs were near misses but caused some damage.

Carlisle and the two convoys were joined early the next morning by Vian's cruisers and destroyers. The fleet was then subjected to continuous enemy air attacks throughout the day, and U-boats were also detected. Speed had to be reduced to eight knots so that *Rowallan Castle* could keep up.

At 1345 a number of Ju.88s attacked the convoy from astern. *Clan Chattan* was hit, a fire started and she stopped. *Carlisle* was ordered to stand by to provide AA cover as the aft part of the ship was burning furiously, whilst *Southwold* and other destroyers took off survivors. While still being bombed at 1500, the empty merchant ships from Malta, *Clan Ferguson*, *City of Calcutta*, *Ajax* and *Breconshire*, were exchanged for the heavily loaded *Rowallan Castle* with much needed stores for Malta, whilst *Carlisle* protected *Decoy* as she sank *Clan Chattan*.

The Ju.88s now pounced on *Rowallan Castle*. As one crew member recalled:

Several Ju.88s came from different directions, dropping their loads all around until one put a stick of bombs right along our port side. An enormous wall of water rose. It felt as if the ship had taken a leap in the water.

Like *Clan Chattan*, *Rowallan Castle* slowed to a stop, her fuel lines fractured. Cunningham gave the order for her to be torpedoed to deny the enemy the satisfaction of sinking her. The westbound convoy had now ceased to exist, and no desperately needed cargo got through to Malta.

Carlisle, together with the cruiser and destroyer escorts, had turned back for Alexandria, still subject to continuous high-level bombing attacks. Worse was now to befall *Carlisle*. At 1750 on 14 February a main steam pipe fractured and she could produce no power. She thus became a sitting target for the expert Luftwaffe pilots. Captain Neame's Letter of Proceedings, typed later by Paymaster Stoke, reads:

Whilst stationed on the starboard quarter of Convoy ME10, a steam pipe fractured in *Carlisle*'s forward engine room, necessitating the abandonment of the engine room and the shutting off of main steam in order to locate the damage in position 34.54N 20.58E. *Eridge* and *Beaufort* were ordered to stand by.

Between 1800 and 1850 three attacks were carried out on *Carlisle* while stopped. During these attacks *Carlisle* was straddled amidships by two 500lb delayed action bombs, both of which near missed, causing engine-room damage, and aft by four smaller bombs. A further stick fell in the sea two cables ahead. At 1830 five more aircraft attacked the three ships, and *Eridge* and *Beaufort* were also near missed by four small bombs.

The defect was made good by 1853 and *Carlisle* was able to proceed at 20kts to rejoin the other ships returning to Alexandria. At 2000, during the last enemy attack of the day, *Eridge* was again near missed.

With the power restored, *Carlisle* and her crew had had a very lucky escape. They continued at Action Stations for the next twenty-four hours against both high level bombers and U-boats; a number of fast emergency turns were required to avoid the latter's torpedoes.

Cunningham noted that after four days of almost continuous action, the three cruisers *Naiad*, *Dido* and *Euryalus* had expended some 3,700 rounds of 5.25-inch ammunition, which represented a serious depletion of the reserves available in Alexandria. He wrote to the First Sea Lord:

I fear our attempt to run a convoy into Malta has failed and has cost us two valuable merchant ships. It appears useless to try to pass a convoy until the air situation in Malta and military situation in Cyrenaica have been restored.

*   *   *

18 February

I am sorry that this letter is a little late being written but as you may remember when this does reach you, we have just returned from another Malta job. The papers have given it a big write-up both here and at home. They say that we lost two merchant ships and one of HM Ships suffered a little minor damage. That was quite correct. It was the good ship *Carlisle*. This is the story.

We had been shaken about quite a deal by many bombing attacks and then at 1750 on the return part of the trip, a main steam pipe in our forward engine room burst. To locate the damage, main steam had to be cut off. We were therefore motionless for over an hour. The convoy and escort steamed on so that we were alone for this period with two small destroyers. All our gunnery control went as power went.

The ship was in darkness between decks for the same reason. During this period the guns – already fired over their safety limit – fired in local control i.e. by eye! We were straddled at least twice by two sticks of 500lb bomb but not hit. We eventually got going again and managed to rejoin the convoy. We had fired over 1,500 round of 4-inch in the afternoon.

When we got back to harbour, we learnt that the two destroyers were sent to stand by us to pick up survivors! They thought we had no chance. And nor did we. Still you can see how successful we have been in the paper. I am enclosing a newspaper cutting from the local rag, though it's against the regulations. We are at Action Stations all the time being an AA cruiser and all our meals are just bully beef sandwiches.

I have been a little unlucky lately. I got a game of rugger against a far bigger cruiser the other day and we won. I scored four tries, but in running through their entire team to score my last I hurt my left ankle. The bone is rather badly bruised and I have been hobbling now for ten days. I am having it X-rayed tomorrow to confirm it is quite sound.

20 February
I have been having a fairly exciting time out here. Our principal job is protecting convoys to and from Malta. We have unfortunately no fighter protection for the majority of the trip. Last time we had fifty-four bombing attacks and for one hour we were stationary, alone, whilst the Fleet carried on without us! We were near missed and only sustained slight damage except to my expectation of life!

*   *   *

Another eyewitness account of the action was recorded sixty years later by Vic Chanter, a signal rating onboard *Eridge*, which stood by *Carlisle*. Chanter was only four months older than Stoke:

Two days before my twenty-first birthday, on 7 February 1942, I was drafted to HMS *Eridge* to relieve the senior visual signal rating aboard. We put to sea from Alexandria with the cruiser HMS *Carlisle*. We were to escort two merchant vessels westwards. The next day we met up with the main convoy, and enemy aircraft soon spotted and attacked us. The supply ships were obviously the main targets for destruction, whilst the escorts were there to protect with their lives. With such pickings for the enemy, we attracted a sky full of high-level bombers all day. It soon became difficult to spot the aircraft among the ever-increasing black puffs of exploding anti-aircraft shell bursts from *Carlisle*. I witnessed the distressing sight of the supply ship *Clan Chattan* being hit and quickly sinking. At 1900 we were the target for a full stick of bombs, which straddled us, covering us on the bridge with grey gunge. It was the nearest in a crop of near misses throughout the day.

Another rating, Able Seaman John Ellis, was on the destroyer *Jervis*, in Rear-Admiral Vian's covering force:

14 February. Convoy escorted by six Hunt class and the AA cruiser *Carlisle* are being attacked by aircraft. We 'pinged' a sub and drop depth charges, pass several floating mines on the starboard beam. Action stations from 1330 to dusk. Dive bombed all through the night aided by dropping flares. One merchant ship, *Clan Chattan*, hit and set on fire. *Carlisle* and one Hunt stand by to rescue crew.

15 February. At dawn we meet up with convoy from Malta. We are continuously being dive bombed whilst the convoys are changing over. Shrapnel is falling down on us like rain, several are hurt; a stick of bombs from Stukas drops near our stern and shakes the ship from stem to stern. When darkness falls the German bombers keep dropping some hundreds of flares and bomb us endlessly. The sea is all lit up making a beautiful picture together with Ack-Ack fire, especially the Breda colours. We remain at Action Stations all night. All next day attacked by Ju.88s, one bomb drops near our stern. At 1600, three torpedo bombers came in very low and almost catch us by surprise. Captain goes full ahead. I saw the torpedoes leave the plane. I thought we'd had it, but the torpedoes just passed under us. Very lucky that was. Savoia bombers come in and machine gun us, but no casualties.

The 'official' version, released at that time, painted a rather different picture! The Admiralty issued a press release that was upbeat and very economical with the truth, as reported on the front page of the *Egyptian Mail* of 19 February:

British Convoys Get Through Mediterranean– Navy Foils All Attacks

Admiralty communiqué

The operations took place between 13–16 February. No casualties in personnel were suffered either by His Majesty's ships or merchant ships in the convoy. Only superficial damage was caused to one of His Majesty's ships. Two merchant ships were damaged and were subsequently sunk by our forces. During the air attacks, the enemy lost five planes for certain, and four more were probably destroyed.

The *Egyptian Mail* devoted a whole page to an eyewitness account of the action by John Nixon, Reuter's Special Correspondent with the Mediterranean Fleet:

From the bridge of Rear-Admiral Vian's Flagship *Naiad*, I saw warships for hour after hour put up a terrific barrage which so disconcerted the German and Italian airmen that they only superficially damaged one of the Naval units. In this latest sea and air battle, Britain scored heavily over the Axis. Our total losses were only two merchant ships lost and one slightly damaged, and no casualties in either the warships or merchantmen.

The superstitious amongst us noted we sailed on Friday 13th. The next day, enemy planes were with us from soon after dawn until after dark and gun-crews had little respite throughout twelve hours. We also had submarine alerts, accompanied by the 'crump' of our depth charges. Luncheon consisted of a cup of soup and a roll filled with cold tongue munched standing at action stations, while watching six enemy aircraft hovering above the convoy. Another attack developed. Our bridge quaked as our guns hurled steel skywards. Bombs were falling all round and the sky was plastered with bursting shells, which prevented any other bombers aiming accurately. The bombers tried new tactics as the light failed, dropping flares to light up the convoy.

The next day, on the return, we were eating lunch when the soft, plaintive bugle notes of 'Action Stations' came over the loudspeakers sending us to our posts. First a submarine alert, then three Savoia 79 torpedo-bombers on our starboard beam launched their 'tin fish' and hurried away. An hour later, another three attacked.

Honour the men of the Royal and Merchant Navies who take their ships through these much-bombed waters, subject also to submarines, surface ships and mines. During a brief lull, I heard a pom-pom gunner playing a mouth organ softly to himself. That expressed the attitude of these men to one of the world's most dangerous sea routes.

Another paper, the *Sphere*, reported on the same convoy a couple of weeks later on 14 March 1942. A correspondent who was onboard one of the merchant vessels, *Clan Chattan*, described how he actually witnessed the whole scene from the opening of the bomb doors to the actual explosion of the bombs:

> It was at 1335 in the afternoon when the twin-engined enemy aircraft came plunging out of the clouds: at 4,000 feet it was plain its bombs were labelled for us. *Carlisle* and the other ships, including our own, poured fire on him. But he was a determined devil. With a spine-stiffening whistle, two plump bombs headed straight for our after-deck. Both struck home. They sent a flash of red flame as high as the masts. Peering over the bridge parapet, I watched the bombs during their entire flight, and saw the plane wheel off at a rakish angle and escape. The ship shuddered like a rat shaken by a terrier. Instantly black clouds of smoke began billowing from the rear half of the ship. When it was reported by the ship's officers that the fire was beyond control and that the boilers had cracked, myself and the crew abandoned ship.

Carlisle remained in Alexandria for the next four weeks for repairs, before the next big Malta convoy in mid-March. This gave Stoke the opportunity for a well needed rest, some rugger, music and thoughts on his post-war future.

*   *   *

23 February
As a result of the last party, we have had to undergo a small refit for the next ten days for repairs to the ship and some machinery. I must confess that we all feel that a little rest would not be amiss.

My ankle is still most painful. Still I hope it will be all right soon as I am playing for a combined cruisers team at rugger versus a battleship [name censored]. The ground is getting very hard as the 'rainy' season is over. We had a shower last November!

These near misses, apart from shaking up the ship's company, have played havoc with several pieces of equipment. For example, the ship's galley has had to be taken down. It first started cooking in 1917 and as far as I know has never been touched since. The whole ship is easily the most uncomfortable I've been on, especially the lower deck. All I have is a chest of drawers in a passage underneath a hatch which leaks at sea and no place to stow my bags.

My old boss, Captain Poland, is shortly to be relieved of his job in the desert and I have asked him by letter if he will want a Secretary in his next appointment. His next job is to be Captain (D), in charge of the 14th Destroyer Flotilla here in Alexandria – a sea-going job. It would mean I would be in a destroyer and it would complete my line of ships – battleship and flagship, large cruiser, smaller AA cruiser and shore jobs, including trips in minesweepers etc. Not bad variety for just two years of service! [Poland joined destroyer *Jervis* less than a month later, a few days before the Second Battle of Sirte.]

I am wondering what I shall do at the end of the war. At the moment I do feel that I have made quite a good start in the Navy, so that I should probably get to a brass hat. If I do well in my exams in September, it would reinforce that. On the other hand, I feel that after the war there will be many most interesting jobs of reconstruction, though whether at my age with no qualifications or experience I shall get what I think I should deserve is another matter!

7 March

The other interesting thing of late was that a gully-gully man asked if he could give a show onboard. Local pidgin for conjuror. He was very good. He swallowed a sword of course. He did one or two tricks that baffled all of us. He had two officers hold three discs each in their hands. Then one threw his lot over the side. When the other opened his hand … there were six discs! All really first class with a clever patter. He made no charge but passed his fez round.

The Western Desert seems to have quietened down, but still unsatisfactory from the Navy's point of view. We are expected to run convoys to Malta successfully in the teeth of the Hun Air Force based in Cyrenaica, Crete and Sicily and with no fighter support at all. We can and are doing it but sooner or later someone is going to buy it. A look at the map can show you how long an ordinary merchant ship convoy takes to run from Malta to Alex or vice versa. I could devise many better ways of passing the week!

15 March

I see you are sorry I left the *QE*! Of course, she is now as safe as houses and there is no likelihood of danger, whereas in the *Carlisle* we rather feel surprised to see Alexandria again when we manage to hobble back into port.

About the present job and ship. At the moment I am in charge of Stores and the Pay side with a Cash Account. However, shortly, I shall be promoted Secretary and probably stay with *Carlisle* until I get my stripe on 1 September. The *Carlisle* is most uncomfortable and still leaks horribly. Still, I am quite happy, although I would rather be Secretary to Capt. (D) Fourteenth Flotilla – Poland!

Today we had the honour to be inspected at Divisions by no less than the C-in-C, Cunningham. He made a short speech saying we had been through some hard times and should expect harder, until we can stabilize the Far East. Pleasant eh!

*   *   *

Operations MF3, 4 and 5 were preludes to the next operation, MG1, during which the famous Second Battle of Sirte was fought against a vastly superior Italian battle fleet, regarded by Cunningham as 'one of the finest, if not the finest, sea actions of the Second World War'.

Chapter 8

Malta Convoy MG1

The Second Battle of Sirte and Bombed in Malta

Operation MG1 in March 1942 was to escort convoy MW10 of four merchant ships (*Breconshire, Talabot, Pampas and Clan Campbell*) with urgently needed stores, fuel and ammunition for Malta. Paymaster Midshipman Stoke was still on the cruiser *Carlisle*, which was providing the major anti-aircraft protection with the Hunt class destroyers. The covering force was just three cruisers from Rear-Admiral Vian's Fifteenth Squadron (CS15), as Cunningham's Mediterranean Fleet was now without aircraft carriers, battleships or even heavy cruisers with which to oppose the Italian Fleet, and at the mercy of the Luftwaffe and Italian pilots based in Cyrenaica, Sicily, Greece and Crete. Even Cunningham, ever the optimist, was showing concern for the next convoy. On 15 March, he wrote to Pound:

> I can't conceal from you that I look on this next Malta convoy operation which starts tomorrow with some apprehension. If we are lucky with the weather, all may be well, but if not, we may easily lose the convoy and a ship or two as well. The cruisers' AA ammunition is a cause for anxiety. If the Italians in strength make contact with Rear-Admiral Vian's CS15 in the middle is another risk.

The Italian Battle Fleet did make contact during MG1 and with much bigger ships and heavier guns. However, after a harrowing encounter on Sunday, 22 March 1942, in gale force winds and heavy rolling seas, the big Italian battleships and cruisers were outfaced by the smaller, more manoeuvrable and courageous British cruisers and destroyers, protected by a smokescreen laid by *Carlisle* and *Avon Vale*. The actions of the cruisers and destroyers prevented the vastly superior Italian ships from engaging with the convoy. This was later named the Second Battle of Sirte, regarded by Cunningham as one of the finest, if not the finest, sea action in the Second World War.

The Operational Orders for MG1 were planned and issued directly by Admiral Cunningham, headed 'Most Secret – To be destroyed by fire when complied with'. The Orders demonstrate the clear thinking and anticipation of events by Cunningham's team:

Convoy MW10 is most urgently required at Malta. It is the intention to use all available forces to escort the convoy to within a night's run of Malta. Enemy surface forces may endeavour to intercept convoy during Day 3. The enemy should be brought to action by Force B, whilst the convoy should be sent on to Malta with destroyer escort. The convoy should only be turned back if it is evident that the enemy will intercept in daylight.

A speed of advance of twelve knots has been allowed. On D-1, the Fifth Destroyer Flotilla will carry out an anti-submarine sweep. MW10 will then leave at 0700 escorted by *Carlisle* and six destroyers. CS15 plus destroyers (Force B) will sail to rendezvous with MW10 on D+2. The Fifth Destroyer Flotilla is to refuel at Tobruk and meet up with MW10 on D+2. Force K (*Penelope* and *Legion)* will leave Malta after dark to meet the convoy at sea the next morning.

About 1800 on D+3, *Carlisle* and two destroyers are to be detached to return to Alexandria at their best speed. After dark on D+3, Force K and the Fifth Destroyer Flotilla are to escort MW10 to Malta. Submarines have been requested in the approaches to Messina and the approaches to Taranto to look out for any movement by the Italian Navy. As diversionary tactics, the C-in-C Middle East Forces to arrange a military diversion in Cyrenaica and an air offensive.

Over the previous weeks, Vian's force had practised and rehearsed tactics that Vian planned to use on any convoy that was intercepted by the Italian surface forces – he wanted divisions of his ships acting independently to a large extent, with a minimum of signals and using smoke to cover themselves and the convoy. Captain McCall on the cruiser *Dido* said, 'What was achieved was only made possible by teamwork and a complete and utter trust in our leader and he in us.'

At the start of the action, Vian only had to make the signals 'Enemy in sight' and 'Engage the enemy' – the Nelson touch. One of the issues facing the anti-aircraft duties of the close escort group when having to deal with both air and surface attack, was the quick decision as to which target was the more important to engage, because switching from one to the other caused momentary delay. 'Never before', said McCall, 'had we to switch so frequently from surface to anti-aircraft fire.'

The distance between Alexandria and Malta was approximately 900 miles, divided roughly into three sections of 300 miles each. At an average freighter speed of twelve knots this was conveniently divided into three periods of twenty-four hours. Leaving Alexandria at daybreak on D-Day should have meant the convoy arriving in Malta just before dawn on D+3. The route would necessarily pass through 'Bomb Alley' between enemy airfields in Crete and Cyrenaica. Some fighter protection would be provided through the daylight hours of the first two days, but the risk (as already foreseen by Cunningham) was the Italian Fleet during daylight on Day 3, Sunday, 22 March – Passion Sunday!

In summary, Vian's plan in the event of sighting the enemy was to have a striking force (Force B and K) to attack and harass the enemy warship, a division laying smoke to hide the convoy and a close anti-aircraft escort for the convoy. Paymaster Stoke was in the anti-aircraft and smoke-laying division that would protect the convoy, consisting of just two ships, *Carlisle* and *Avon Vale*.

In another typical Nelson touch, Vian dined his Captains in the *Cleopatra* the night before sailing. One had arrived just three days before from his previous twelve months' posting as Senior Naval Officer Inshore Squadron – none other than Captain Poland, Midshipman Stoke's boss in Tobruk. He had been appointed to take command of *Jervis* and to lead the Fourteenth Destroyer Flotilla, and 'his unflappable professionalism and modest personality had made a lasting impression on those in the Tobruk garrisons and the Inshore Squadron.'

The operation got off to a bad start. The six Hunt class destroyers had put to sea on D-1 to carry out the anti-submarine patrol between Alexandria and Bardia, the first leg of the convoy's passage to Malta. Shortly after 1130 on 20 March, *U-652* (under the command of Georg-Werner Fraatz) struck *Heythrop* with four torpedoes from just 1,000 yards. *Eridge* closed to take her in tow, but by 1600 the pumps could not cope and, after transferring the crew, *Eridge* dispatched *Heythrop*. Vic Chanter, a signal rating on *Eridge*, recalled sixty years later for the BBC's *People's War*:

We slipped on 19 March, and, along with the other Hunt class destroyers – *Southwold*, *Dulverton*, *Heythrop* and *Hurworth* – we put to sea for a 'biggie'. This was no convoy up the coast into the ports of Benghazi and Tobruk with supplies for the troops fighting in North Africa. This time we were about to meet up with a far larger force. At 1135 *Heythrop* was struck by torpedoes, the effect of which broke the ship's back. *Heythrop* was finally abandoned. Towlines were slipped and *Dulverton* delivered the *coup de grâce*. It is an awe-inspiring, chilling feeling to see a proud ship go to its grave, and I don't have the words to describe that feeling.

The next day, *Carlisle* cast off at 0740 as main escort for the convoy, led by Captain Hutchinson in *Breconshire*, together with the 22nd Destroyer Flotilla. The day passed quietly as the convoy steamed westward at a bit over 12 knots.

The following morning at 0730, the convoy was joined by the remaining five Hunt class destroyers that had refuelled in Tobruk overnight. At 0834, CS15 – *Cleopatra*, *Dido* and *Euryalus* – together with the 14th Destroyer Flotilla (D14), led by Captain Poland in *Jervis*, were sighted on schedule. So, by the morning of 21 March the combined forces of the cruiser and destroyer flotillas had met up with the convoy, escorted by *Carlisle*, and proceeded west on a zig-zag course, but at a slower speed than anticipated due to engine issues on *Clan Campbell*.

Unfortunately, during the day four unexpected troop-carrying Axis planes flew overhead and reported the position of the convoy, so that Italian and German aircraft at various airfields were alerted.

Meanwhile, light cruiser *Penelope* had departed Malta with destroyer *Legion* to meet up with the convoy. Vian's orders for the convoy were flown to Captain Nicholls in *Penelope*, but she sailed before they arrived. Captain Nicholls, therefore, fought the whole battle, with its fast moving and intricate actions, without having received one word of written or spoken instructions from his Admiral. Yet he was never in doubt as to what was required of him.

That evening, the Italian Messina Fleet (closer to the convoy) left harbour; two heavy cruisers and a light cruiser, escorted by four destroyers. A little later, the Italian Taranto Fleet sailed; battleship *Littorio* (Admiral Iachino), plus six destroyers. British submarine *P36* spotted *Littorio* that night and reported her position to the Mediterranean Fleet. The Messina Fleet was not detected and therefore not reported.

At 0518 on 22 March Rear-Admiral Vian received *P36*'s signal that an Italian battle squadron from Taranto was at sea. The wind was getting up and the Italians were making 22 knots into a head sea with some difficulty. At 0750 Vian altered the course of the convoy a little further south to give more time before he expected enemy ships to be in sight, a little after 1600. Captain Frank Gregory-Smith on *Eridge* thought the escort force looked very impressive:

Three light cruisers, one anti-aircraft cruiser (*Carlisle*), eleven fleet destroyers and six 'Hunts'. In reality it was weak against a superior Italian Navy and the Luftwaffe air superiority, with no fighter protection of our own. The weather was poor, with wind and a rising sea from the southeast. Already our ships were pitching and rolling in the heavy seas. The Italians would be fighting into the wind but might reach the convoy by mid-afternoon. There was no reconnaissance plane available from Malta so we did not know the composition of the Italian fleet. However, it was clear the convoy had to be got through to Malta. I addressed the ship over the tannoy: 'The Hunts and *Carlisle* will stay with the convoy, so we'll probably get a bellyful of bombing.' There would be no turning back.

At 1035 the first torpedo-bombing attacks were made on *Carlisle* and the convoy, but as a result of excellent manoeuvring neither convoy nor escorts were damaged. Lieutenant Commander J. Wright, Naval Liaison Officer onboard SS *Pampas* in ADM 199/681, reported: 'There was a peaceful spell about lunch time and we were able to get a meal in comfort.'

That was short-lived, as about 150 torpedo-, dive- and high level bombers were concentrated during the rest of that day on the convoy, which was protected only by anti-aircraft fire from *Carlisle* and the destroyer escorts. At 1410, smoke from the enemy fleet was sighted, much earlier than expected, by Captain Eric Bush on *Euryalus*, and by 1417 three ships were identified.

Puzzled by the earlier than expected arrival of the Italians, Vian signalled the convoy to continue its course southward to delay contact with the enemy for as long as possible. So, at 1430 Vian's cruisers and destroyers headed north to engage the enemy, while *Carlisle* and *Avon Vale* made smoke to hide the stern of the convoy.

At 1436 the Italians opened fire on *Euryalus* but their shots fell short. The fleets were closing at 50 knots, so the British were soon firing their own guns but finding it difficult to aim accurately as the ships rolled, twisted and plunged through the heavy seas. At 1450 the main combined Italian/German air assault intensified on *Carlisle* and the convoy, reinforcing high level bombing with low, fast torpedo runs. Sixteen attacks were made, predominantly by Ju.88s. Chanter, the signal rating on *Eridge*, recalled:

Oddly enough we had to wait one hour before all hell broke loose. Being such a large convoy invited everything that the Axis powers could throw at us: high-level Ju.88s, dive-bombing Ju.87s, Stukas and torpedo-bombers, and the Italian Fleet for good measure. From the air, the attack was in excess of anything we had so far experienced. Enemy aircraft filled the air like swarms of locusts, whilst the anti-aircraft shell bursts pockmarked the sky above the convoy. As torpedo bombers came in low to discharge their lethal loads, the decision to open fire on them at such low altitudes, across the convoy, was a highly calculated risk. An escort vessel under maximum speed and helm – to evade missiles – gave little help to the gun crews manning the pom-poms and Oerlikons, trying to keep the enemy aircraft in their sights.

Carlisle, with *Avon Vale* in company, was making smoke to cover the convoy and as a result of her movements to avoid the deluge of bombs at 1507, in the smoky murk, the two ships had a glancing collision, but fortunately neither suffered any major damage.

By 1530, after various skirmishes, Vian appeared to have driven off the enemy, signalled the same to Cunningham back in his Ops. Room in Alexandria and returned towards the convoy and *Carlisle*, which had been near missed by the Axis aircraft, which 'didn't come over in ones or twos, they came in thirties and forties!' By mid-afternoon, *Carlisle* had already shot off a third of her anti-aircraft shells, and *Southwold* only had 40 per cent of hers left.

Captain Bush on *Euryalus* recalled:

At 1535 the Italians withdrew and we returned to the convoy. In our absence they had been having an unpleasant time driving off wave after wave of dive-bombers but had suffered no damage, thanks to the fine gunnery of *Carlisle* and her destroyers, and to the admirable handling of the merchant ships by their masters. But at 1637, a larger Italian fleet was sighted, including a battleship. 'Stand by again', I said into the loudspeaker. 'There's more to come!'

This time the attackers included the newly arrived Taranto Fleet. The 15-inch guns of the Italian battleship *Littorio* and the 8-inch guns of three cruisers should have easily seen off the much lighter British ships. They looked a truly formidable force. The Italians under Admiral Iachino had a total broadside of 24,000lbs as against Rear-Admiral Vian's 5,900lbs, part of which was committed to supporting the escort.

The Italian fleet was also greatly helped by their aircraft, unhindered and able to report the movement and position of the convoy. Vian's force continued to lay more smoke, and the Italians, although faster, did not dare penetrate it, as the British destroyers dashed in and out taking quick pot-shots. The *Littorio* opened fire on the flagship cruiser *Cleopatra*, which received a direct hit at 1644. The *Daily Express* correspondent recorded:

> We used our three forward turrets for firing at enemy ships and the two after turrets for firing at aircraft. We were hit on the starboard fore-corner of the bridge, where Admiral Vian normally stood; he was luckily having a quick look at our position in the charthouse. That shell killed an officer and fourteen men and brought down all our radio aerials and signal masts.

At one point, Vian led part of his force east to check the Italians were not trying to get to windward of the smoke. This left *Carlisle* and the convoy exposed to any of the Italian ships sailing westward between the convoy and Malta. Paymaster Stoke on *Carlisle* could see the Italian battleship was within 10 miles of the convoy and would annihilate the convoy and *Carlisle* if the enemy pressed home their advantage. The *Littorio*'s heavy shells then began to appear between the convoy and *Carlisle*. He wrote in a letter after the battle: 'We were the sole HM Ship between the battleship and the convoy! We made smoke and prepared to die valiantly as we were straddled by 15″ bricks, which fortunately missed.'

Not far from *Carlisle*, Lieutenant T.J. McFarlane (ADM 199/681) was on *Talabot*:

> Occasionally glimpses of a cruiser or a destroyer coming through the smoke which were alarming. One was never sure at first whether it was one of our own or an enemy ship. We could also see gun flashes on the horizon to the west of the smokescreen, the direction the convoy was heading. Combined with the columns of water thrown up by the plunging 15-inch shells from *Littorio*, we thought we were for it. We took a very pessimistic view of our prospects of reaching Malta.

Vian's cruisers returned just in time to position themselves between the convoy and the *Littorio* and the other Italian ships. However, the Ju.88s 'were now diving much lower before releasing their bombs' wrote Captain Edkins of the Hampshire Regiment, also on *Talabot* and manning a Bren gun in the action:

> Bombs were fairly whistling down. I saw another stick of bombs pitch almost certainly on the stern of *Clan Campbell*. The weather had really turned foul and we were bouncing all over the place. A stick of four came

crashing down to starboard. The 15-inch splashes were all over the place. Then, directly above us at about 12,000 feet we saw six Ju.88s. They peeled off for a dive–bombing attack. My Brens were loaded. I followed the Ju.88 down the length of the ship. One of our Bredas got him – our first kill. Another Ju.88 came down in a vertical dive; smoke was pouring out from one engine ... the light began to fade and what looked like a torpedo attack came in out of the sun very low. We couldn't see any 'fish' but the Savoia came straight at us, only a couple of hundred feet above the sea. He began to wobble, banked round our bows and went straight into the sea. Shortly afterwards another Ju.88 was shot down to end the party.

Euryalus darted in and out of the smoke, but the Italians were reluctant to make a bold move into the smoke to find the convoy. At 1841 the battleship *Littorio* spotted *Euryalus* through the smoke and sent salvos from her 15-inch guns towards her. Captain Bush was on the bridge:

We were straddled as they plunged into the water all round us, engulfing the ship in columns of water masthead high. The thought of my wife left a widow flashed through my mind but in twenty seconds I was myself again. 'Starboard twenty', I said down the voice-pipe. I knew the only way to save the ship was to alter the range before the next salvo arrived. The situation was critical again, but was turned to our advantage by a most determined torpedo attack at 1845 by Captain Poland and his Fourteenth Flotilla, under cover of our guns and *Cleopatra*'s.

Poland led his destroyers toward the enemy at over 25 knots. At this speed in the gale force wind and high seas, the destroyers were swept from end to end by breaking seas, guard rails went and boats were smashed, as men clung for their lives at action stations. John Mosse recalls trying to keep a track of the enemy movements on *Jervis*:

We fired a broadside, all the lights went out ... the ship heeled over, everything was rattling when a voice behind me said, 'Have a toffee!' The Padre had brought a bag of sweets from the canteen and was distributing them as tranquillisers! By all the rules we should have been blown out of the water.

Poland later recalled the events:

The main impression I have is of quantities of smoke – everywhere – which blocked all view of what was going on. Our smoke was being carried by the wind, forming an impenetrable pall which blotted out everything to the north and west of us. We could see the convoy was being heavily attacked time and time again by large formations of Ju.88s. It seemed inevitable that before long the ships would be damaged or even destroyed, but after each rain of bombs they emerged steaming steadily on towards their destination. There is no doubt they owed their escape to the terrific and accurate fire of *Carlisle* and the escorts which kept attacking planes up high and put them off their aim when they attempted to attack.

Vian, on his flagship *Cleopatra*, had made a general signal to 'attack with torpedoes through smoke if opportunity offers'. Around 1830, the moment seemed propitious. When we emerged through the smoke we saw one enemy ship, larger than expected (later identified as the battleship *Littorio*), and I ordered the flotilla to take up formation for a torpedo attack and speed was increased to twenty-eight knots. Soon after, a second enemy ship appeared out of the haze, also looking remarkably large and then a third and a fourth. They were steaming south-south-west in line ahead. They opened fire with their much bigger guns.

My flotilla returned fire with all the guns that we could bear. We went onto the attack. The range seem to take an unconsciously long time to shorten. When the range of the nearest enemy from *Jervis* was about 7,000 yards, it was grand to see the second ship in the enemy line turning away from us as she lost her nerve. Eventually the range was down to 6,000 yards. We turned all at once – and some twenty-four torpedoes started off towards the enemy line. As soon as we turned to the prearranged course for retiring, our ships started to make smoke to cover our get away, which unfortunately obscured our view of what the enemy was doing.

As dusk fell about 1900, with the Italians having retreated, the convoy headed on to Malta, and Admiral Vian's cruisers and destroyers, who were desperately short of fuel, headed directly back to Alexandria into the teeth of the howling SE gale. The night was most unpleasant. The whole ship was completely flooded and the mess decks feet deep in water. However, it had to be done as we were still very much in 'Tom Tiddler's Ground' and could expect heavy air attacks as long as we were there.

When the last enemy aircraft withdrew at 1850, the convoy was still unscathed, but by now the wind was SSE 7, and as *Carlisle* took station astern again 'she was washing down for'd, though the gun crews were still sticking to their posts.' Whilst the convoy had been protected, the afternoon's battle had pushed them too far south, and it was unlikely that any of the ships would reach Malta before dawn, as had been previously planned. The Axis bombers would have another chance at daybreak.

At 1900 Hutchinson had on his own initiative dispersed the convoy to take different routes to Malta. *Breconshire* increased speed to 17 knots and in the company of *Southwold* and *Beaufort* could have made Malta by dawn, but she swung away further south again, to leave the slow and damaged *Clan Campbell*, escorted by *Eridge*, to head directly for Malta on the shortest route. This detour was to prove fatal.

On *Eridge* that evening, the gun crews found they had nearly used up all their ammunition. 'Fill the lockers with blanks, starshell, smoke and practice shot', the gun crews were instructed. 'They'll at least make a noise if nothing else.' Down in *Eridge*'s forward mess deck, conditions were not any better. Water was coming down the ammunition chutes. Lockers and crockery had been torn from the bulkheads, and broken plates, cups and saucers were piled into a mobile mass amongst a heap of sodden clothing. The deck stank of vomit and funnel fumes. Ratings, sitting or lying in duffel coats or oilskins, were coughing and retching in the foul air. The cook was handing round cordite-covered sandwiches which were not being received with any degree of enthusiasm.

The original orders were for *Carlisle* to return to Alexandria, and so at 1948, she disengaged from the convoy and turned east into the Force 8 SE wind, losing some deck equipment over the side as she rolled in the heavy seas. As dark fell, Cunningham, in Alexandria signalled Vian to detach *Carlisle* from the returning fleet and turn back west to provide AA cover for the rest of the convoy's journey. At 2145 she rejoined *Breconshire*.

Neame now had to take over as senior officer of the convoy, as Vian and his fleet headed east for Alexandria. A very heavy sea was running by this time, making it extremely uncomfortable for the much smaller destroyers. *Carlisle*'s log records: 'Midnight – Wind SSE 9', and at 0400 – 'SSE 7'.

During the night, as the weather was growing steadily worse, two Italian destroyers capsized and sank off Sicily. Heavy cruiser *Trento* was forced away from rescuing the destroyers' crews due to the heavy seas. All the men were lost.

At dawn the next morning, the officers aboard *Pampas* felt the psychological effects of dispersal, observing with a certain amount of trepidation that they were alone. At 0715 a Ju.88 attacked low, out of the haze. One 500lb bomb damaged the forward derricks before bursting over the side, the second dented the funnel but shot over the side unexploded. From then on the *Pampas* was continuously harried by Ju.88s. As Lieutenant Commander Wright of *Pampas* wrote:

> Finding us alone, [they] often came down to below 1,000 feet and sprayed us with machine-gun fire. One Ju.88s came in from the port side and released a bomb not more than ten yards from the ship's side. It exploded under No 4 hold and shook the ship, but she continued to steam and steer. Our spirits rose when at 0830 the *Talabot* with two destroyers were sighted.

On *Talabot*, land had been sighted at 0815, and 'two Hurricanes from Malta appeared over us – a most welcome sight.' *Talabot* passed up the swept channel and was off Ricasoli point, within half a mile of the harbour mole, when she was attacked by Me109s, which dropped small bombs on her without effect. She entered Grand Harbour at 0915, and *Pampas* followed at 0930. Wright wrote:

> The terraces were lined with cheering Maltese and I felt a lump in my throat at our reception. The damaged destroyers *Havock* and *Kingston* passed up the harbour to more cheers from the populace.

Breconshire, meanwhile, with *Carlisle*, *Southwold* and *Dulverton*, had also had a rough start to the morning. At 0755 a Ju.88 dived on her, its bombs exploding in the ship's wake. A second sped in at 0817 to be met with a hail of fire and was driven off. Then at 0920, when the slower *Pampas* and *Talabot* were already in Grand Harbour, and with Delimara Point in sight, the same three Me109s flew just over the ship from port to starboard. All their bombs hit, and the engine room began to flood. Twenty minutes later, a Ju.88 dropped a bomb which exploded beneath *Breconshire* and her engines stopped. She was just 7.6 miles east of Grand Harbour. One rating on *Carlisle* was killed during the action.

If *Breconshire* had carried on at her normal speed direct to Malta she would have arrived safely into Grand Harbour at the same time or ahead of *Pampas* and *Talabot*. The detour was indeed fatal.

At 1000 another Ju.88 made a bombing and strafing run, her bombs passing over the ship to detonate close alongside and further damage her. *Carlisle* stood by in the heavy swell. *Carlisle* was desperately short of ammunition, so left air defence to *Southwold*. Neame manoeuvred to pass a tow wire, but was unsuccessful. *Penelope* emerged from Grand Harbour, having taken on fuel and ammunition during the night, and managed to get a tow secured. However, with the wind having backed slightly to NE 8, in the heavy seas this soon parted and *Breconshire* had to let her two anchors go to prevent her drifting to leeward into a minefield. *Carlisle* entered Grand Harbour, securing at No. 2 berth at 1350.

Carlisle's log at 1600 reported the wind had eased to NE 3, and at 1615 the officer on watch noted in the log that *Eridge* and *Dulverton* entered harbour. The body of the rating killed in the earlier action in the morning on *Carlisle* was disembarked a short time later. *Carlisle's* Commanding Officer, Captain Neame, sat down to write his own rather understated Letter of Proceedings of the encounter on 22/23 March 1942, typed by Paymaster Midshipman Stoke:

At 1429 on 22 March, CS15 hoisted 'ZLG' and altered course to 360 degrees. *Carlisle* commenced making smoke and gave orders to *Avon Vale* to follow astern. Smoke was laid between the convoy and the enemy, my intention being to keep, if possible, within visual touch of the cruisers and at the same time lay as much smoke as possible to cover the withdrawal of the convoy.

At 1459 *Carlisle* started making smoke. Shortly afterwards *Carlisle* was attacked by a Ju.88 which dived from a height of 9,000 feet. *Carlisle* took avoiding action on bomb release by altering to port. As a result of this alteration *Avon Vale* became enveloped in *Carlisle's* smoke and collided with *Carlisle's* port side. Immediately afterwards another two Ju.88s were driven off. In all cases the bombs dropped into the sea some distance away. At 1530, *Carlisle* rejoined the convoy, who were being incessantly attacked by both high-level and torpedo bombers from 9,000 to 5,000 feet.

At 1645 enemy battleships were reported to the NW and CS15 turned away from the convoy. Whilst laying another smoke screen the convoy was repeatedly attacked by Ju.88s and torpedo bombers until 1910. There were so many attacks taking place that it would be impossible to analyze them all. As my ammunition was getting very short and in accordance with Orders, I made a signal to CS15 that it was my intention to return to Alexandria after dark. I disengaged from the convoy at 1948, and headed east. At 2000 orders were received to return to the convoy and I rejoined *Breconshire* at 2145 to escort her to Malta in company with *Southwold* and *Beaufort*.

At dawn, we were only forty miles from Malta. The weather was very overcast. However, at 0730 the first hostile aircraft was sighted. About eighteen attacks were made on *Breconshire* and *Carlisle* by Ju.88s, followed by attacks from seven Me109s who near missed *Carlisle* and killed one rating and wounded another with machine gun fire.

Breconshire appeared to be hit below the water-line and shortly after, she had a near miss with a Ju.88. *Breconshire* stopped at 0917 and I prepared to take her in tow while circling round to offer her AA protection. More air attacks took place during this period. At 1026 *Penelope* arrived but it took an hour for her to get a tow on *Breconshire*. Very shortly afterwards the tow parted and it was quite clear that the weather conditions were impossible for towing.

With no ammunition or fuel remaining, *Carlisle* entered Grand Harbour finally securing to No 2 buoy. It was a great pleasure and surprise to find both *Pampas* and *Talabot*. I consider the behaviour of the convoy, throughout that most difficult period on Sunday, 22 March between 1520 and dusk, was magnificent. In spite of repeated alterations of course and in poor conditions, all ships kept station extremely well and even *Clan Campbell* managed to keep up by intelligent anticipation of courses steered. I am sure that this good station keeping by the Masters largely saved the convoy.

The escort of Hunts was admirable too. The weather conditions made things most difficult for them and yet their shooting was excellent and handling of ships all that could be desired. It seemed the greatest of misfortune that after surviving so many bombing attacks the *Breconshire* should have been damaged by almost the last attack when within such a short distance of her goal.

The *Parade*, the local newspaper in Alexandria, had the following rather more romanticized report a few days later filed by J.L. Cooper, the *Daily Express* Naval Correspondent, who was on Vian's Flagship, *Cleopatra*:

Thanks to a gallant and brilliant delaying action fought against the odds by Admiral Cunningham's light forces under Rear-Admiral Vian, the convoy got through with the loss of only one merchantman.

I was the only staff reporter in the action and I am now in the charthouse of Vian's flagship writing this story of how, with only a few light cruisers and destroyers protecting the convoy to Malta, we drove off a fleet led by a *Littorio* battleship, five heavy cruisers and six destroyers and did it in the face of every form of air attack, including dive–bombing Junkers 87s, high-level attacking Junkers 88s and torpedo after torpedo from Savoia 79s.

Yet it was the Italians who turned away. Before they turned, we hit the battleship and my last glimpse was a red flame at the aft of the battleship. A spark at 13,000 yards is a pretty big fire on a ship!

We were hit under the bridge five feet from where I stood, but it did no structural damage and impaired neither our fighting power nor speed. We had had five hours of torpedo bombing and about sixteen torpedoes fired at us by 1410, when we first saw smoke on the horizon, at that time 150 miles south-east of Malta. Vian stood unprotected on the bridge and rapped out orders. A south-east gale was whipping the seas and the spray drenched us as we increased speed to thirty knots. Out of the smokescreen I could see at least two ships. Their guns appeared to be aiming straight at me.

The lookout identified four cruisers, two 8-inch and two 6-inch. All this time aircraft were overhead dropping bombs. I could see the sun glint on the windscreen of a Junkers close overhead. The horizon swirled as we changed our course with criss-crossing wakes and the smokescreen turned the storm grey waters black. The Italians turned away and by 1515 we had stopped firing. In the next hour we had several more air attacks.

1640 brought a report of more enemy ships ten miles away. At 1642 I found myself knocked on the deck. We had been hit. But the Admiral was still there straining to see over the wind-barrier; and the Captain still with a pipe in his mouth, though he had seen the shell coming towards him as 'big as a football'. The Gunnery Officer was at his speaking tube as calm as if it was a Mediterranean cruise.

At 1745 we again dash towards the enemy through the smokescreen in battle formation, white ensigns ironed straight in the gale. Shells whine overhead. 'Fifteen inches', shouts the Gunnery Officer, who has nothing heavier than 5.25-inch with which to respond. Our destroyers are racing ahead, hopelessly outmatched in gunpower but seeking a chance to launch torpedoes. And over us there are still aircraft dropping bombs. The Axis must have devoted 150 aircraft to this celebration of Passion Sunday.

It is 1857 and the Italians turn rapidly north away from us. The convoy continues to Malta and we turn back for Alexandria, and despite eleven more air attacks as we pass through Bomb Alley between Derna and Crete, we reach port to the welcoming sirens of other ships who have run out flags in our honour.

Poland concluded afterwards:

> The lesson is that good training, good discipline and good leadership will always lead to victory. The Italians had fine fast ships but they had neither the training nor the will to win. We did what we had spent years learning to do. I only joined my ship two days before we sailed. The last time I had been in destroyers was in 1934 but I knew exactly what to do. Under the then Rear-Admiral Cunningham I had been trained in dummy torpedo runs against our own fleet.
>
> On 24 March 1942, when Cunningham came on board *Jervis* after our arrival back in Alexandria, he said to me, 'I see you haven't forgotten what I taught you eight years ago.'

Having originally thought they would be returning to Alexandria, *Carlisle*'s crew must have been very disappointed to have had to rejoin the convoy, but relieved to finally reach the comparative safety of Malta the following morning. However, their ordeal was not over and about to become considerably worse, as the Luftwaffe unleashed an even more severe blitz on the ships and quays surrounding Grand Harbour over the next forty-eight hours.

Blitz-bombed in Malta, then back to Alexandria

In the early afternoon *Legion*, *Eridge* and *Beaufort* entered harbour, followed by a very heavy air raid at 1625. Later that afternoon, after clearing up the ship from the tumult and chaos resulting from the last few days, Paymaster Midshipman Stoke settled down to write a short letter home.

HMS Carlisle
Grand Harbour, Valletta
23 March
This letter may come as a shock. We can only send one letter of one sheet. We arrived here after a terrific trip which I suppose has taken about ten years off my life. We have been attacked by at least seventy planes and had no fighter protection for us or our convoy of four ships. Then we had the misfortune to run into the Italian Fleet! As you can imagine with no main armament or torpedoes we didn't have a dog's chance. We were escorted by three cruisers who had gone off to attack the Italian cruisers and destroyers.

They arrived back just in time to divert the Italian Battleship's attention from us. We were straddled by one 15-inch salvo! All the time we were laying a smokescreen to protect the convoy. On top of the surface action, we then had to contend with air attacks which were the heaviest since Crete. So we were glad to arrive in harbour. There have been some rather nasty blitzes all day and we have been very lucky. We have just had thirty-three Hun visitors who have left several traces of their presence. Moreover, I gather we are going to leave harbour very shortly. In the engagement above, one our destroyers got a torpedo hit on the Italian battleship. And now I must close as the postman is waiting for the letter.

*   *   *

The rest of the evening was relatively free of air raids. Regrettably, no unloading of either of the merchant ships that had arrived safely was started, with dire consequences in the following days, as both *Pampas* and *Talabot* were later savagely bombed and only 5,000 of the 26,000 tons of stores were saved. *Carlisle* was asked to stay longer to provide additional anti-aircraft cover in the harbour, so didn't leave as expected in the letter.

By the following morning, the wind had died right down to a light north-easterly and by 1220 more air raids started, with red and yellow warnings every subsequent hour. *Carlisle*'s log records the ship's crew were called again to Action Stations whilst still moored in the harbour at 1615 and 1700. There was then a short lull till later in the evening when there were air raid warnings at 2115, 2300, 2338 and 2350!

The morning of 25 March commenced with the usual air raid warning at 0715. It was decided that, due to the continuous heavy raids, those ships that could raise steam should depart that evening. The Vice-Admiral Malta sent a signal in mid-afternoon to Cunningham:

We are having a hectic time. Since this morning there have been the heaviest raids I have yet experienced and I hope to get the ships away tonight without further damage. Yesterday when HQ was demolished, one bomb fell on a newly decorated office and sitting room for me which is now a heap of ruins under which are my few cases of clothes not yet unpacked. They are probably well pressed now! Regrettably, Brigadier Clinch was smothered and killed in his office.

It was estimated that in March more than 2,000 tons of bombs were dropped on Malta. The city of Coventry was blitzed and reduced to rubble by just 500 tons.

At 2036 *Carlisle* slipped her moorings and proceeded to leave with destroyers *Eridge*, *Beaufort*, *Dulverton* and *Hurworth*. The wind was a lot kinder than on the journey up to Malta as they plotted a feint course initially westward and then turned east and further south to avoid enemy air detection. At 0800 on 28 March, Carlisle's crew gratefully secured alongside in Alexandria harbour.

Captain Neame wrote his second Letter of Proceedings for the period in Grand Harbour and the three-day return, typed again by Paymaster Stoke:

During our time in Malta the following air raids took place on 24 March:

(1) 1220. About twenty Ju.88s dropped bombs on the harbour area, diving from a height of 12,000 to 14,000 feet to about 6,000 feet before bomb release.

(2) 1615. A number of attacks were made on the Island by Ju.88s and Ju.87s. A large formation of the former made a determined attack on the harbour, *Carlisle* appearing to be the main target.

(3) 1625. A heavy attack was made on the harbour by two successive formations of twenty to thirty Ju.88s in each. *Carlisle* appeared to be the principal target again.

Carlisle was near missed on the following occasions:

(1) 1615. Four bombs, possibly 500lbs about 100 yards on the port bow and four bombs, possibly 500lbs, about 100 yards ahead.

(2) 1625. Two bombs, delayed action, possibly 500lbs or larger, one twenty feet on the port quarter, and one twenty feet on the starboard quarter. Various other bombs of similar type fell within 100 yards ahead and astern.

(3) About midnight. One or more bombs about 200 yards ahead.

At 1128 on 27 March, a Ju.88 passed over *Carlisle* and dropped bombs from a height of 14,000 feet. Our fighters were called up and the bomber disappeared above the clouds. From about 1300 to 1930, *Carlisle* was shadowed by two aircraft. When both attempted to close the range, we called up non-existent fighters to search for them. The ruse proved successful. It was thought the shadowing planes were listening out on our Fighter Direction Wave.

Among the many signals of congratulation on the recent engagement, the following was received by the C-in-C from Churchill:

> I shall be glad if you will convey to Admiral Vian and all who sailed with him the admiration which I feel at this resolute and brilliant action by which the Malta convoy was saved. That one of the most powerful modern battleships afloat attended by two heavy and four light cruisers and a flotilla should have been routed and put to flight with severe torpedo and gunfire injury in broad daylight by a force of five British light cruisers and destroyers constitutes a naval episode of highest distinction and entitles all ranks and ratings concerned, and above all their commander, to the compliments of the British Nation.

*   *   *

Two days after returning from the Battle of Sirte and the blitz bombing for two days in Malta, Stoke was able to write a fuller account to his parents.

Alexandria
29 March
I hope you got my hurried note of last week. Actually, it was rather a fraud since at the very last minute our sailing was delayed for another two days. And what a two days!! I hope not to have another two days like them.

I'll attempt to give you a rough idea of what the trip was like. As you know the Press certainly gave a large write up to the party. As you may have gathered from previous letters the trip has never been exactly a pleasure cruise. In fact, the *Carlisle* has been very lucky to get back several times. However, we left Alexandria with the convoy and some destroyers. The first two days were ominously quiet. Only sporadic attacks instead of the usual steady bombing. Day three we were caught up by Rear-Admiral Vian in *Cleopatra*, following the torpedoing of his previous flagship, *Naiad*, just 10 days previously and two other light cruisers (*Dido* and *Euryalus*), all with 5.25" guns and were met by one cruiser from Malta with 6" guns, *Penelope*.

We were bombed all morning. Then at 1429 one cruiser sighted masts away to northward, when we were about 150 miles from Malta. The cruisers, now four in number, turned away to engage them, while we made smoke to cover the convoy. Of course, we were no use in a surface action having no tubes and our puny guns. We thought that these ships were battleships but they proved to be 6-inch cruisers, including 8-inch ones.

Stephen Stoke, Mick's father.

Barbara Stoke, Mick's mother.

G.A. (Mick) Stoke MBE, DSC RN, October 1943.

Westcliff High School motto.

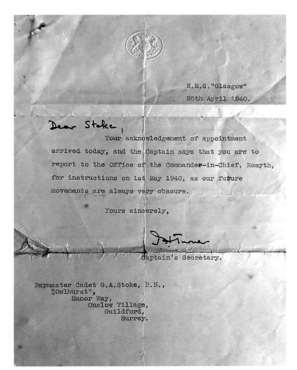

CERTIFICATE AT END OF COURSE IN TRAINING SHIP.

This is to certify that Mr. Gordan Alexander STOKE

Paymaster Cadet has been through a course of training on board this ship at RN College Dartmouth

His knowledge and ability are :—

In Ship's Office— 143/150
In Victualling— 147/150
In Central Stores— 80/100
In Captain's Office— 123/150
In Cyphering— 92/100
In other subjects— 220/300
In special subjects (languages, etc.)—

He has shown marked attention to his work, and his Officer-like

qualities have been assessed as 8 .*

Result of examination on passing out of training ship (K.R. 302).

Maximum marks— 950
Marks obtained— 805
Class of Certificate awarded— First
Swimming qualification— PPT Good
Completed Gas Course— Not undergone

Given on board His Majesty's Ship " Britannia "

this 30th day of April 1940

R.S.Ginnaffe Captain.

*To be shown as in form S.206 (1 to 9).

Passing out certificate First Class, April 1940.

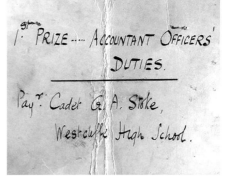

1ˢᵗ PRIZE ---- ACCOUNTANT OFFICERS'
DUTIES.

Payr Cadet G.A. Stoke,
Westcliff High School.

First Prize, Dartmouth Royal Naval College, March 1940.

Paymaster Cadet G.A. Stoke, December 1939.

H.M.S. "Glasgow"
26th April 1940.

Dear Stoke,

Your acknowledgement of appointment arrived today, and the Captain says that you are to report to the Office of the Commander-in-Chief, Rosyth, for instructions on 1st May 1940, as our future movements are always very obscure.

Yours sincerely,

J.T.Turner
Captain's Secretary.

Paymaster Cadet G.A.Stoke, R.N.,
"Owlhurst",
Manor Way,
Onslow Village,
Guildford,
Surrey.

Appointment to first ship, HMS *Glasgow*.

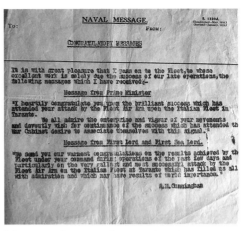

Messages of congratulations after the success at Taranto, November 1940.

Promotion to Midshipman, 1 September 1940.

Captain Pegram, Captain Hickling and Commander Cuthbert, HMS *Glasgow*.

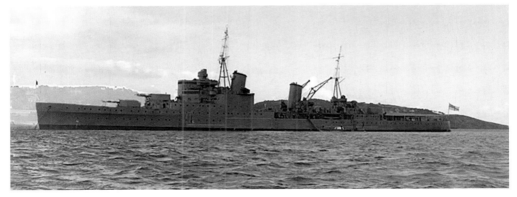

HMS *Glasgow*, 1940.

No. P.8.

6th January 1941

This is to Certify that _Mr G.A. Stoke, Royal Navy_
has served as _Paymaster Midshipman_ in
HMS "Glasgow" under my command, from the _6th_ day
of _June_ 19 40 , to the _6th_ day of _February_ 1941 , during which
period he has conducted himself* _Entirely to my satisfaction._
_A hard working, painstaking & competent officer who
promises very well. As my secretary & staff officer
while SNO Inshore Squadron & in the Western desert
he has shown marked efficiency & common sense.
His manner & manners are excellent._

Harold Hickling { Captain H.M.S. _Glasgow_

* Here the Captain is to insert in his own handwriting the conduct of the Officer   S. 450

Stoke's 'flimsy' signed by Captain Hickling, January 1941.

Douglas V. Duff, author of *May the Winds Blow*.

Tobruk Harbour, 1941. Admiralty House is the large, isolated building near the water's edge.

AUSSIES

AFTER CRETE DISASTER ANZAC TROOPS ARE NOW BEING RUTHLESSLY SACRIFICED BY ENGLAND IN TOBRUCH AND SYRIA.

TURKEY HAS CONCLUDED PACT OF FRIENDSHIP WITH GERMANY. ENGLAND WILL SHORTLY BE DRIVEN OUT OF THE MEDITERRANEAN. OFFENSIVE FROM EGYPT TO RELIEVE YOU TOTALLY SMASHED.

YOU CANNOT ESCAPE.

OUR DIVE BOMBERS ARE WAITING TO SINK YOUR TRANSPORTS. THINK OF YOUR FUTURE AND YOUR PEOPLE AT HOME.

COME FORWARD - SHOW WHITE FLAGS AND YOU WILL BE OUT OF DANGER !

SURRENDER !

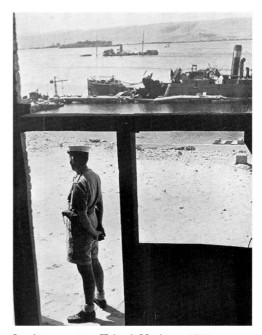

German propaganda leaflet, Tobruk, April 1941. Looking out into Tobruk Harbour, 1941.

4370   SUPPLEMENT TO THE LONDON GAZETTE, 29 JULY, 1941

The KING has also been graciously pleased to give orders for the following Appointments to the Distinguished Service Order, and to approve the following Awards:—

For courage, skill and devotion to duty in operations off the Libyan Coast:

To be Companions of the Distinguished Service Order:

Lieutenant-Commander John Fulford Blackburn, Royal Navy (Retired).
Lieutenant-Commander John Oliver Campbell, D.S.C., Royal Navy (Retired).

Bar to the Distinguished Service Cross.

Commander Richard Borthwick Jennings, D.S.C., Royal Navy.

The Distinguished Service Cross.

Commander Arthur Harold Hildreth Griffith, R.D., R.N.R.
Lieutenant-Commander Alexander John McHattie, R.N.R.
Temporary Lieutenant-Commander Alistair Macintosh, R.N.R.
Lieutenant John Bevan Cox, Royal Navy.
Lieutenant Alexander Henderson Diack, Royal Navy.
Lieutenant John Bruce Lamb, Royal Navy.
Lieutenant John Russell Phillimore, Royal Navy.
Lieutenant Henry Herbert Dietrich Mackillican, R.N.R.
Lieutenant Charles Donavan Smith, R.N.R.
Temporary Lieutenant Alfred Brian Palmer, R.N.R.
Surgeon Lieutenant Gerald Lipson Ward, M.B., B.Ch., M.R.C.S., L.R.C.P., R.N.V.R.
Mr. Alexander Charles Grant, Commissioned Engineer, Royal Navy.

The Conspicuous Gallantry Medal.

Acting Petty Officer Leslie Roy Poore, P/J.111050.

Leading Telegraphist Nelson George Wilfred Squires, P/JX.133737.
Able Seaman Rochford John Boyd, P/J.71360.
Able Seaman William Arthur Phillpotts, P/SSX.14433.
Stoker First Class George Edward Daley, P/K.59444.
Signalman Leonard White, C/JX.131740.
Ordinary Seaman William Stanley Wiltshire, C/JX.181559.
Cook (S) Albert Frederick Birch, P/M.61045.
Fireman Serang Gafoor Meah, 2174.

Mention in Despatches (Posthumous).

Chief Petty Officer Frank Howard Arnsby, P/J.95263.

Mention in Despatches.

Captain Hector Macdonald Laws Waller, D.S.O., Royal Australian Navy.
Acting Captain William Power Garne, Royal Navy.
Commander James Cairns Morrow, D.S.O., Royal Australian Navy.
Lieutenant-Commander Rodney Rhoades, Royal Australian Navy.
Lieutenant Vincent George Palmer, Royal Navy.
Lieutenant Herbert Douglas Gordon, R.N.R.
Lieutenant Charles Edward Oehley, R.N.R.
Temporary Lieutenant Frederick Heywood Thomas, R.N.R.
Temporary Engineer Lieutenant James Dorrance, R.N.R.
Paymaster Lieutenant Norman Steel Grant, Royal Navy.
Temporary Sub-Lieutenant Richard Baggott Laing, R.N.V.R.
Temporary Paymaster Sub-Lieutenant Norman Cassleton Elliott, R.N.V.R.
Paymaster Midshipman Gordon Alexander Stoke, Royal Navy.
Chief Petty Officer John Francis Day, P/J.59888.
Chief Petty Officer Edward John Hill, D/J.10945.

By the KING'S Order the name of
Paymaster Midshipman Gordon A. Stoke, R.N.
was published in the London Gazette on
29 July, 1941,
as mentioned in a Despatch for distinguished service.
I am charged to record
His Majesty's high appreciation.

First Lord of the Admiralty

King George VI's Order recognizing the Mention in Despatches.

Letter from Stoke (aged nineteen) recommending honours for ratings who assisted him during heavy enemy air attacks on Tobruk harbour during April and May 1941.

Confidential

Admiralty House,
Tobruk,
15th May, 1941.

Sir,

I have the honour to report the meritorious conduct of the following three ratings:-

Leading Seaman James C. McAlonan Official Number C/SS.X 15653
Able Seaman Frederic J. Williams Official Number C/SS.X 25983
Signalman Gordon C. Hewitt Official Number C/J.X 144264

2.   The circumstances are as follows:-
At approximately 1500 on the 12th May, 1941, " H.M.S. Ladybird " lying in the west end of the harbour was seen to be struck by two bombs on her stern. Immediately the above named three ratings followed me down into the Fleming lifeboat. There was following on the initial attack on " H.M.S. Ladybird " a lull and three soldiers joined the party as we ran to the jetty. However, when the attack was renewed with redoubled vigour the three soldiers fled back to their " funk-hole ". Unmoved by this display, the ratings remained undeterred by the sound and effect of bombs and the barrage of shrapnel falling in the harbour and though many enemy planes could be seen overhead at low heights, apparently machine-gunning and firing cannon.

3.   In particular, I would bring to your notice Signalman Gordon C. Hewitt Official Number C/J.X 144264 as he has been away during air attacks in my boat on every occasion since the " blitz " started when ships have been sunk in the harbour.

I have the Honour to be,
Sir,
Your Obedient Servant,

Paymaster Midshipman, Royal Navy.

The Naval Officer in Charge,
Tobruk.
(Copy to The Senior Naval Officer, Inshore Squadron.)

Announcement of DSC in *The London Gazette*, 25 November 1941.

SUPPLEMENT to the LONDON GAZETTE, 25 NOVEMBER, 1941   6773

For courage and devotion to duty while serving in the Mediterranean:

The Distinguished Service Cross.

Lieutenant Herbert Douglas Gordon, R.N.R., H.M.S. Chakla.
Lieutenant Joseph William Robinson, R.N.R., H.M.S. Stoke.
Paymaster Midshipman Gordon Alexander Stoke, Royal Navy.

The Conspicuous Gallantry Medal.

Stoker First Class René Sethren, S.D.F.71240, H.M.S.A.S. Southern Isles,
for his steadfast bearing when his ship was attacked by an Enemy aircraft which machine-gunned the deck. Though eleven times wounded, he stood to his gun and turned a steady fire on the aircraft until it fell in flames into the sea.

The Distinguished Service Medal.

Chief Engine Room Artificer Cornelius George O'Halloran, P/M.35029, H.M.S. Stoke.
Engine Room Artificer First Class George William Hammond, C/MX.58134.
Petty Officer Walter Robert Riglar, D/J.108517, H.M.S. Stoke.
Leading Stoker Harry McDonald Jewell, S.D.F.69617, H.M.S.A.S. Southern Isles.
Able Seaman Frederick Arthur Bissmire, C/JX.171472, H.M.S. Chakla.

Able Seaman Charles H. Beavington, C/SS.11573.
Able Seaman Reginald Francis Marshall, D/J.107295, H.M.S. Stoke.
Able Seaman Robert Walter Sutton, C/JX.157637, H.M.S. Kipling.

For bravery, endurance and devotion to duty when H.M.S. Fiona was lost:

The Distinguished Service Cross.

Temporary Sub-Lieutenant William Macleod Hogg, R.N.V.R., H.M.S. Fiona.

The Distinguished Service Medal.

Chief Petty Officer Edward John Hill, D/J.19945, H.M.S. Fiona.
Able Seaman David Knox, D/JX.177841, H.M.S. Fiona.
Able Seaman George Edward Patterson, D/J.46225, H.M.S. Fiona.

Mention in Despatches.

Chief Petty Officer Stanley Bate Collings, D.S.M., D/J.28241, H.M.S. Fiona.

For good services and devotion to duty:

Mention in Despatches.

Temporary Acting Leading Seaman William Leslie Arter, C/JX.147257.

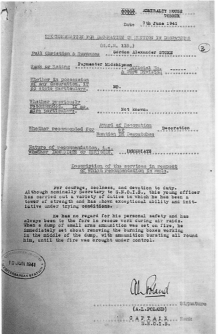

Admiralty noticeboard, Alexandria. Stoke's DSC.

Captain A.L. Poland's personal recommendation for Stoke's DSC, 7 June 1941.

Recuperating in Alexandria after five months in the Western Desert and the Siege of Tobruk, 1941.

Gully-gully man entertaining naval officers, Alexandria, 1941.

HMS *Queen Elizabeth* in the Eastern Mediterranean, 1941.

HMS *Queen Elizabeth* firing a broadside in the Eastern Mediterranean, 1941.

HMS *Queen Elizabeth* 'taking it green' in the Eastern Mediterranean, 1941.

HMS *Jervis* refuelling alongside HMS *Queen Elizabeth*, 1941.

HMS *Barham* at anchor in Alexandria harbour, 1941.

HMS *Barham* following a zig-zag course shortly before being torpedoed, November 1941.

HMS *Barham* explodes as her 15-inch magazine ignites after being hit by three torpedoes, November 1941.

HMS *Queen Elizabeth* surrounded by anti-submarine nets installed the day before the human torpedo attack.

Ratings rapidly unload 15-inch shells from the stricken HMS *Queen Elizabeth* shortly after she was severely damaged by human torpedoes, December 1941.

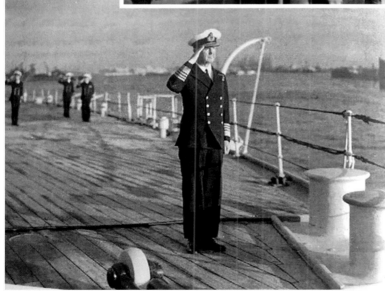

Admiral Cunningham saluting the colours on board HMS *Queen Elizabeth* after she was severely damaged by human torpedoes, December 1941.

HMS *Carlisle* at anchor in Alexandria harbour, 1942.

Message of thanks from the Governor of Malta, 23 January 1942.

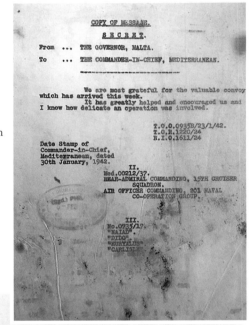

COPY OF MESSAGE.

S E C R E T.

From ... THE GOVERNOR, MALTA.

To ... THE COMMANDER-IN-CHIEF, MEDITERRANEAN.

We are most grateful for the valuable convoy which has arrived this week.
It has greatly helped and encouraged us and I know how delicate an operation was involved.

T.O.O.0935B/23/1/42.
T.O.R.1220/24
R.I.O.1611/24

Date Stamp of Commander-in-Chief, Mediterranean, dated 30th January, 1942.

II.
Med.00212/37.
REAR-ADMIRAL COMMANDING, 15TH CRUISER SQUADRON.
AIR OFFICER COMMANDING, 201 NAVAL CO-OPERATION GROUP.

III.
No.0935/17.
"NAIAD".
"DIDO".
"EURYALUS".
"CARLISLE".

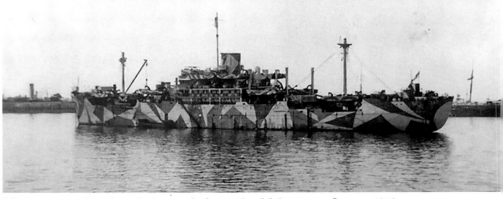

SS *Glengyle*, auxiliary/assault ship, ready for another Malta convoy, January 1942.

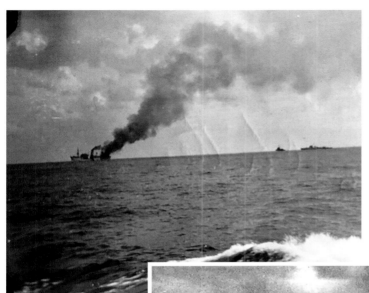

SS *Clan Chattan* hit by Ju-87 bombers, Malta Convoy MF5, February 1942.

HMS *Carlisle* trying to assist SS *Clan Chattan*, Malta Convoy MF5, February 1942.

The last moments of SS *Clan Chattan*, Malta Convoy MF5, February 1942.

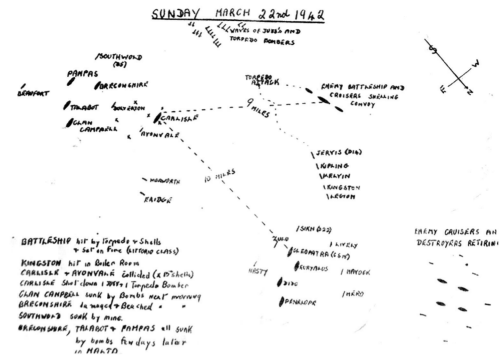

SUNDAY MARCH 22nd 1942

WAVES OF JU88's AND
TORPEDO BOMBERS

/SOUTHWOLD (35)
PAMPAS
/BRECONSHIRE
/BEAUFORT
/TALABOT   /HAVY JASON
/CLAN CAMPBELL   /CARLISLE
  /AVONVALE

TORPEDO ATTACK ... ENEMY BATTLESHIP AND CRUISERS SHELLING CONVOY

9 MILES

/HARWORTH
/ERIDGE
10 MILES

/JERVIS (D14)
/KIPLING
/KELVIN
/KINGSTON
/LEGION

/SIKH (D22)
ZULO   /LIVELY
/CLEOPATRA (C.S.15)
/HASTY   /EURYALUS   /HAVOCK
/DIDO   /HERO
/PENELOPE

ENEMY CRUISERS AN DESTROYERS RETIRIN

BATTLESHIP hit by Torpedo & Shells & Set on Fire (LITTORIO CLASS)
KINGSTON hit in Boiler Room
CARLISLE & AVONVALE collided (x 15" shells)
CARLISLE Shot down 1 JU88 & 1 Torpedo Bomber
CLAN CAMPBELL sunk by Bombs next morning
BRECONSHIRE damaged & Beached "
SOUTHWOLD sonk by mine.
BRECONSHIRE, TALABOT & PAMPAS all sunk
    by bombs few days later
    in MALTA

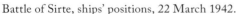

Battle of Sirte, ships' positions, 22 March 1942.

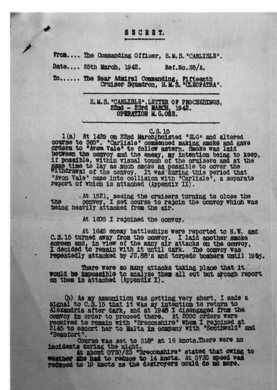

SECRET.

From.... The Commanding Officer, H.M.S. "CARLISLE".

Date.... 25th March, 1942.   Ref.No.55/A.

To...... The Rear Admiral Commanding, Fifteenth
         Cruiser Squadron, H.M.S. "CLEOPATRA".

H.M.S. "CARLISLE" LETTER OF PROCEEDINGS,
22nd - 23rd MARCH, 1942.
OPERATION M.G. ONE.

C.S. 15

1 (a) At 1429 on 22nd March)hoisted "ZG" and altered
course to 360°. "Carlisle" commenced making smoke and gave
orders to "Avon Vale" to follow astern. Smoke was laid
between the convoy and the enemy, my intention being to keep,
if possible, within visual touch of the cruisers and at the
same time to lay as much smoke as possible to cover the
withdrawal of the convoy. It was during this period that
"Avon Vale" came into collision with "Carlisle", a separate
report of which is attached (Appendix II).

    At 1521, seeing the cruisers turning to close the
the convoy, I set course to rejoin the convoy which was
being heavily attacked from the air.

    At 1600 I rejoined the convoy.

    At 1645 enemy battleships were reported to N.W. and
C.S.15 turned away from the convoy. I laid another smoke
screen and, in view of the many air attacks on the convoy,
I decided to remain with it until dark. The convoy was
repeatedly attacked by JU.88's and torpedo bombers until 1935.

    There were so many attacks taking place that it
would be impossible to analyse them all out but a rough report
on them is attached (Appendix I).

    (b) As my ammunition was getting very short, I made a
signal to C.S.15 that it was my intention to return to
Alexandria after dark, and at 1945 I disengaged from the
convoy in order to proceed there. At 2000 orders were
received to remain with "Breconshire" whom I rejoined at
2145 to escort her to Malta in company with "Southwold" and
"Beaufort".
    Course was set to 318° at 16 knots. There were no
incidents during the night.
    At about 0730/23 "Breconshire" stated that owing to
weather she had to reduce to 14 knots. At 0730 speed was
reduced to 10 knots as the destroyers could do no more.

Captain D.M.L Neame's Letter of
Proceedings, Battle of Sirte, 22 March 1942.

The NELSON TOUCH

Thanks to a gallant and brilliant delaying action fought against odds by Admiral Cunningham's light forces under Rear-Admiral Vian, the convoy got through with the loss of one merchantman. The graphic story is by J. L. Cooper, the "Daily Express" naval correspondent with the Mediterranean Fleet.

The Nelson Touch. Newspaper report of the Battle of Sirte, 23 March 1942. Captain A.L. Poland on the right.

HMS *Carlisle* ship's officers, 1942.

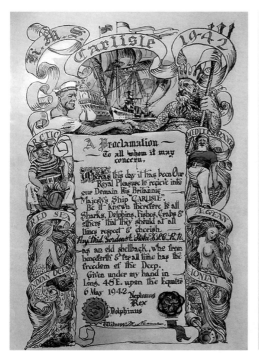

'Crossing the line' certificate, 6 May 1942.

Promotion to Sub-Lieutenant, 1 September 1942.

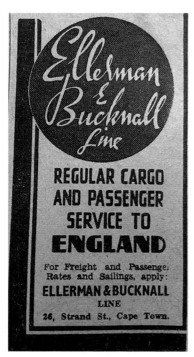

Advertisement for the Ellerman & Bucknall shipping line. Stephen Stoke worked for Ellerman for 40 years.

Third Officer Doreen Le Poidevin, 1942.

The London Gazette, 4 May 1943, announcing Stoke's MBE.

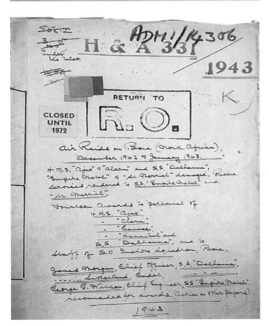

ADM 1/14306 held at the National Archives (Kew), with the recommendation for Stoke's MBE.

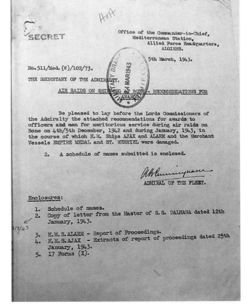

Admiral Cunningham's recommendations for awards and honours for meritorious service during the air raids on the port of Bone 4/5 December 1942 and during January 1943, including Stoke's MBE.

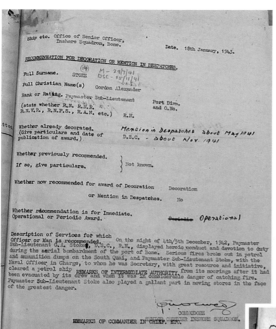

Commodore G.N. Oliver's recommendation for Stoke's MBE during air raids on 4/5 December 1942.

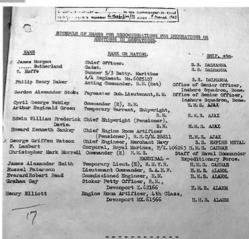

Personnel in the port of Bone, Algeria (including Stoke) recommended for honours following the savage air raids in December 1942 and January 1943.

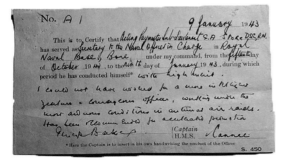

Stoke's 'flimsy' from Commander Philip Baker (9 January 1943) plus announcement of his specially accelerated promotion for 'meritorious war service' in Bone, Algeria, 22 July 1943.

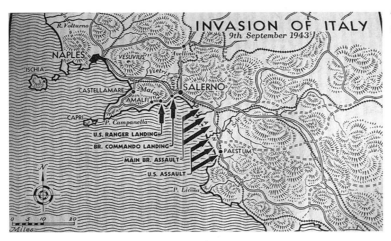

The Salerno landings, 9 September 1943.

Commodore G.N. Oliver.

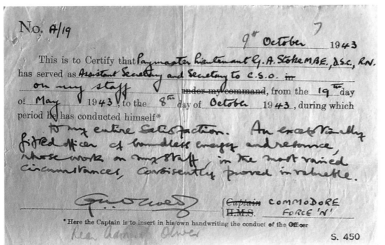

Stoke's 'flimsy' from Commodore G.N. Oliver, Commodore Force 'N' at Salerno.

Paymaster Lieutenant G.A. Stoke MBE, DSC
RN, October 1943.

Doreen Le Poidevin, his fiancée (1942), later
married, November 1944.

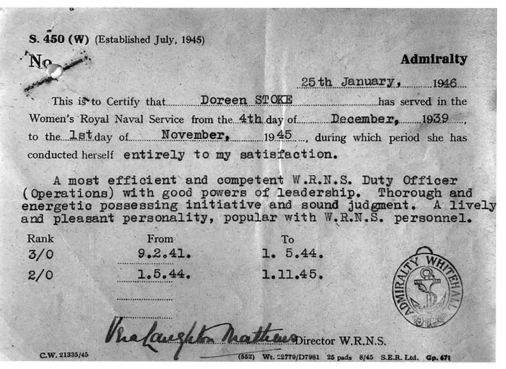

Doreen Le Poidevin's 'flimsy' on leaving the WRNS, November 1945.

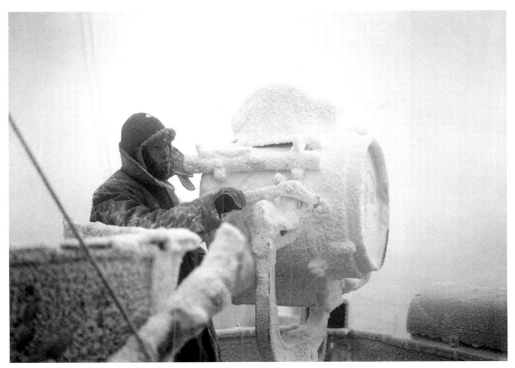

Signalling was difficult with the snow and ice on a Russian convoy.

A destroyer on the Russian convoys in bad weather.

HMS *Kempenfelt*, which took over from the torpedoed HMS *Hardy*, April 1944.

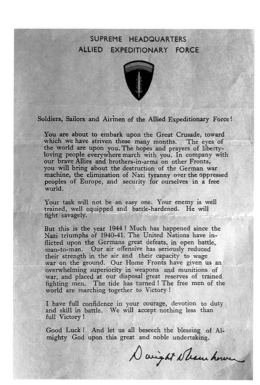

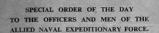
General Eisenhower's message to the Allied Expeditionary Force on D-Day, 6 June 1944.

Admiral Ramsay's message on D-Day, 6 June 1944.

Paymaster Lieutenant G.A. Stoke and his father, Stephen Stoke, wedding day, 16 November 1944, Glasgow.

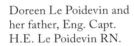

Doreen Le Poidevin and her father, Eng. Capt. H.E. Le Poidevin RN.

Paymaster Lieutenant G.A. Stoke and Doreen Le Poidevin. Just married!

HMS *Rajah*. A Ruler-class aircraft escort carrier in the Pacific between San Diego and Pearl Harbor, 1945.

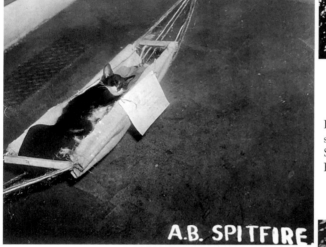

A.B. SPITFIRE

HMS *Rajah*'s ship's cat in a specially designed hammock. A B Spitfire kept the crew safe in the Pacific.

Stoke (far left) with US Navy personnel in the Pacific, 1945.

While this action was in progress, suddenly an Italian battleship (*Littorio*) came up out of the west and sighted by us about ten miles away. We were the sole HM Ship between him and the convoy! We made smoke and prepared to die valiantly. We were straddled by 15″ bricks but fortunately before it was too late, our four cruisers came to our rescue. You know the results. One enemy battleship hit by a torpedo and afire from shell fire and two enemy cruisers hit, for very slight damage to our own forces. They had at least seven cruisers!

All that afternoon we were being attacked i.e. the convoy and *Carlisle* protecting them – by waves of torpedo bombers and Ju.88s! More near misses. We went on to Malta and arrived there with practically no ammo left, and having been attacked from mast high by Me109s.

We expected to leave there after loading fuel and ammunition but did not as I have said. We stayed for two more days and were the main target for the full German blitz. How we survived I do not know. It was a miracle. We eventually arrived in Alexandria having been bombed on the way back. All through the operation the weather was gale force and we leaked like a sieve. There was over six inches of water in the after flats and swilling around my chest. Truly a pleasant trip in a pleasant ship. The only bright spark was that it was so tremendously successful. Many planes shot down and enemy ships in superior force were beaten up.

*   *   *

Carlisle's Captain Mortimer Neame DSO was awarded a second DSO during this battle for his handling of *Carlisle*. Her manoeuvring and steering, whilst maintaining position under constant enemy attack, was of the highest order, and Neame's navigating officer Commander John West was awarded the DSC. Following the action of the previous week, young Paymaster Midshipman Stoke was promoted Captain's Secretary to Neame.

Carlisle remained in Alexandria for a couple of weeks for repairs (to the ship and the crew!). It was normal for officers of the ships in harbour to visit others that they knew. On Sunday, 5 April, Captain Poland's diary notes that he paid a visit to *Carlisle* to meet Stoke, whom he hadn't seen since early June 1941, and Captain Neame.

Jackson, one of *Carlisle*'s stokers, recalled the repairs:

The *Carlisle* took a lot of pounding during the convoys. I remember her holed up in dry dock with tremendous damage to her bow. Huge pieces of shrapnel had caused tremendous damage to the ship. She looked so vulnerable, just as if she were made of butter. We managed to come through much of the conflict. Many times facing a barrage of dive-bombing Stukas.

* * *

5 April

We are at present doing a little repair to our noble ship and so have not been to sea since last week. I note you say that my present ship seems a fearful tub!

I am now promoted to Captain's Secretary. I took over last Monday and have been working very late all this week to try and get the job square. Captain Neame is very pleasant to work for but I have not got a cabin and in fact am the least well off since I came to sea.

Your query about sea time is easily answered. We do the Malta run up 'Bomb Alley' (between Cyrenaica and Crete) and that's all. And that's enough. It's a week's job (about five days). As for a refit? We MAY get one and we may go to South Africa for it. It's very unlikely.

I note you refer to concentrated attacks on Malta! And don't I know it. I feel that an attempt will shortly be made to take the island. It's the old trouble all over again. No air support for the Fleet out here because of the Far East. We will play along and succeed, but I'm afraid will have our losses. It will really be nothing short of a marvel when we have as many fighters as we want for our ships.

The strain at the moment is terrific. It's no good blinking the facts. Our morale at the moment can still stand these runs but it's a very trying business, those days in constant air attack. However, I have no doubt but that we will do our job and that right well. It's not a custom of the Senior Service [the Royal Navy] to go back on its obligations. Malta will be supplied.

* * *

Despite Paymaster Midshipman Stoke's good intentions to continue the Malta convoys, due to lack of air cover there were no more planned for a couple of months, so *Carlisle* remained in Alexandria for the rest of April.

Chapter 9

Return to England and Sub-Lieutenant Exams

Alexandria and the visit of HRH Duke of Gloucester

At the end of March, Admiral Cunningham handed over as C-in-C Mediterranean to Admiral Harwood. On 1 April 1942 Cunningham hand-wrote his farewell signal to the Mediterranean Fleet:

You will understand, one and all, the deep regret with which I lay down command of the Mediterranean Station. It has been my greatest pride that throughout the war, the Mediterranean Fleet has consistently shown itself the master of the enemy in every branch of naval warfare, whether in the air, in submarine warfare or surface fighting. It is this factor which has enabled us during the last two years to impose our will on the enemy to a very high degree, despite his superiority in every class of ship and his almost overwhelming strength in the air. This achievement of the officers and men of the Mediterranean Fleet in some two years of the most strenuous naval fighting on record, is one which I greatly treasure, as greatly I do the privilege of having led the Fleet during that period.

The enemy knows we are masters on the sea, and we must strain every nerve to keep our standard of fighting so high that that lesson never fails to be borne in on him.

Our worldwide commitments at present mean that we have not, at times, as large forces as we would like to carry the war to the enemy's front door. This will not always be so, and I look forward to the day when the Mediterranean Fleet will sweep the sea clear and re-establish our age-old control of this waterway so vital to the British Empire. I am confident that day is not too far distant and meanwhile I wish you all good fortune and Godspeed.

The war continued as usual after his departure. In the early morning of 7 April about twenty enemy aircraft attacked Alexandria, concentrating on the *Queen*

Elizabeth in the floating dock. On the same day, hospital ship *Somersetshire* was torpedoed by a U-boat while on passage to Tobruk. Early in the morning of the next day, another twenty enemy aircraft again attacked the floating dock in Alexandria. Two ships were hit and sunk, and the torpedo depot was severely damaged and had to be evacuated.

The 15th Cruiser Squadron and all available destroyers carried out large scale exercises in the Eastern Med during the day and night of 11 April. This was to be Stoke's last major outing in the Med, until he returned six months later for Operation Torch and the landings in Algeria in November 1942.

* * *

12 April
I have had rather a hard time of it lately. We have had a lot of sea time in the most dangerous waters that there are, in a ship that will fall to bits as soon as it is hit by anything, in filthy weather conditions. Moreover, I have taken over as Captain's Secretary to Neame with a lot of leeway to make up. However, it is quite a joy at times to have a lot of work to do as it prevents Alexandria getting too much of a bore. I have not been ashore for quite a time. Incidentally, I volunteered four weeks ago for a very special service (so the blurb said) and was recommended by my Captain. Happy Birthday, Mummy and I hope you are healthy, wealthy and wise.

* * *

Alexandria may not have been a home from home, but for many service personnel it provided some welcome distractions from being at permanent Action Stations and continually under the threat of bombs, mines and torpedoes. Captain Gregory-Smith gave a flavour of Alexandria:

> If one had to fight a war overseas, Alexandria was one of the best places on which to be based. It possessed clubs, bars, restaurants, cinemas and excellent facilities for sports. For those so inclined, there were establishments of a more sordid nature. The place catered for every taste from the exotic to the erotic. Altogether, it was a fascinating city possessing a definite character of its own. It was the junction between the eastern and western worlds. People of every nationality jostled each other on its crowded pavements; the mysticism of the ancient east with its veiled

women, muezzins, smells and beggars mingled with the cinemas, trams, cocktails and plumbing of the modern west.

War and peace stalked each other side by side. Allied troops, airmen from the desert and seamen from the convoy routes rubbed shoulders with wealthy, well-dressed women to whom the war was utterly remote. In the harbour, ancient feluccas sailed past modern fighting ships while trim yachts glided amongst men of war and rust stained merchant ships, some still bearing the scars of some bitter convoy battle.

Quite often we would play tennis in the afternoon, followed by tea on the balcony, where members would forgather for their evening gossip. This provided great entertainment as the tennis courts were right next door to the swimming pool, offering ring side views of scantily clad bathing beauties. Consequently, a few days without having to be constantly keyed up to deal with a sudden attack by submarine or aircraft seemed the most wonderful reward.

Captain Poland's diary shows that when not on escort duty or in action, he also spent a lot of time in Alexandria. His distractions included much golf, tennis, bathing and reading and writing letters home, interspersed with lunch, drinks and dinner at the Club, the Union Bar, the Casino, the Metropolitan, Fourmi or Pastroudis every other day! However, young Midshipman Stoke, from his letters home, seems to have only frequented the rugger pitch and the concert hall!

*   *   *

19 April
I expect I told you that I had received a book of prayers from the United Congregational Church and that one book was missing. Well it has just arrived. It is a New Testament with leather covers and vest pocket size. It vividly brings home to me how much I have missed the Bible. Not only from a religious angle but also from enjoyment and fascination. I find it makes a very good bedside book.

I have only been ashore to play rugger and to a couple of concerts by the Palestine Symphony Orchestra this last four weeks. The first concert was Gluck's Overture *Iphigenia in Aulis*, Beethoven's Fourth Symphony followed by Ravel's *Mother Goose* and Stravinsky's *Petruska*. Not too good a selection. In fact, I disliked the second half. The Gluck was tuneful if not striking, whilst the Beethoven was competent.

Today's concert was Handel's *Water Music*, the *Emperor* and Brahms' Fourth Symphony. The *Emperor* was played by a fifteen-year-old girl. A most amazing show. She was quite alright as far as fingering went. She blurred some passages but on the whole, she managed. But tone was altogether beyond her. She put her soul into it but I'm afraid her maidenly youth did not make up for what I wanted. The rest of the audience seemed quite content to applaud because of the performer's youth. But I want to listen to the *Emperor*, not to marvel at technical prodigies. Still enough of this.

I note with irony that you say I seem happier on my new ship. Actually, I am about the only RN officer besides the Captain. I find it exasperating because of the others' inefficiency and slovenliness. The mess is as selfish and childish as a school cricket team. However, I am doing my job and I trust doing it well. Captain Neame says he is pleased. You need not worry that I am learning bad habits re drinking. It's still cider for me and gin or liquors on special occasions. I have been able to defy *Carlisle* at her worst and have survived with honour her 30-degree continuous roll. We have done another trip and once again are surprised to get back! Without being a prig, I can say that on these trips I worry far more about you than I do for myself.

*   *   *

HRH Duke of Gloucester visited the Fleet in Alexandria on 20 April, despite it being subject to air attack at short notice. The Orders and Programme for his visit, headed 'Most Secret', read:

HRH arrives on Monday, 20 April 1942 to be received by a very high-ranking delegation of senior Allied Commanders and local dignitaries. At 1430 on Tuesday afternoon, 21 April 1942, HRH will be received by Rear-Admiral Vian, Commanding Officer Fifteenth Cruiser Squadron on board his flagship *Cleopatra*. HRH is allowed 20 minutes per ship and visits the cruisers *Euryalus* and *Dido*, before arriving at *Carlisle* at 1545 where the Guard of Honour and Band will be paraded, as the ship's company marches past.

The Orders emphasized that ships' companies will give 'Three cheers' for HRH on his departure from each ship and that dress for the programme on both days for Officers will be No 5s without swords or gloves, and for Ratings No 2.

*   *   *

26 April

I think that this will be the last letter from this part of the world. The Duke of Gloucester is out here, reviewing the Med Fleet and he came on our quarter deck. You may remember I had a flight on a Walrus and then a Fulmar. Well I have now had a flight in a Beaufort. They are twin-engined fighters with four cannon and six machine guns firing forward. It was only a spin for three hours but I thoroughly enjoyed it, although it still confirms my impression that I would not like to fly. Occasionally and in different types of plane for the thrill – yes … but regularly – no!

*   *   *

Shortly afterwards, *Carlisle* was nominated to return to UK for a refit, departing on 24 April via the Suez Canal, Mombasa, Durban and the Cape of Good Hope.

The C-in-C sent *Carlisle* a signal on their departure:

Carlisle is leaving the Mediterranean after a long period of excellent and arduous service culminating in her admirable performance in the recent Malta Convoy operation. I am very sorry to lose a ship which has fought so well and wish you all goodbye and good luck.

*   *   *

2 May
Off the East Coast of Africa
The heat here is terrific. I am sweltering and living in a perpetual bath. Still, it's all in a good cause. I hope to see some new places shortly. I shan't be sorry for a change. This Wardroom as I may have said before is old reservists. Their impression is that they've done me (i.e. the RN) a great service by being RNVR officers. My goodness, if they weren't here they would be footsloggers in the army they profess to despise. I'm afraid I've spoken my mind about this, so we're not quite such a happy family. Still, I get on all right with the Captain and the ratings, so I suppose I can't be completely wrong. Perhaps it's the heat!

*   *   *

On 6 May, *Carlisle* crossed the equator and, despite the war, observed the nautical tradition of the 'Crossing the Line' ceremony. The 'Proclamation by Neptune' stated:

> Whereas this day it has been our Royal Pleasure to receive into our domain His Britannic Majesty's Ship *Carlisle*, be it known therefore to all Sharks, Dolphins, Fishes, Crabs and others that they should at all times respect and cherish
>
> Paymaster Midshipman G.A. Stoke DSC RN
>
> as an old shellback, who from henceforth & for all time has the freedom of the Deep
>
> Given under my hand in Long 48 E upon the Equator
> Dated 6 May, 1942
> Neptunus Rex Dolphinus

A day later, *Carlisle* stopped briefly in Mombasa to refuel, where Stoke picked up a copy of the *Mombasa Times* which contained this report:

> Heavy air raids on Malta have fallen off but ruthless machine-gunning attacks have again been made. The Director General of the Army Welfare Services compared Malta with Tobruk. He described the morale as fantastically high, the men supremely uncomfortable but supremely happy.

Carlisle departed Mombasa in the early morning of 8 May and anchored in Durban five days later. During this leg of their trip, Stoke listened to Churchill making a speech on 11 May that was relayed via South African radio stations. He obtained a typed extract which demonstrated Churchill's ability to give leadership and a vision to the nation, whether at home or in the Services:

> Here at home in this island, invasion was near, the Mediterranean was closed to us. Our small ill-equipped forces in Egypt seemed to await destruction. All the world, even our friends thought our end had come. Accordingly, we prepared ourselves to conquer or perish, we cast calculation to the winds, no wavering voice was heard, we hurled defiance at our foes, we faced our duty and by the mercy of God we were preserved.

For a whole year after the fall of France we stood alone, keeping the flag of freedom flying and hopes of the world alive.

We suffered grievous reverses in going to the aid of heroic Greece. We bore unflinchingly many heavy blows abroad and still more in our cities at home. We have only to endure and persevere to conquer. Now we are no longer unarmed, we are well armed, now we are not alone, we have mighty Allies bound irrevocably by solemn faith and common interests to stand with us in the ranks of united nations.

There can only be one end, when it will come or how it will come I cannot tell, but when we survey the overwhelming resources which are now at our disposal, once they are fully marshalled and developed as they can be, we may stride forward into the unknown with growing confidence.

Stoke also picked up a copy of the previous Sunday edition of the *Durban Daily News* dated 9 May 1942, in which was an advertisement issued by the South African Bureau of Information in conjunction with the Naval authorities urging the population to be very careful:

Don't talk about ships or shipping!

It never stops at that. The names and destinations of nine-tenths of the ships in port would remain unknown if nobody talked. The lads from an arriving troopship may have told you more than they should. Tell them about South Africa but DON'T ASK QUESTIONS about their ships, or their regiments. The less you know – the less you risk a slip of the tongue.

There were 'neutral' spies everywhere who could supply crucial shipping information that might find its way to help the U-boats in their search for easy targets.

After leaving Durban for Simonstown at the Cape, *Carlisle* was diverted back to Durban to provide escort cover to a delayed 'Winston Special' convoy (WS18) carrying troops to the East, before that convoy continued on to India.

Carlisle rounded the Cape of Good Hope and had a longer stopover in Capetown from 21 to 26 May. Lewis John Jackson, a stoker on board *Carlisle*, recorded his memories for the BBC's *People's War*:

I joined as a stoker and was assigned to the HMS *Carlisle*. We were one of many ships involved in the Malta Convoys. I stayed on *Carlisle* and we sailed down to Cape Town. We were involved in taking on board millions of pounds worth of gold bars. The decks were crawling with Marine sentries. It was all hands on deck to load the staggeringly heavy cargo of boxes on board. I joked with one of the sentries whilst carrying one of the boxes that this one was for the stokers' mess – he soon gave me short shrift. The *Carlisle* didn't have submarine detectors or devices. This made us extremely vulnerable to attacks from such vessels. We were guided safely back to Plymouth by a Dutch destroyer – *Isaac Sweers*.

Paymaster Stoke makes no mention of any gold in any of his subsequent letters but he did bring back a copy of the *Cape Argus* newspaper dated Monday, 25 May 1942 which includes an advertisement for 'The Ellerman & Bucknall Line – Regular Cargo and Passenger Service to England' – the organization his father was employed by for over forty years.

On leaving South Africa there were brief oiling stops up the west coast of Africa before finally reaching the naval port of Devonport in the West Country. On 20 June at 1800 *Carlisle* moored alongside for a refit.

On the same day, back in the Western Desert, Tobruk again faced a targeted German onslaught. But this time, short of troops and air support, Allied troops in Tobruk surrendered after less than two days on 22 June. Captain Frank Mortem Smith, NOIC Tobruk for the past eighteen months and a mentor to the young Midshipman Stoke on his arrival in the Western Desert, was fatally shot while standing in the cockpit of the last ship departing Tobruk harbour.

*   *   *

Carlisle was ready for service again in September 1942, but another Paymaster took over from Stoke as Captain's Secretary – Robert Clarkson, who had also joined up just before Stoke in 1939. They were of similar age but Clarkson had had a slightly less exciting career to date. In his autobiography he recalled *Carlisle*'s recent reputation:

I was relieved to get a letter at last, appointing me Captain's Secretary of HMS *Carlisle*, and ordering me to join at Devonport on 20 September 1942.

I was delighted to be on board. My endless training whilst I had been posted to the Far East would end and I could expect to be a full member of the side.

Her record was second to none. She had been in the front line from the start. She began in Norway and moved permanently to the Mediterranean for the Malta convoy battles, Sirte, Greece, the Tobruk run and the Crete battles. She was not known to the newspapers because she did not sink the enemy but did the dirty work of repelling aircraft. She had a reputation in the Mediterranean for survival.

I learnt this from the Officer of the Day, an RN Lieutenant who had previously served on her. He talked about enemy aircraft, Ju.87s and 88s, He111s and SM79s with a sinister familiarity, seemingly anxious to ensure that I realized how lucky he was to be alive.

'The snares of death compassed me round about: and the pains of hell got hold of me. Thank Christ,' he said, 'that I'm not going back for some more.'

One of my first jobs was to answer a letter from a sailor's mother, who had been killed onboard, and she enquired about his funeral. I sought out the Chief Gunner's Mate who had been there and remembered the occasion and the man. He was in No 2 gun's crew and killed when a bomb near missed amidships. I asked him about the funeral. He said there had not been one. Like a fool I asked why.

'It was a hose and squeegee job', he said … I wrote to the mother that her son had been buried at sunset off Crete with full naval honours.

Besides being a fine Commander, Neame was also a natural athlete, having represented Great Britain in the hurdles event at the Amsterdam Olympics in 1928. He also played cricket, rugby and hockey for the Navy. He completed Paymaster Midshipman Stoke's S.206, marking his skills as follows:

Professional and Administrative abilities – 9 each, Personal qualities, Leadership and Intellectual ability – 8 each. A most able and energetic young officer who has well lived up to the reputation with which he joined this ship from the *QE*. A fine rugger player who plays all games well, a good pianist with a sound knowledge of music and well read. Carries himself well in a Wardroom of which he is by several years the youngest member. Possesses personality and is well above the average of his contemporaries. Has volunteered for special services of an arduous and dangerous type.

Captain Neame also completed Stoke's 'flimsy' on leaving the *Carlisle* on 21 July 1942:

Stoke served with marked ability. A most keen, energetic and capable officer who should go a long way. An enthusiastic sportsman and a fine rugger player.

Then much needed Home Leave followed, the first since leaving the Clyde in October 1940 just under two years previously. Stoke was still only a midshipman, just turned twenty-one, but already with a Mention in Dispatches and the gallantry award of the Distinguished Service Cross from the Siege of Tobruk, and a survivor of multiple bombing and torpedo attacks in the Eastern Mediterranean and on some of the most challenging and dangerous Malta convoys.

Adrian Holloway, another midshipman who had been on the battleship *Valiant*, summed up his departure from the Mediterranean in early 1942:

We had left England as raw schoolboys of seventeen. We returned in early 1942 as battle-hardened veterans of nineteen. We had seen enough action to last many a man a lifetime. Some never made it home. They lie in steel coffins off the coasts of Greece, Crete, Libya and Cyrenaica, in the depths of the eastern Mediterranean. This book is dedicated to their memory.

* * *

It would have been no surprise if Stoke had found it difficult to concentrate on his Sub-Lieutenant Exams in two months! But first he had much to catch up at home and see his old school master, Ivan Brown.

Leigh on Sea
13 July
Dear Ivan,

I am so delighted that I have at last closed the distance and managed to establish speedy communication with you. I hope shortly to be in signalling distance! I anticipate a week's leave within a few days. I return to my ship this Wednesday and would be most grateful if I could come up and see you when my next leave starts between 20–27 July. Naturally for the present, my mother does not like me out of her sight!

Stoke left *Carlisle* and travelled north to Belper to stay with Ivan and his wife for a few days, after which he wrote to thank them:

Leigh on Sea
30 July
Dear Mrs. Brown,

I am just beginning to recover from your splendid hospitality! I never thought that I could ever have spent so wonderful a time in these war-time days or even in normal times. I really did enjoy myself most thoroughly. Not only at the baser level of good feeding but also the joy of seeing such friends again. I travelled home all right though air raids followed me. There was an alert at Derby and at other places. Last night we had over two hours of alarms with heavy gunfire. So, I'm told, as I slept through it! In fact, I didn't stir till 1200.

The rest of August was spent at home, catching up with his parents and his brother John prior to his next posting, which arrived by telegram dated 17 September 1942:

From: B.S. Mallory, Captain's Secretary HMS *Merlin*, Donibristle, Scotland.
     Will you please note that you have been appointed as shown: Merlin – for temporary duty in Commodore's office (CW list of 14.9.42).

He received confirmation of his promotion to Acting Paymaster Sub-Lieutenant dating from 1 September 1942, just prior to taking his exams and getting ready for his next (unknown) posting.

RNAS Donibristle
20 September
Dear Ivan,

Shortly after I got your letter I was moved to the above address in a hurry for a temporary job before a permanent posting as soon as I have finished my exams, which start tomorrow and continue for five days. I am now a highly exalted person – a Sub-Lieutenant with one gold stripe. I was told after staying with you that in all probability my next job would be the Far East. I was rather annoyed having just got home, but how can one move the heart of a stone. But for this temporary position in Donibristle, I might have been on the way now! I feel like Micawber – the longer I'm here, the more possible something may turn up to deliver me! The Russian news is still extraordinary. How the Russians have held Stalingrad should go down as one of the great feats of 'guts'. I managed to go sailing for a couple of hours yesterday evening on the Firth of

Forth, in a cutter. There wasn't really enough wind but I found it extraordinary pleasant.

The next week, Stoke sat his Sub-Lieutenant exams, which covered a number of subjects. These questions are taken from the original exam papers:

Captain's Secretary Work

Q3 (b) Your Captain logs a Sub-Lieutenant for exceeding his wine bill and says he wishes the logging to be permanently recorded. Draft any necessary correspondence.

Q8 What advice would you give in the following circumstances:
   (a) A Bishop takes passage in your ship and the Captain wishes to know what amount he is allowed for his entertainment
   (b) An officer informs you he has recently married a Chilean
   (c) The Torpedo Officer wants to know if a certain mark of torpedo is still on the 'Secret' list

Ship's Office Work

Q2 Forms S.161 and S.165. What are the purposes of these forms, and when are they rendered? What action is taken with the duplicate forms?

Other exams included 'Victualling and Naval Stores', 'Naval Discipline & Court Martial Procedure', 'Naval History', 'Typewriting', and 'French'.

The results of the exams would not be known for six months. Although he did not know it, Stoke's temporary position in Scotland was in readiness for Operation Torch – the invasion and retaking of North Africa, for which large numbers of ships had been arriving in the Clyde, before starting to depart in various convoys from early October.

In his last few days before departing Stoke had met Doreen Le Poidevin, a Third Officer WRNS in the naval signals branch at Donibristle, where she was a cypher operator. Her father, Engineer Captain H.E. Le Poidevin, was Admiralty Engineering Overseer at Yarrow's shipbuilding yard on the Clyde. Captain Le Poidevin was originally from Guernsey, had served since 1905 and was present at the Battle of Jutland in the First World War. He was an Engineer Officer on HMS *Renown* that took the Duke and Duchess of York (the future King George VI and Queen Elizabeth, later the Queen Mother) to Australia and New Zealand on a Royal Tour in 1926. Le Poidevin had taken his wife (Winnie) and Doreen with him on one of his postings to Malta in 1935, so Doreen knew about service life.

News of the results of his exams would not appear until June 1943, when Stoke was still in North Africa, as described in the following letters to Doreen:

18 June

I picked up news in Algiers that I managed a First in my Subs exams last September. I am very relieved and rather pleased as only one other fellow has managed Firsts in both the Cadet and Subs exams, so I shall definitely get my 2nd stripe, promotion to Lieutenant, on 1 November 1943.

5 July

I have received a pleasant note from my old Pay in the *Glasgow* – Paymaster Captain Boutwood. He is now at the Admiralty as Secretary to Hickling, my old Captain of the *Glasgow,* who is now a Vice-Admiral in the Fourth Sea Lord's Office. He says he had noticed my exam results and was glad to see his tuition had successfully come home to roost!

*   *   *

Despite having known Doreen for just a few days, Stoke was definitely smitten. Unfortunately, at the same time, he received his confidential instructions for Operation Torch. He was in Naval Party 623, which would immediately embark on the SS *Duchess of Richmond,* part of KMF2, the last convoy to leave the Clyde on 1 November 1942. He was to undertake another key role in the North African Inshore Squadron, based in the exposed and forward port of Bone on the Algerian/Tunisian border just 50 miles from the German lines, 180 miles from the German and Italian airfields in Sicily and 230 miles east of the safety of the main Allied naval base at Algiers.

Chapter 10

Operation Torch, the Retaking of North Africa

Decorated again

Admiral Cunningham was in overall command of the naval side of Operation Torch but had only recently returned from his posting in Washington, and the detailed naval plan had not yet been fully written. So it was not until the middle of October 1942 that he was able to really get down to the detailed arrangements for the Allied landings in North Africa. Time was very short. He wrote:

I augmented my team with a fourth, from my Mediterranean staff, Commander Power,* who had written many a plan for us and was a master of clear and concise exposition. Our Orders involved the sailing, routing, exact timing and arrival at their respective landing places inside the Mediterranean at Oran and Algiers of two advance convoys of some forty-five ships, to be followed by a main body of more than two hundred vessels with a hundred escorts carrying some 38,500 British and American troops.

Over and above this, the orders laid down the movements and duties of all the naval forces inside the Mediterranean, which, apart from more than a hundred vessels at Gibraltar, meant another one hundred and seventy-six vessels of all types from battleships and aircraft carriers to submarines, sloops, corvettes and motor launches. To ensure the passage of more than four hundred vessels through the eight-mile wide Gibraltar Straits undetected, within a limited period of time, was the problem upon which all else depended.

Additionally, the French Navy manned most of the coastal defences in North Africa. It was highly important that the harbour installations and

---

* Stoke was appointed Captain's Secretary to Captain Manley Power in HMS *Kempenfelt* at the D-Day landings in June 1944 (*see* Chapter 14).

shipping in the ports of Algiers and Oran should not be destroyed before our forces gained control of them.

In view of the huge number of small craft involved, Cunningham applied for and secured the services of Captain Geoffrey Oliver, whom he had known for years and in whose outstanding ability and personality he had good reason to have complete confidence. Oliver arrived in Gibraltar promoted to Commodore.

By the beginning of November Cunningham was ensconced in Gibraltar with General Eisenhower. The procession of large convoys had started moving south, converging on the Straits of Gibraltar and passing close to concentrations of U-boats, but remarkably getting through undetected. It is extraordinary that they were not attacked. The Germans had assessed that the Allied expeditionary forces would land further south, near Dakar on the West African coast, and had massed some sixty U-boats around the Azores and Madeira.

By 3 November the Eighth Army under Montgomery had beaten the Axis forces at El Alamein and Rommel was under heavy land and air attack, retreating westwards towards Tripoli and Tunis. The convoys passed through the Straits on the night of 6/7 November 1942 under complete wireless silence. The main Algiers convoy was spotted, but the Germans thought it was just an extra-large convoy for Malta and subsequently massed their aircraft in Sardinia and Sicily to deliver the usual concentrated attacks.

*   *   *

Back on the Clyde, Paymaster Stoke appears to have already decided that Doreen was the one for him, as evidenced in his first handwritten letter-cum-diary that he wrote each evening on the *Duchess of Richmond* as she made her way down to Gibraltar. He found out on board that he would share a cabin with Commander Philip Baker, who would be his boss as NOIC when they arrived in Bone, under the overall command of the recently appointed Commodore Geoffrey Oliver, SNOIS.

SS Duchess of Richmond
2 November
My dearest,
    When I left you yesterday I had no heart for anything but sauntered back to the club so as to avoid having to speak to anyone. I shall always adore you come

what may and I only ask that at least I may be allowed to be around to do what I can for you.

3 November: Reading what I have written yesterday, it seems highly presumptuous of me to assume you will at all be interested in my odd doings or thoughts – but I still worship you.

You may remember I told you about the size of my apartment (cabin)! It's on the third floor, on the right-hand side, facing the blunt end (i.e. stern). Yesterday I discovered this sign 'Certified to accommodate one seaman'. Whether the Commander is the one seaman and I his shadow is not as yet quite certain.

We have three war correspondents on board, including that very well-known and informed reporter Philip Jordan. He writes in the *News Chronicle*. He has just returned to UK from the Middle and Far East where he covered the Fronts with another *News Chronicle* man – James Lansdale Hodson – who has written a book called 'War in the Sun' which has just come out. The Commander has lent it to me. I found it very interesting as it has a lot about Tobruk in it. It mentions many people I knew very well – the aged NOIC, Frank Mortem Smith, the Australian Lieutenant who kept the Air Raid Log, and he mentions my efforts at repelling the Huns.

4 November (2100): My thumb is still hurting badly so I have turned in so I can take the sling off and try and write. Blast and hell's teeth, the Boss has just arrived with two friends and it will be impossible to think. He has a propensity for whisky. He was drunk before dinner the other night and I shan't be surprised if he is again tonight. And the ship's supposed to be dry! However, I have great admiration for his brain and abilities. If we do not do well at our Port, it won't be his fault. The Commander is well and truly pickled now.

5 November: Most of the officers' bunks are erected in the old cabins of the ship that have been ruthlessly partitioned. The troops are in what were the lounges and smoke rooms. We have just run into dense fog and owing to the Commodore of the convoy making a mess of his signals there have been several frighteningly near collisions. I have just heard the BBC news of the Eighth Army's great success – Montgomery beating Rommel at El Alamein.

7 November (1300): Yesterday (Friday) was not a good day. My thumb got very bad and I was unable to write. This morning we were within twenty yards of ramming the ship abreast of us – our fault too. As a result, we have been sent from being leading ship of our column to the rear!

There are 253 officers and 4,000 troops on board. The ship's staff have given me one of their offices, so my own work is progressing well and all our organization will be on paper by the time we arrive. We hope to have provided for every contingency. The greatest snag is that the German aerodrome of

Cagliari in Sicily is only 180 miles from Bone i.e. well within fighter and fighter bomber range.

8 November (2345): We have just put the clocks forward one hour, so technically it's 0045. I have just turned in, after a rather wearying day. Commander Baker has had to go to the hospital onboard with a strained back, so I am running the show alone. Today was D-Day for Operation Torch. The BBC News is good so far. We are still 650 miles west of Gibraltar so are not yet actually at the scene of operations. The Libyan news is most comforting as we have great hopes of really smashing the Axis.

Philip Jordan gave a lecture today on Russia. It was most informative, witty and interesting. He put it over remarkably well. His principal point was that Russia is looking after No 1 and still suspicious of us. Oh Doreen, I do indeed love you so much it's beyond rhyme or reason.

9 November (2345): As we are now 250 west of Gibraltar the atmosphere is distinctly warmer. The ship is of course too overcrowded. The Commander invited Philip Jordan down to his place of sickness tonight for a talk. I could listen to him for hours. Extraordinarily well informed and has a most acute judgement … I miss you terribly. It's now eight whole days.

10 November (midnight): I have just finished the Bone Planning Memorandum and the Provisional Bone Standing Orders. This has entailed pencil draft, rough typed draft and now wax masters. The boss being ill has not eased the situation. I've also produced posters on health precautions etc. Though we don't arrive for another thirty-six hours, the mail is closing so I will start afresh tomorrow. My thumb should now get better as the doctor dug deep and found a large splinter and extracted it.

The news today is again splendid. Oran (in Algeria) has fallen so all seems to be well. Of one thing I am certain, whatever happens to me, I shall be able to see it through, as I have you to spur me on and guide me as an inspiration. Oh Doreen, you mean so much to me.

All my Love
Mick

11 November
My dearest,

This is the last day on the ship. And what a day! I'm writing this in what has become the customary time of 0130 (on the 12th). We are due in A [Algiers] at 0800. I've had a really hectic day as you can imagine, making all last preparations. I've just realized from the date that today is Armistice Day or was anyway. It makes me feel very cynical that those fellows, who were afterwards betrayed, should have their names mocked, by keeping Armistice Day in the midst of another war. What their sons feel who are now serving or what their widows feel, who have sons in danger, I shudder to think.

The actual war news continues to be good. The North African situation will become interesting now that we are in Algeria and the Boche in Tunisia. My port is only fifty miles from the Tunisian border! However, it's no use imagining anything until I get some facts. I should be in the C-in-C's office in another eight hours. We have changed our English money today into what is termed BMA – British Military Authority – currency until we get sufficient local francs.

The Commander's back is by no means right yet but he hopes to stagger ashore to find out our next move. He's certainly got guts.

Last night I saw again the lights of Spain – always fascinating to see lights again on a shore and La Linea, especially as it silhouettes the Rock. Naturally, most people on board had not seen them before and were excited. Meddlesome Mick after two years previously in the Mediterranean was, of course, very blasé … I still love you more than I can say.

* * *

Arrival in North Africa

An unopposed landing at Bone took place at 0300 on 12 November, when 200 British commandos were put ashore from the destroyers *Lamerton* and *Wheatland*. Though frequently dive-bombed during the day both these ships escaped undamaged. Bone was 250 miles further east than the nearest main landing at Algiers, near the Algerian border with Tunisia and closest to the German Luftwaffe based in Sicily.

* * *

Algiers
12 November
1530

As I should have known, things have gone completely differently to schedule. We arrived off the port of Algiers at 0800 but are only just berthing now at 1500. So far there's only been one air raid. We – the naval party – have been told to remain aboard pending our next move, as apparently accommodation and food ashore is very scarce. So, it looks as if this afternoon will be wasted.

The port is undamaged as far as I can see and the French are very friendly and only wish we had come earlier. The Hun has taken everything he can out of the country. Casualties so far have been light at Algiers but heavier in Oran. That's all I know until I get contact with Rear-Admiral Burrough.

Later at 2330. The BBC have announced tonight that Bone has been occupied, so I wouldn't be at all surprised if I move off tomorrow. We took a walk ashore tonight. You wouldn't have thought an assault had taken place four days ago. All the innumerable French pubs-cum-cafes were open as usual, the population drinking and reading the evening paper. The trams were all packed. The people were most helpful and friendly. The streets are clean and tidy and free of cars as there is no petrol. The Army is breakfasting at 0430 tomorrow and then disembarking, as are the RAF, but I'm glad to say the Navy is breakfasting at 0800 as usual! The only snag that has now cropped up so far I gather is that the locals won't have any truck with the 'fake' BMA money.

Bone, Algeria
17 November
My sweet,
It is certainly is a far cry from England, Home and You to Bone. And perhaps I'm nearer crying than you think! As you can see from the date I have missed several days. I think you will appreciate why when I give you a bare outline of my last few days.

As far as I can remember, we arrived in Algiers on 12 November. Dates are very mixed at the moment as time matters for nothing here. The Commander and myself went ashore that evening to report but it was too dark to find the Naval HQs. We reported the next morning and ever since then life has been hectic. The same day I collected a party of communication ratings and got arms for them, collected CBs etc. and a million other things such as arrangements for W/T traffic, moving the Commander's baggage, until we embarked that afternoon in one of the two assault ships – *Princess Beatrix* and *Queen Emma*. I naturally had a busy evening as we hoped to be in Bone the next morning. I managed to collect nine old RNVR codgers and two Subs for ciphering, but they know nothing of the job.

I didn't turn in till late and was up at 0400 as we expected trouble. This didn't materialize and we entered Bone harbour at 0602 – my official timing. We were the front line – 400 troops, five Naval Officers and twenty-six signal staff, with 4,000 Huns in Tunisia, fifty miles up the coast. Comforting in the extreme!! This I think was 14 November. I had an extremely trying day arranging a naval base and signal station and talking my pseudo French. I finally established my W/T contact with Algiers and turned in at 0300 – a fairly long day.

The two cypher subs are useless – they've only had a two-week course on being commissioned and have no interest in their job. The old codgers have gone to a hotel and are just awaiting events. So NOIC and myself are the 'Marine Anglaise'. We were only lightly bombed this first day and the assault ship returned to Algiers. We felt very lonely – an outpost of the Empire with no guns save our revolvers to face these 4,000 Huns.

The next day was spent arranging accommodation and offices for the rest of our party when they arrive, surveying the port and preparing for a convoy. I was extremely tired by the evening – I was up at 0700 – only four hours sleep and by midnight was almost out. I managed to get to bed (my pile of mail bags on the office floor) by 0100 and slept soundly until roused by the Hun at 0630. He arrived in force with Ju.87s and 88s and really hotted us up. He continued this all day and hampered us considerably. I had to do all the night cyphering as NOIC won't trust the two cypher subs to decipher or make signals on their own authority. Unfortunately, last night was full of signals as a convoy was due today – the first convoy. So, I only got three hours sleep.

Today the convoy arrived and the Hun has really got going. It isn't up to the Tobruk scale yet by far but it's still most nasty. So far, I've been hit only once, but my seaman's knife luckily saved me from a serious wound. The Hun is not over now (2200) and so I'm chucking work for a minute or so in this lull to write this in peace. Unfortunately, our offices are in the port – in fact fifty yards from the quays in one direction and on the quay in the opposite direction. For the moment, the house has only rocked!! I'm on duty again tonight and am expecting a busy night. I may have to become a Florence Nightingale yet!

As far as the job goes, the Commander has made me his right-hand man and lets me act on my own initiative for him. As far as the advance goes, we have I believe now 400 troops ahead of us and 1,600 in the town. The Hun may yet decide to have a go at us. I trust not, however! I rather fancy the odds are against us – their guns versus our five revolvers!! We have no heavy AA guns and only a very few light guns. By day we are pretty naked and by night defenceless against their bombing.

At the moment I'm still just, but only just, contriving to walk about as if this was an every-day affair, air raid shelters are no use to me and there's no danger. It requires great strength of will not to run when the Hun starts machine gunning and to try and put on a brave face before the French. The Hun is overhead again now and so I must stop and get on with my job, ma petite (notice the French fluency) …

The Boche – beg pardon, Le Sale Boche – has gone away and here I am again. That at any rate is another raid over. Owing to my pressing work I have not yet seen any of Bone except the quays!! It is backed by hills which form a plateau to the North and West and has the sea to the East and South. [A sketch plan of Bone harbour was included in the letter]. You can see how our Admiralty House is situated. Eventually, when the rest of our party arrives and the supporting army as well, I am moving everything next door except the signal station – W/T office, SDO, Cypher Office etc. – so it can be self-contained.

The town lies to the north of the harbour. The fellows who have been up there say the wine is cheap and fruit plentiful, but food is in acute shortage. We are living on bully beef and biscuits. The water requires chlorination or boiling before drinking. The French I have met are very friendly indeed and only say why didn't we come earlier to save them. The Italians have pinched everything – all the petrol, car batteries, tyres, typewriters, duplicating machinery ad infinitum. Anyway, we get on quite well. Though I've not 'thought' French for seven and a half years I can already get myself understood and understand them. It's not grammatical, of that I am certain, but still it suffices.

So far, I have slept every night on the floor of the cypher office, as combined duty NOIC and Cypher Officer. I should be honoured to be NOIC's opposite number but it is needing intense concentration to continue to function in the early hours of the morning. Still, enough of my petty griefs. How are you all bearing up in that mighty city of Greenock?

22 November
My angel,

It's now five days since I last wrote to you, but I haven't had time to think or write. It's a long day from 0600 to 0130, when it involves both mental and physical effort. The last five days have been a blur of continuous activity – air raids, running hither and thither, berthing ships in the early hours, pacifying the French and acting as the complete staff until the fifty other naval officers arrive.

On Thursday morning a white object was sighted in the harbour at dawn after a heavy night of raids. It was considered to be a parachute with a mine attached. I volunteered to swim out with a cord to attach to it, so that an attempt could be made to tow it to a less vulnerable spot. I swam in fear and trembling not relishing the idea of a kick in the pants from a mine. However, on my arrival at the mine it turned out to be only a bit of white wreckage. If I hadn't been in the water I think I might have fainted from the anti-climax!

*   *   *

Following the landings at Algiers, Bougie and Bone, the British First Army, under the command of General Anderson, was to then move eastwards to capture Tunis and Bizerta. Within three days they had captured the inland towns of Setif and Constantine and the small port of Tabarka, sixty miles from Bizerta. But within two weeks they were bogged down by the wet winter weather, as it turned out, for the next four months.

Bone, some 250 miles east of Algiers, was quite a good port with several excellent berths for unloading, so it naturally became the advance base for the First Army. It also had an airfield with a good runway from which fighters could operate in most weathers, and was within range of the enemy's supply route by sea from Sicily to Tunis, so well suited to night operations by the cruisers and destroyers of Force 'Q' which based itself in Bone. To be in overall charge of the port of Bone itself and as Senior Officer Inshore Squadron North Africa (SOIS), Cunningham brought Commodore Oliver forward from Gibraltar. As Cunningham wrote:

> His drive and quiet determination proved him to be a veritable tower of strength in a situation that was always difficult and sometimes dangerous. No better man could have been chosen for what was a very trying and difficult job.

The enemy was fully aware of the value of Bone as a supply base for the First Army in Tunisia. The Germans had air superiority and organized savage attacks on Bone every day and night during the rest of November. On the night of 27/28 November there was continuous bombing for five and a half hours. At about 0500 two bombs fell close to *Ithuriel*. The first plunged into the sea a few feet from the ship and exploded beneath the after magazine and shell room. The second fell abreast of the engine room, exploding under the ship. It was apparent that her back was broken in two places, and she had to be beached the next day outside the port to ensure she didn't sink at a valuable berth alongside the quay.

During 1 December 1942 a convoy of four Axis ships loaded with armoured vehicles, munitions and a number of troops was located by Allied reconnaissance planes. Force 'Q' consisting of the cruisers *Aurora*, commanded by Rear-Admiral Harcourt, *Argonaut* and *Sirius*, and the destroyers *Quentin* and *Quiberon*, swiftly departed Bone. With the advantage of superior radar and gunfire, Force 'Q' fell upon the enemy in devastating fashion. The convoy and one destroyer escort were wiped out in a brief overwhelming cannonade, while Force 'Q' suffered no damage.

* * *

1 December

My dearest,

You can see it's been eight days since I last wrote. I don't think I have ever spent so much time up and awake at one continuous spell since the hectic days of Tobruk. Since last writing I have missed completely two nights of sleep. Our main party has arrived and live about three miles away from the port area. But NOIC and myself still live in an ex-Italian house right on the quayside. Here, we get the full benefit of the Hun's twenty-four hour display! So far, I have had my car lifted off the ground while driving and been covered in bricks in bed! I am enclosing a report by a newspaper correspondent on Bone. NOIC and I are up for every air raid.

I am in addition to my now official title of Chief of Staff to NOIC also running his office, as the other Paymaster has gone back to the UK sick. It's going to be a full-time job! If you don't mind I must stop now as my head feels as if my eyes were ton weights. Good night my lovely.

2 December

My dearest,

I am able to write this comparatively early tonight – 0100, as today has been very free of air raids – only two and so I have managed to get more work done. Admittedly one raid straddled our house and destroyed the electric supply, but we are still kicking. I feel very bewildered through only having one-way touch with you at the moment. How I long for the mail. It should bring word from you – perhaps an abrupt order for me to stop writing to you or even perhaps a little encouragement. Nevertheless, nothing can destroy my thoughts and feelings towards you, even if you ignore them. Now if you'll excuse me I must try and get some sleep. All love to you.

3 December

Today's great news was of the great success of Force 'Q' against a Hun convoy. They are based here, so it's peculiarly satisfying to me – Chief of Staff, Bone!!! Oh Doreen, it's all so unreal this present existence. Here, I am trying to do a job which has no precedents or rules, under unnatural conditions. Sleep? Well I have averaged four hours a night. It's hard to maintain a level outlook. It becomes so easy to give in and relax one's standards and become unkempt, bad tempered and tyrannical. Your photograph, with a smile of complete tranquillity, provides me with the essential stimulus to keep going – an incalculable effect … I have had my spies go into Bone but found no

stockings or lipstick. I have found some wool so will send that instead.
All love

Mick

*   *   *

Paymaster Sub-Lieutenant Stoke DSC RN awarded the MBE

Due to the success of the naval action on 1 December, the enemy launched even
heavier air attacks on Bone before dawn on 4 December and that night from
2000 till 0400 the next day. The quays and jetties of the port were congested with
ammunition, petrol and stores. There were many fires and multiple explosions,
with considerable loss of ammunition and valuable material, and fairly heavy
casualties. It was during this action that Stoke was later recommended for and
awarded the MBE. It was just eighteen months since his previous Mention in
Dispatches and the award of the DSC in Tobruk in 1941.

The recommendation was made by Commodore Geoffrey Oliver DSO,
Senior Naval Officer Inshore Squadron, based in Bone, dated 18 January, 1943
(TNA – ADM 1/14306):

> On the night of 4/5 December, 1942, Paymaster Sub-Lieutenant G.A.
> Stoke DSC RN displayed heroic conduct and devotion to duty during
> an aerial bombardment of the port of Bone. Serious fires broke out in
> petrol and ammunition dumps on the South Quay, and Paymaster Sub-
> Lieutenant Stoke, with the Naval Officer in Charge, to whom he was
> Secretary, with great resource and initiative, cleared a petrol ship ——
> [censored]* from its moorings after it had been evacuated by its crew
> and when it was in considerable danger of catching fire. Paymaster Sub-
> Lieutenant Stoke also played a gallant part in moving stores in the face of
> the greatest of dangers.

This recommendation was signed off by both Vice-Admiral Burrough and the
C-in-C Mediterranean, Admiral Cunningham. The award was confirmed by
the Admiralty and the King and published in the *London Gazette* No 36001,
Third Supplement dated Tuesday, 4 May 1943:

---

* SS *Alpera*

Paymaster Sub-Lieutenant Stoke DSC to be an Additional Member of the Military Division of the Most Excellent Order of the British Empire (MBE): for bravery during enemy air attacks in North African waters.

Stoke also received a letter from the Admiralty confirming his appointment as a Member of the Excellent Order of the British Empire for:

Outstanding bravery, resource and devotion to duty during the night of 4/5 December 1942, when the enemy heavily attacked the port of Bone from the air.

*   *   *

7 December
My darling Doreen,
Since last writing I have had simply an awful time. It all started on the night of 4 December. We were blitzed from dusk to dawn continuously – in fact a raid almost of RAF size on an area just 1,100 yards by 400 yards!!! I was up all night and had an active time with fires etc. The next night was worse and a huge fire started. I was engrossed in casting off the bow ropes of a ship, which was catching fire, when I was attacked by a sailor with a knife – he had been concussed and thought I was stealing the ship! I managed to survive him, the bombs and the exploding ammunition and we got the ship safe. She had been deserted by her crew, so NOIC and myself managed the job alone. So that was another two nights without any sleep whatsoever. I never want to have such a period again.
You provide the only means I have of keeping my nerve from breaking. When I am in these fires and raids, I feel like running out of the docks in to a safe area. I merely have to say to myself – 'You can't face Doreen if you bolt' – and so I stay. During the heaviest bombing the night before last, I took refuge from machine gunning by sitting under a railway truck. I felt more than jittery. There was only a bare dozen of us – army and navy – out fighting the fires. But the Hun dropped enough flares to make it as bright as day. I spent a few minutes with your photographs and was able to imagine myself in Greenock again and not in Bone!
My days are full. I am officially NOIC's Chief of Staff and Port Gunnery Officer. I know it sounds incredible but it's true at aged just twenty-one!! These duties are sandwiched between my 'normal' job as Secretary. The Hun is overhead again so I hope I can finish this and get some sleep – I've some days to

catch up!! Remember I am always thinking of you. I shall soon be in Greenock again to disturb a hardworking Cypher Officer from her arduous duties. Good night and Happy Xmas Mick

25 December

My dearest and sweetest Doreen,

I scarcely have the courage to write to you after such another lamentable lapse. I haven't even had time to write home yet since before I last wrote to you. Where to start? The best start is to say that I love you more than ever. You may not know it but the greatest moment of my life was a very small event. It was on that Sunday in Greenock when you allowed me to take your arm. I've never felt so happy. All my fervent ambition right now is to be so lucky for the rest of my life.

Dates have rather ceased to have any meaning these days. Today (or rather yesterday as it is now 0330!) was Xmas Day and has been the worst of many b––y days here. Life has really been hectic, not only with the bombing but also work. My temper – never angelic – has now to be firmly secured before attempting another day. Nerves of all of us are strained and little things get so easily magnified. For example, whereas I found it amusing, in a very small sardonic way, to see the Commander a little unsteady on the troop ship on the way down, it now tries my temper (and discretion!!) considerably. Especially so today, on Xmas Day I had hoped to have a good meal – not bully beef and biscuits – for the festive board. But after the round of the messes he was incapable. My Xmas meal was off and I was left alone to hold the fort.

My position here actually is most entertaining. I'm officially referred to as the Staff, GT&N by the Cruiser Squadron (Force 'Q') here as I run the port AA Defence, Signals and Telephones, as well as acting as CSO [Chief Staff Officer] to NOIC. In my spare moments, I run my own office. My only staff is a writer. He has been described by our Administrative Authority as being of abnormally low intelligence. In fact, I can't even trust him to sharpen a pencil. All I have him for is cleaning the office. As a result, I am averaging a nineteen-hour day. In addition, I am on air-raid duty as 'oppo' to the NOIC, every other night.

I'm rather vague as to what I told you about my being chased by a lunatic with a knife on the burning petrol ship! This event, though nearly curtailing my natural days, must have been very amusing to any third party!

The war seems to be going very well (except here). The Russians seem to have got their steam roller into top gear, whilst the Eighth Army are cracking away. The First Army is not doing too well – the weather here is being difficult and the Luftwaffe is busy. I had the greatest joy yesterday of receiving two letters from you. I have already read and reread them several times and they are true lights of yourself. So, my dear, good night. Whatever the future holds for me, it can never be bleak whilst I have hope or memories to fall back on.

*   *   *

There were particularly heavy daylight air attacks on Bone and the aerodrome at New Year 1943. About one hundred aircraft came over on 1 January, attacking in waves of five. The cruiser *Ajax*, which had only joined Force 'Q' the day before, was severely mauled by a 500kg bomb dropped by Ju.87s escorted by German FW190s, two merchant ships were also damaged and the berthing facilities were much hampered by the grounding of stricken ships. Another sharp attack took place the next day, when *Ajax* was again near missed; the minesweeper *Alarm* had her back broken and had to be beached, while four merchant ships were hit and caught fire. Two of them, which carried petrol, were lost. A report on the damage to *Alarm* describes the initial incident (TNA – ADM 1/14306):

> At 0830 on 2 January *Alarm* was berthed alongside SS *Dalhanna*, when the harbour of Bone was attacked by enemy aircraft. Ship's company went to Action Stations and fire was opened on attacking aircraft. At 0839 a bomb exploded under the stern and it was discovered that the hull had been holed. The ship was moved firstly to a quay where extra pumping could be provided but later the ship had to be beached in the outer harbour.

Meanwhile the SS *Merriel*, a petrol tanker, was bombed and set on fire, her plight exacerbated by burning oil on the water. A second petrol tanker SS *Empire Metal* was also set on fire. Stoke then led a shore party to try and save the SS *Dalhanna* that caught fire later the same evening. In letters written nine months afterwards he refers to that dreadful night at the height of the Luftwaffe bombing.

9 September
I saw recently in a WIR, dated 25 June 1943, a description of damage to the SS *Dalhanna* on 2 January 1943 in Bone written by the Master. If I could lay hands on him I would speak my mind in no uncertain manner. He makes himself out to be a great hero. The facts are that he left his ship as soon as the air raid started and that I was the first person to board his ship during the air raid when she was well ablaze. With assistance from the destroyer *Lightning* and some sailors, we fought the blaze from 1915 till 0300 and eventually got the fires under control and put out. It was during this that I ruined my suit,

although I did get compensation for it! We would have scragged him if we had had the time at that moment. By Jove, it does make me angry to see accounts like that when the RN is dismissed in the phrase that 'the NOIC then sent along a working party who put the fires out.'

* * *

13 January

Dear Mummy and Daddy,

I have just heard the most disappointing news that all my letters to you have gone down to be read by Mr Davy Jones. I shall try to tell you what has happened to me since landing at Algiers, over two months ago. Life has been most strange and strenuous since 12 November. I arrived at Algiers that evening and set off to Bone the next day. It had never been the original intention to take Bone until about another three weeks, so the Army could give us no support. I landed with the NOIC, some signal ratings, two cypher officers and some elderly RNVR gentlemen.

200 Commandos had also just landed and we were the front line. About 80 miles away were the Huns – 4,000 of them armed to the teeth. All that we had to defend Bone with were three revolvers, some rifles and our ingenuity. We were alone in the place for some days until eventually a few army people arrived. We were then, as we have been continuously ever since, blitzed both by day and by night almost on Tobruk proportions. It has been a most wearying time for me.

I have been combining the duties of Port Gunnery Officer, Port Signals Officer and Secretary, with permanently one officer assistant and one rating short. It has meant about a twenty-hour day ever since we arrived, and many nights with no sleep at all, when air attack has been particularly intense or damage to ships and fires have occurred. I have so far myself led two parties and saved two ships from being a total loss.

I live, work and try and sleep in the same building, which is about forty yards from the main quay. That is, right in the target area. So far, we have not been hit, though you would be surprised to hear how many have just missed us!! We have no windows, gas, electricity, or water. Still, we make do. At night, we – i.e. NOIC and myself and one or two hardy souls are the only people in the port area. Everyone else flies to the hills for safety. Now after two months, the scale of attack is diminishing and I think that the worst is definitely past.

The war has not gone too badly here for us, but we have faced tremendous difficulties. The weather is badly bogging us down at the present. The French are still waiting to see who is going to win in North Africa before they show their hands too fully. They are quite happy to see us and certainly seem to prefer us to the Americans.

I myself have been averaging quite a varied job of work. I am in reality Chief of Staff to the NOIC, as well as Secretary, and in charge of the defence arrangements for the port. I was complimented by a cruiser captain on my gunnery and anti-invasion orders. He did not realize that I not only wrote them – but typed and duplicated them as well!

13 January
Dearest Doreen,

Your letter I received today is of course the most important as in it you lay down your 'policy'. You explained things in a way that I could never have put down on paper, though naturally I can't subscribe to it all. For myself, and as you wish it, I won't say this again, I shall continue to feel the same way about you, but shall endeavour to keep it to myself. I don't want to do anything that could possibly hurt or annoy you, but I must make it plain that as long as you will allow me to write to you and IF I am in visiting range to make a fuss of you, I shall be the happiest man in the whole wide world.

The most cheering event so far since I have been in Bone, except for your letters, has been that I have survived!!! It may sound strange to you but as I have been living in what the RAF call the 'target range', it is quite remarkable. I feel always that I am living in a false world. Nothing is real. My work, the air raids, and the strain of the hours etc. all seem to recede and I seem to be living so that I see in a mirror some other Mick who is existing. I am rapidly approaching the stage when I could cheerfully say that I have no further interest in worrying about tomorrow. Though this may annoy you, it's the thought of letting you down that has kept me from showing my complete and utter funk on numerous occasions when I pop off to fight fires in ships and on the quays during air raids.

Commander Baker has had to return to Algiers as a result of a breakdown. He could not keep up the ceaseless grind of almost twenty-four hours a day and worked himself into a frazzle. Actually, the doctor tried to send me back too, but I just managed to evade his clutches. Every time he sees me he tries to take my temperature or my pulse, looks grave and says that I must catch the next boat. However, the job has to be done. My main trouble is I am short of one officer and one writer in my office for its normal duties. My one and only assistant is a Welshman who sings his phrases rather than speaks them.

The armies, both ours and the Huns, are bogged down and show no immediate sign of moving. The Hun Air Force is operating in full force and calls on us frequently. The other night in particular he annoyed me. As a result of his activities I lost a perfectly good suit of clothes in putting out a fire in a ship, which every seaman had deserted. I got together a volunteer crowd and we succeeded in quelling the fire [the SS *Dalhanna* incident].

On the night of 5 December, we had to save a ship in the harbour from a fire, and when I went aboard to throw off her mooring lines, and throw a heaving line to the tug who was going to tow her clear, I was chased by a lunatic armed with a large sized knife. However, I managed to elude him, the fire, the exploding ammo and the bombing Hun [for which Mick was awarded the MBE].

I had rather a nice compliment paid to me today by the Captain of one of the cruisers in port. He is quite a senior bird, and he said my orders for the Gunnery and anti-invasion defence of Bone were better than those of Algiers, where the whole of the C-in-C's staff are based. When he said this, he did not know that I had written them, he thought the present NOIC had!

* * *

Commander Baker replaced as NOIC, Bone

On 9 January Commander Baker had effectively been relieved as NOIC to be sent home on sick leave. He was replaced by a very competent, energetic and engaging man, Captain N.V. Dickinson, who had been in charge of some of the first Algiers Landings of Operation Torch.

As can be seen from the letters home, Baker had relied very heavily on the young Stoke (and alcohol) for support in his seven weeks at Bone, and he wrote on Stoke's 'flimsy':

Acting Paymaster Sub-Lieutenant Stoke DSC has conducted himself with high merit. I could not have wished for a more intelligent, zealous and courageous officer, working under the most arduous conditions in continuous air raids. He has been recommended for accelerated promotion.

Commander Philip Baker arrived in Algiers on 10 January and wrote a personal letter to Stoke's parents from the Hotel Aletti:

Your son asked me to send you a cable saying that he is fit and well, but I find there is no cable service here, so I am sending his message by air mail. I should, of course, explain that I am his Captain at Bone, but I am here in Algiers for a few days. I should like you to know what wonderful work he has done, the reward for which I hope is coming to him by way of accelerated promotion. I can say without exaggeration that I have never come across a more efficient and at the same time charming young man. He is working very hard and long hours, which explains why he has not had much time to write to you. I hope, however, that soon he will be able to get some sort of relief, as we have been through a pretty strenuous time at Bone. I am sure you must be very proud of him. We certainly are.

Commander Baker later wrote an eyewitness account of a typical day in Bone for the popular periodical *Blackwood's Magazine*:

At a Port in Algeria

The dawn raid on Bone was over. The last screeching bomb, driving one flat on an empty and quivering tummy, had fallen; not far from HQ, but far enough, thank heavens, from the ships and quays piled with ammunition and petrol. The sun's first rays were lighting the eastern hills. From the signal station of my office, as Naval Officer in Charge, Bone, we looked over our port and sighed with both exhaustion and relief; our ships were all there, our quays untouched.

The first of the queue of important visitors arrived as the steward brought in the kedgeree. A batch of convoy signals was flung to Staff Officer Operations to analyze. We note they intend for a convoy to arrive at 2200, just in time for another night air raid! Ten ships will scream for but three available pilots, and those which are not bombed, torpedoed or mined will ram the breakwater. Each day a horde of people invade us, unheralded and unasked for. Stoke, my Secretary, groans into his coffee. Bone, two months ago a silent waste, is now as busy as the Liverpool docks.

The daily Port Committee Meeting is attended by the naval and military officers whose job it is to clear the convoys and get their cargoes forward to the fighting line. It is a good team for we cannot afford to delay the turn-round of ships, especially in this much bombed port. As though to emphasize the point, the sirens scream; we disperse. A wave of twenty-five aircraft are reported. They are drawing nearer and lower. We can hear the roar of their engines now. 'Enemy aircraft over the harbour. No limit to gun-fire.' The 5.5s of our cruisers, the 3.7s of the shore batteries, pompoms, Bofors, Oerlikons, rockets – they're all at it.

There are three of the swine tearing down the harbour now. We see their bombs fall slowly – it seems so slowly – in a parabolic curve. Will they hit that line of ships along the quay? Two great splashes leap from the Outer Harbour. A rush of flame erupts out of a merchant ship. 'Away fire-float; call up the ambulance; order the tug to stand by!' For four long hours the raid continues. As dusk falls the enemy fades away. Two ships are burning furiously. Two other ships are damaged, a trawler sunk and an escort vessel with a broken back from a near–miss. It is Bone's fifty-second air raid in less than two months.

In a remarkable coincidence, on 8 January Captain Poland, Stoke's boss in Tobruk eighteen months earlier, stepped down as Captain (D) of *Jervis* (of the Battle of Sirte fame), then based in Malta. Poland records in his diary that he flew to Algiers, eventually taking off from Malta at 0300 early Monday morning, 11 January, arriving in Algiers at 0815. He straightaway took off for Gibraltar but due to bad weather had to return. After much trouble he got a room at the same Hotel Aletti, recording:

Had a few drinks in the bar. Met Baker on sick leave from Bone there. Fed with him and four airmen at Café Oasis – food not bad.

An hour earlier, Baker had written the letter to Stoke's parents in the same hotel, and two days earlier, had recommended him for accelerated promotion. One wonders what they said over drinks and dinner about the young man, as Poland had also recommended him for both his Mention in Despatches and his DSC whilst in Tobruk! Both men were fortunate to return to the safety of England, whilst Paymaster Stoke had another five months to endure in Bone.

Chapter 11

The Turn of the Tide in North Africa

Bone
17 January 1943

Dear Mummy and Daddy,

Mail is very frustrating as I have only received four letters since leaving England in mid-October. The war news is on the whole, as far as we can see from our limited perspective good, though our own sector is causing a little anxiety. The Eighth Army, under Montgomery, travelling rapidly west through Libya after victory at El Alamein, are certainly going great guns and by the time you get this they should no doubt be in Tripoli and well entrenched. In fact, it is said in rather a laughing mood, that the Eighth and not the First Army is to take Tunis and Bizerta, which is, as you may know, only about 100 miles from Bone. We shall have to keep a careful watch in case the Hun does one of his spectacular breakthroughs in our direction. Still, I suppose it can't be worse than when we arrived here, all six of us to face 4,000 Huns.

Naturally, as the foremost base, we must expect a lot of attention from enemy aircraft. But the Hun is not getting the results he expects. The number of his casualties over Bone in the air now runs well over three figures, so that gives you an idea of the scale of his effort. At the beginning, when our defences were non-existent, raids by night of sixty machines were not uncommon and the port area, where I live on the North Quay, is their only target and it is only 1,100 yards long by 400 yards wide. I live on the North Quay.

17 January

My dearest Doreen,

At Bone the routine is not yet established and things are still all improvisation and hand to mouth. Still, the port has functioned and done its job. I gather that Cunningham has expressed his satisfaction. The routine bombing and E-boat attacks have continued. My great ambition at the moment is to lie in and relax for as long as I desire, in a really hot bath. I have not had a hot fresh water bath since before leaving England. Coming down we only had salt water to bath in.

Since arriving in Bone, I have only had a daily cold shower, which though it keeps me fresh, does not give me that joy of relaxation. It has always been one of my simple pleasures to lie in hot water.

I had a short note from Commander Baker yesterday from Algiers. He is apparently a very sick man and I don't think he will return to Bone. I can't say I am over sorry. He was always a most charming man but he was not easy to get on with towards the end. He took more and more to the bottle and as a result it was quite a strain hiding him from people who wanted to see him, when he was not in a fit state to be seen. Xmas Day was his worst. He mentioned in his letter that he had seen Captain Poland in Algiers, though I am not sure why or how.

24 January
Dear Mummy and Daddy,

Thank you so much for the Xmas Greetings. Though belated, they do recompense for a rather miserable Xmas. My boss (Baker) was drunk for the majority of the day. I had not only his job and mine to carry out but also to conceal the fact to the outside world that he was incapable. However …

Anyway, he has gone, not to return and we now have a new NOIC who is an Active Service Captain – N.V. Dickinson. He is really competent and has a good sense of humour. More than anything else, that is required on this job. For here, things never go as expected. Still, the port is functioning despite tremendous air attacks by the Hun. Tobruk scale has been reached at times. Actually, the NOIC and myself are the only people who have to face all the bombing. Because we live and work in the docks and so are plumb in the target area. Everyone else lives well out in the country so are safe at night. Still, the job has to be done. My chief trouble still continues to be lack of sleep as it is a working day of twenty hours.

In addition to what would be my ordinary duties, I have, of course, these extra staff duties – gunnery, signals and operations. This entails duty on alternate nights, which has been recognized by Commodore Oliver, who is in charge of all the ports and the ships operating from them – the Inshore Squadron, the same organization as I was in the Western Desert, only far bigger – that things are difficult for me and he has made many requests for extra staff.

The Eighth Army has taken Tripoli. That certainly is a great achievement. Admittedly, the Hun is smashing at the First Army and they have had to give a little ground. Great will be the relief at Bone, however, when the Hun is out of Tunisia as his air attack and possibly ground attack is a constant threat. I hope that in another couple of months we may have reached the end in Tunisia.

The death of Darlan [a Vichy French admiral who struck a controversial deal with the Allies] has relieved a lot of tension out here. We have had some very sticky times with the French and I don't think that the average person who has had to deal with the French authorities will be very cordial, though the fraternization between troops and population is excellent.

Daddy, thank you very much for the book 'Years of Endurance'. Is this supposed to be a hint of the extent of time I am going to be in Bone? I hope not!!

24 January
Dearest Doreen,

Yes, it's that man again to plague the life out of you! As usual the chief complaint at Bone continues to be about mail. It's very extraordinary how the lack of mail brings us all to one common level. The half-wit or the Rear-Admiral all want letters and even a tailor's bill can be gratefully received at times.

The war here has taken a new turn. The Huns are managing to make progress against our right flank where the French are. I don't think we will have to get out of Bone, but it is a situation that must forever be present in our minds. The enemy airforce continues to be very active over Bone. It has been up to the Tobruk standard at times. My personal trouble is that living in the port area day and night there is never any let up or relaxation from the worry that one day my nerve may break. Funnily enough, that is always my fear. Not so much the actual bombing, but that I will disgrace myself and my friends by not being able to take any more of it. Still, it is only when I get depressed that this really preys on me.

I am still hoping to get an assistant. If and when he comes and also sufficient other officers to relieve my gunnery, signals and staff duties, I shall be able to live a more regular life and get out to see Bone and its environs.

I believe that Commander Baker is returning to England. It is a pity for him as it may mean he loses his third (acting) stripe, but Commodore Oliver thinks that he is not quite suited for the job, in view of his likeness for the bottle (so I am told!).

31 January
The Hun has not left us alone but his efforts are not on his original scale. We have nearly as many alerts as before but as many aircraft do not materialize as often as they did. But it does not relieve one of the mental worry that you do not know that any particular raid is not going to be a heavy one. Still, I think the worst is over.

31 January

You will have noticed that the address is now HMS *Cannae*. It has taken overlong to be decided by Their Lordships what we were going to be called. They have now produced some quite respectable and well-known classical names – *Cannae*, *Scipio* and *Hannibal* being Bone, Oran and Algiers respectively. I think I remember the date of the Battle of Cannae. Is it 216 BC? This resulted in the defeat of the Romans by Hannibal and historians say if he had only gone on he could have captured Rome. However …

This week I took my first spell away from Bone. The medical men said that if I did not go away for at least a day they would send me back to Algiers. As I am the only original Bone 'assault' party left of the three services, I took a very dim view of this. So, I went up to Tabarka. It is a little port about sixty miles to the east of Bone and is just in Tunisia, whereas Bone is in Algeria. The only snag is that Tabarka is only a very few miles from strong enemy positions and really at the moment is in no-man's-land. Air raids are quite nasty being mainly of the fighter bomber variety with FW.190s. Still, it was good to be merely a spectator (or victim) without having to worry about the port and ships. I was only away for the day but I think that the small change of twelve hours may help a lot.

I drove there in a requisitioned Citroen with a front wheel drive. It is a most peculiar sensation especially as the gear lever is in the dashboard, in a most awkward place. The lights had been so very well blacked out that it was impossible to see the kerb on either side of the road. The road is abominable and one crawls around the face of the mountainside with a steep precipice on the left-hand side. We traversed this in pitch black darkness with no moon. The car eventually stopped as the petrol had been watered down. We had to hitch the last twenty kilometres back. So ended my picnic.

7 February

Ivan's letter says he spent two nights with you and had a good time. He has a hearty respect for Daddy's debating powers. He remarks that Daddy's range of reading and his memory are phenomenal. He seems to think Daddy is more liberal than him. I think this is true. Ivan has to me always seemed to be cynical towards real democracy and believed in benevolent despotism. Mummy he calls kindly, bright and breezy. I have also received a letter from ten months ago, dated 12 April 1942 re-directed via the *Queen Elizabeth*, *Carlisle*, *Merlin* and home!

7 February

Dearest,

Tonight was a red-letter night. For the first time since arriving at Bone, I took a little time off. I went across to the cruiser *Sirius* in the harbour and saw the Noel Coward film 'In Which We Serve'. It was extraordinary that your letter should have arrived only two days before describing your reactions on seeing it. For myself, I was frightfully impressed and thought it marvellous. The whole atmosphere was exact to the last detail, and the words and actions of every member of the ship's company were true to life, as indeed was the whole story, which was not a bit over-pitched. The ship only shot down one plane and the heroes did not get any medals. You can find those officers and men on any ship of the fleet.

It makes me feel ashamed to be afraid of death in Bone, when such experiences come to folks in Plymouth, Greenock and small ships. I agree with you that the speech of the Commanding Officer's wife was a highlight and I trust that you will pardon my remark, but I seemed to see you in every action and word. After all, if you are not a Captain's wife, you are a Captain's daughter. I feel very humble as it is people like her who have the bitterest burden. They have the continual suspense, whereas the chap at sea has only the momentary qualms of actual danger. It is the first film that has ever moved me.

The change in my mood was terrific and the civilizing atmosphere of a ship, fresh faces, a drink of Drambuie – that particularly – and the spirit of being truant, all combined to make me feel a brighter man.

I am feeling very hopeful of the war in North Africa. Once the Hun is thrown out of Africa our next moves are speculative. Personally, I think we shouldn't attack Italy. If we attack through Greece or the Balkans we shall have enthusiastic supporters immediately. Then Italy will fall as a natural consequence without much further ado. All I hope is that I don't get stuck to vegetate in Bone until the affair in Southern Europe is over.

14 February 1943

Randolph Churchill has been into lunch with us. Our mess – consisting of NOIC, our SOO and myself – have achieved a certain notoriety in North African circles for its feeding and so he pops in on us when he is passing. He had met our new NOIC, Captain Dickinson, when they were both at Tabarka. Dickinson was in command of the landing craft and Randolph is in the Commandos. He is not a bit like his father, Winston, and I for one, would never have connected him with the PM.

The second time he arrived with Ward-Price. Unless my memory is at fault, he is the *Daily Express* correspondent, but whether he is a good man I do not know, for Randolph talks most of the time and so Ward-Price didn't have much chance to shine.

Dickinson was in charge of the assault parties at the beginning of Operation Torch. He then moved the Commandos up the coast to their raids near Bizerta. He was on his way back to England, passing through Bone, when Commander Baker went sick, and Dickinson was detailed to be temporary NOIC. He is a young destroyer Captain – about forty-two.

The food situation is improving. I have discovered that the American cargo ships that are arriving at Bone seem to have insufficient liquor on board for the excessive requirements of their American seamen. For the good of the mess, I have been giving up my rations of spirits to these ships in return for fresh meat, butter and fish. In addition, I have some French contacts whom I have been cultivating since the beginning, who obtain for me supplies of fresh food, such as lettuce and cabbage. For eggs we have encouraged some twelve hens to live in a wire pen constructed in the back of the house, who manage to produce four eggs a day. We have moreover persuaded one hen to be broody over twelve eggs, so we may soon have an increase in our flock. I am also contriving to get some chocolate from Gibraltar from one of the escorts that run back and forth, which is one of my weaknesses. Regrettably I have had no letters from home since 28 December.

21 February

The rain has been torrential for a few days. Lakes have been springing up as fast as you look out of the … I was going to say window, but of course my dwelling has none. Lately here, the bombing has died down. The Hun seems unable to decide whether to make a valiant effort to try and retrieve Tunisia, or whether to cut his losses as he has done in Tripolitania.

24 February

Dearest Doreen,

I am writing this mid-week as I have been thinking about you all day. The workmen are in our house. I have had a tame French contractor here since we landed and he does us proud, much to the envy of all of Bone, as he is under contract only to <u>me</u>. He has built my Signal Station, SDO, Cypher Office, all to my design and my French orders! His latest effort is our galley complete with H&C, built-in cupboards, saucepan racks etc.

25 February

I have a chance to send this letter back by an officer returning home – Commander Stoker (no relation!). He is part of the Ministry of Information and goes around the country telling everyone what wonderful heroes there are in the Navy. He has come out here to North Africa to get some local colour into his talks. He expressed a wish to the NOIC to see the Church of Saint Augustine and the NOIC asked me to drive him there. So, we have had a very pleasant afternoon.

28 February

I am getting very restless here because the job is now organized, as far as my meagre ability can take it. I am rapidly losing interest in Bone because there is nothing new and the rough and nervous excitement of the first three months is running down, leaving monotonous work with no joy. It is reported locally that in the first two months at Bone, we have shot down one hundred and fifty-eight enemy planes. In addition, another hundred are claimed as 'probables'. It gives an idea of how many enemy planes have been over us at times. The dock area is now completely flattened except, remarkably, our house on the quay!

1 March

A most interesting visitor this week caused quite a sensation. I was in my office when a very flustered Brigadier blew in and said, 'The C-in-C's outside to see the NOIC.' I thought it must be Admiral Cunningham in person, but in staggering outside saw a mere pongo [Navy slang for army personnel] General, who seemed vaguely familiar. I took him up to NOIC and he said, 'Are you Dickinson, my name's Alexander?' Yes, it was General Alexander in person, with only his COS, ADC and driver. He honoured us by being the first to be called on in Bone, long before he called on his own people. He refused to stay to lunch to eat our rations but went into the dock area and ate his sandwiches with the troops there. A very good man he seemed and most intelligent with his questions.

A war correspondent came to see me this morning, called Devine. I think he is quite well known, and I shall be interested to read the book he is producing on the campaign, including the Navy's part in Bone.

*   *   *

The American war correspondent, A.D. Devine, published *The Road to Tunis* in 1944 about Operation Torch, the American landings and his various visits to key naval locations in the campaign, including meeting the young Paymaster Stoke in Bone:

> I was one of three men in the area for the Allied newspaper group – Kemsley Newspapers. We provided a service for the *Sunday Times*, *Sunday Chronicle*, *Sunday Graphic* and *Empire News* among the Sunday papers; and a number of British regional papers – with a total circulation of over six million.
>
> I had just been recalled from another area to Algiers, in order to provide more naval news. I have always found the sea exquisitely soothing, even in time of war. Clean linen, regular meals, a permanent roof over one's head, armchairs and the possibility of going into battle sitting down, have always appealed to my fundamentally lazy nature.
>
> I arrived on board HMS *Sirius*. Captain Brooking, who commanded *Sirius* on the night of 1/2 December when a whole Axis convoy was destroyed by Force 'Q', addressed a large gathering of War Correspondents after that successful battle: 'Gentlemen, I don't know what the collective noun is for a large gathering of War Correspondents unless it is possibly a 'Flush' of WCs!'
>
> Bone stands as the second great miracle of the naval side of the war in North Africa. On 12 November two destroyers went into the harbour. The next day at dawn two ships (ex-Belgian Channel steamers and now amongst the most famous of all the British assault ships) landed the harbour party of five officers, [one of whom was Paymaster Stoke], twenty-six ratings and 200 commandos to take over the aerodrome.
>
> Enemy air raids immediately started on that first day. In December there were twenty-one daylight raids and forty-seven night-raids. In January thirty-three day raids and fifteen night-raids. The defences fought back magnificently. In those first days there was almost no equipment and the main burden fell on HM Ships.
>
> Bone was a little Malta of its own, and the band of men who ran it were as valiant as the men of Malta – Commander Baker, the first naval officer in charge; Captain Dickinson, who had succeeded him; Commodore Oliver, Senior Naval Officer of the Inshore Squadron; Commander Edwards, his assistant; and Paymaster Sub-Lieutenant Stoke MBE, DSC then at the mature age of twenty, the oldest inhabitant of Bone – an engaging and efficient young man who, if not shot by an infuriated senior officer, will one day become a Paymaster Rear-Admiral of rare qualities.

In Stoke's office I met Commander Walters of the destroyer *Lightning*, and in the middle of the afternoon I went aboard. At 1700 we slipped. We made sorties into the dark Sicilian channel over the next three nights but each time Italian convoys turned for home when realizing the British navy was on the sea at night. To the Malta convoys, to the Murmansk convoys, to the men who ran the Tobruk life-line, must be added the men who ran Bone.

Remarkably, Stoke was involved in and survived all of those key theatres highlighted by Devine.

*   *   *

7 March
This week, one night there was a big fire in the docks and I was wandering my way towards it in the darkness, so I put on a small light. Almost immediately I felt a shot over my head and one of our own sentries shouting 'Put out that f—g light …' Really!!

12 March
Dearest,
    We have been having a quieter time at night recently, with usually only about a dozen Hun aircraft overhead. But the last two nights he has upped this to about twenty-five each time. Tonight, during a lull, I went to fetch the mail. As I was returning, they came over again and I was hit by a piece of shrapnel in my leg, but it was worth it just to get your letters!
    Our farmyard at the back of the house now boasts fourteen chicks and two rabbits. I have never set out to be a country lover, but it's most interesting to watch for a few minutes each day the way in which rabbits, hens, chicks, and pigeons can all live together with no quarrels, strife or enmity between them, unlike us humans!
    Our house on the quayside belonged to an Italian architect and now includes living-quarters and working space for the NOIC, SOO and me. There is one room on the ground floor, which houses my office, my writer and I work in my cabin. On the 2nd floor a lounge/drawing room/dining room plus kitchen area. The 3rd floor has three bedrooms and a bathroom and above a maid's room. By scrounging around for materials, I have organized a number of other erections built by my local French contractor. On top of the maid's room is the Signal

Tower and Yeoman's room. This is quite large. On the balcony I had built an SDO with voice pipe for communication with the Signal Tower. The maid's room is our Ops room. In here we have a long board, 9′ x 3′ with the coastline and longitude etc. painted on. We stretch coloured threads, pinched from some local bunting, to mark the convoy routes! Alongside there is a tracking chart for aircraft. We have built a galley with a big army stove, as the bombing is always cutting off our gas supply. Our bathroom is quite renown up and down the coast as the bath is let into the floor, completely tiled and is 10′ x 4′ x 4′!

14 March
I see Mummy is continuing her preoccupation as to whom I should get entangled to for life. I will say that I have got some idea on the subject but have been warned off for an indefinite period, though a very friendly correspondence is maintained. When I come back I will tell you all about it. Anyway, matters may have sorted themselves out by then.

We had two newspaper men in again this week. One is Rasmussen, a Norwegian broadcasting for the BBC, and the other is George Harrison who is a *News of the World* representative. I believe that Rasmussen is going to try and arrange a broadcast from Bone. It will, of course, be primarily for the sake of ships in the port, which is fair enough, but there may be some message from us as Bone Base.

* * *

There are copies of two newspaper articles written by Rasmussen in the Stoke archives. Handwritten on one of them is: 'To Lieutenant Stoke RN – Guide, Philosopher and Friend. With best wishes A.H. Rasmussen.'

* * *

14 March
I have just heard that my only really close friend of my schooldays is now in Algiers but I don't know his unit yet. When I was at school, and even now, I do not make close friends easily. During my schooldays I got to know numerous folk through my many interests and yet I have only one with whom I am what I consider on close terms of friendship. He's a year older than me – steady and clever, is well read and fond of music and all the arts. With this, he is also an enthusiastic cricketer and a good rugby player. Rather an extraordinary combination.

This afternoon was a social event. The *Capitaine du Port* is sixty-one and has been harbour-master of Bone for thirty-five years, having succeeded his father. He and his wife invited NOIC, myself and the ABO to tea at 1600. It was a terrific effort to make small talk in French with Madame, as my French is not exactly Parisien!

21 March
The Italian radio reported this morning that they had sunk three merchant ships in Bone last night, and wiped out Force 'Q'. It provided another instalment for *Punch*, though it does grow monotonous. The only excuse that could be offered is that with smoke, flames and shells belching forth from ships in the port, it might be mistaken for a hit of some sort.

   This evening was very interesting. Randolph Churchill came to spend the night, as he often does. We put on the news as usual at nine, and we were all most surprised to hear that the Prime Minister was going to make a speech. It was quite fun to hear the man, with his son not a yard away from me. Randolph always refers to his father as Winston or the PM, never as 'my father'. He seems very proud of him – not surprisingly. Randolph talks a lot, especially when he has a certain amount of whisky in him and it was very amusing.

21 March
For the moment I am producing the Port Orders with the SOO. It's rather amusing to think that I am producing orders to control the Rear-Admiral and his Cruiser Squadron based here! So far NOIC has not altered any of my orders. We have had success this week in shooting down the enemy in the air. It makes such a difference when you can see the brutes tumbling from the sky. When I first came into contact with the war, I felt it was an awful pity that brave men had to be shot down. But seeing hospital ships bombed, tented field hospitals machine gunned and survivors in open boats bombed, has turned my kindlier feelings into vindictiveness. It is quite indefensible that I am pleased when hearing enemy aircraft have been shot down with fatal results.

22 March
There is a buzz locally that our beloved NOIC may shortly depart. I hope by now you may have received the small bag of sugar I sent. This evening we heard the Grieg piano concerto on our radio.

24 March

This evening I stumbled on the quayside and whilst saving myself from falling in the water badly sprained my ankle and did no good to my only suit. The other was ruined when fighting a fire in SS [deleted by censor] in early January. I am sending this letter in HMS [deleted by censor] which leaves tonight directly for Home. [It was the SS *Dalhanna*, and this is one of only three letters Stoke wrote which has had parts cut out by the censor.]

28 March

I am feeling much brighter these days, though still rather fatigued, but the pressure of work is steadily declining and as I am expecting my successor soon, I am agitating for a move, even if it implies a move to Algiers. I am not particular where I go, but I have no wish to remain in Bone. The war is a little static here. The First Army's preliminary probe doesn't seem to have found that necessary soft spot so they are going very shortly to try again. With Alexander in command of both Armies and invigorated by his visit to us, all should be well.

28 March

I am writing tonight to Wolsey Hall, Oxford enquiring about a postal Honours History Degree course. I passed my London Intermediate BA back in 1938 and I feel it would be quite fun to finish it off and get a degree.

30 March

My old ship, *Carlisle*, came in with a convoy and although she has been recommissioned, she still had three officers from the old show. They are more than fed up as the new Captain apparently is a tartar. [For more on this visit, see Clarkson R., *Headlong into the Sea*.]

4 April

Still have not found a piano, so my fingers are daily becoming nothing better than bangers of this typewriter. I think that Mummy is unduly hopeful about the war ending soon. After all, the Hun still has a huge slice of Russia and a modest powerful army still in existence. Most of the German casualties are from the satellite states, and I personally do not conceive that the war can possibly be over at least for another winter. I am not at all hopeful that it will finish in Europe before the spring of 1945. And then we will have to contend with the Little Yellow Men. What a thumping they must have to make them learn their lesson. [Very prescient for a young man who had been in North Africa for five months!]

4 April

There is a buzz around here that my days here may be numbered but to where we don't know. We also heard last night that Captain Dickinson has been awarded the DSO for his handling of the assault at Algiers and Bougie.

14 April

Last night I was summoned out to dinner by the local HQ Army Mess. I felt I couldn't refuse an official invitation as the Naval Representative. I chucked work at 2000 and tottered off with my best wing collar and suit. When I arrived, I found the principal guest speaker was none other than General Clarke of the First Army.

18 April

I am sorry, but this is not going to be a good letter as I am feeling lousy, yes lousy is the word. I have an annoying attack of flu or some such malaise, which makes me feel that it would be grand to be blooming well dead. It's unfortunate that this is occurring whilst we undergo a very rapid change of NOIC and so I can't go sick – in fact I have just had to work a night through to finish certain things off before Dickinson goes. I am afraid that now he has gone, I am completely bored with Bone. He was the most gentlemanly and yet most efficient man that I have ever encountered and he was the admiration of the local army. He was whipped away from us suddenly and I have strong hopes of following him up. He has gone to take command of a Landing Craft Base. I feel in my bones, I must stir soon.

Our latest visitor is a Commander Anthony Kimmins, who is staying with us. He has provided national broadcasts from most major naval operations. When I think of the many famous people who pass through here, it makes quite a formidable list.

The war seems to be progressing here quite well. I still think that Bizerta is going to be a mighty bloody affair with all its natural fortifications and the very rough and difficult country involved. The French are still no nearer to winning my affections. I also think that a statement of some of the facts about the British forces would not come amiss. It really is annoying to hear all the slogging of the First Army in filthy conditions, and so forth, ascribed to the gallant Americans. Still, I am on dangerous ground and will be court-martialled!

*   *   *

As he was leaving Bone, Captain Dickinson wrote Stoke's S.206 and his 'flimsy':

> An outstanding young officer with an amazing capacity for work. Not only is he most capable in his own work but can turn his hand to anything. Cheerful, well-mannered and always most considerate and as has been proved, most courageous. I would be very pleased to have him work with me again. Stoke served to my entire satisfaction. An exceptional Officer. Full of energy and a capacity for hard work. He is most efficient in all he does.

Additional comments came from Commodore Oliver:

> An exceptional all-rounder. As the campaign moves forward, he should move with it.

And Commodore Oliver was as good as his word when he was transferred to work with the US on the next major joint operation – Operation Husky. He promoted Stoke on to his staff for the next big strategic operations – the invasion of Sicily and then mainland Italy. Stoke would firstly be based in Bizerta and then the Allied Combined HQ, just outside Algiers.

* * *

20 April
A most extraordinary thing happened the other day. Some of my mail turned up in my old ship – *Carlisle* – which had again arrived here in Bone and so they handed it straight over to me. It turned out to be a Xmas present from my old Sunday school.

* * *

After six months of refit and with new radar equipment, *Carlisle* had arrived in North Africa in April 1943 with Paymaster Clarkson on board, who succeeded Stoke as Captain's Secretary. Clarkson recalled:

> We sailed for Bone, the nearest port to the frontline, where the First Army were engaged with the Afrika Korps. An RAF squadron leader joined to

deter us from engaging friendly aircraft! The convoy of about twenty ships formed up with *Carlisle* in the middle as anti-aircraft guard and as escort for the five Hunt class destroyers and corvettes spread out on the screen.

The first attack came at dawn the day after leaving Algiers. A Heinkel 111 torpedoed a merchant ship and skipped away at wave top height apparently untouched by the barrage from the convoy and its escorts. The attacks became heavier the next day. A mixed force of nine He.111s and three Italian SM.79s came in with torpedoes and were engaged with everything we had. My action station was on the bridge and I watched them at full throttle flying for their lives above the broken sea, trying to get close enough to make sure. Another merchant ship, the *Empire Rowan*, was sunk. The Italian airmen in old slow aircraft, with no armour or adequate defence, showed courage that was an inspiration to see.

Alongside at Bone the shell cases littering our upper deck were thrown into a lighter and replaced with fresh ammunition. After leaving some mail for my predecessor, Stoke, two hours later we were on our way back to Algiers with another convoy. *Carlisle* was escort on seven more convoys running between Algiers and Bone.

By the middle of April Cunningham and his senior team started making plans for Operation Husky – the invasion of Sicily, targeted for early July.

*   *   *

25 April

I am enclosing an account of a sweep by a Coastal Force craft based at Bone that had the benefit of having Rasmussen, the war correspondent onboard. These sweeps are nightly affairs. He is Norwegian and about sixty but spoils for excitement. He is quite a friend of mine and I do endeavour to help these correspondents to get their material away. I am told there is a chance that I may be moving in three weeks' time to an organization that is preparing for the next Front. We added one more distinguished visitor yesterday when General (Ike) Eisenhower came to visit Bone.

Stoke's MBE was published in the *London Gazette* on 4 May 1943, and notification was immediately received in Bone.

6 May

Dear Mummy and Daddy,

I am a very superior person as I am now a Member of the British Empire and so over such ordinary beings who are merely 'de facto' or 'de jure' members. DSC, MBE RN sounds quite senior until you put 'Sub' in front of it!! The other member of our Mess has decreed I be called Dame as being more appropriate, and it will prevent an already swollen head becoming too big.

The war locally is rapidly drawing to a conclusion. Bizerta and Tunis are ours and there's only a mopping up to conclude everything. We have been hectically busy naturally but are beginning to see an end in sight.

*   *   *

By early May the German and Italian forces were retreating in Tunisia, finally being penned into the narrow Cape Bon peninsula to the east of Tunis. Admiral Cunningham recalled:

On 8 May, hearing from Army HQ that Allied troops were in Bizerta (incorrectly), Commodore Oliver at Bone hoisted his broad pennant in a MTB and proceeded thither accompanied by a motor gunboat. Entering the harbour soon after 1000 they were received with heavy, close-range fire from cannon and machine guns and were forced to retire. They were lucky to escape. Oliver's pennant was finally hoisted in Bizerta two days later.

To prevent a Dunkirk-style evacuation by Axis forces from Cape Bon to Sicily, I sent the following signal to my destroyers stationed off the coast of Tunis: 'Sink, burn and destroy. Let nothing pass.' No Axis troops attempted to cross the Sicilian straits!

On 12 May all organized enemy resistance came to an end. Two hundred and fifty thousand Axis troops became PoWs. Just six months after landing in North Africa and three years after Italy had entered the war, the whole of Africa was in Allied hands. Much remained to be done. Bizerta itself was in ruins. Commodore Oliver was the British officer in charge but by the end of May was required for other duties.

*   *   *

9 May

I talked to Commodore Oliver's Secretary that I needed a change and he said he needed an Assistant. So, Oliver has sent in the request to the C-in-C. As

Oliver is going to be in charge of further invasion Operations I shall hopefully be able to keep on the move with him. To answer your question regarding promotion – normally, even if I have wangled a first in my last exam, I will not be promoted till November. However, the C-in-C has recommended to the Admiralty that I should be granted six months accelerated promotion. Their Lordships have replied that 'they will give the matter their earliest and due consideration.'

12 May

I have finally got my new appointment. I leave for Bizerta within a couple of days. Bizerta was taken yesterday so I shall be in the very early flight before the main party arrives. This letter has just been interrupted by the Fleet Engineer Officer (Captain Taylor) arriving back from Bizerta and Tunis tonight. He told me an interesting story as I routed out some food and a drink for him. Apparently Bizerta is bombed and demolished to nothing and he anticipates a long delay in using it to any great extent. Not a house in the old town is undamaged and the water, light, gas and drains are all smashed. There are no civilians there. He says the Tunis Dock area is completely useless but that the town is relatively untouched. What the French will think when they get back to their former main naval base, I shudder to imagine. The entente will not be so cordial!

* * *

The tide had indeed turned in North Africa. The next challenges were the invasion of Sicily and mainland Italy.

Chapter 12

Operation Avalanche, the Salerno Landings

Stoke, still aged just twenty-two, was promoted in May 1943 to work on Commodore Oliver's staff, firstly shore-based in Bizerta (HMS *Hasdrubal*) and then shore-based in Algiers (HMS *Hannibal*).

Bone
17 May
My dearest Doreen,

Rasmussen, the BBC correspondent, is possibly flying home, so I am trying to get this to him so he can post it in the UK. I leave for Bizerta at dawn tomorrow and all my gear has gone by sea tonight. I am going by road, so I shall pass through all the battlefields. I enclose an account by the aforementioned Rass. I gather Commander Kimmins spoke last night on the 9 o'clock news, but I could not hear him as we were in a full-scale air raid. We have now had them for four nights running and on the scale of the earlier months.

Bizerta
20 May
My dearest Doreen,

I am writing this by the rather dim light of my office in Bizerta. The town is flattened. What we hadn't bombed, the Hun blew up. There is one villa still standing which Commodore Oliver has. Our office is in an outhouse which we have re-roofed ourselves. I share with an American captain in the army who is in charge of the harbour defence searchlights. The town is completely empty. There are no civilians, no shops or anything at all. Never have I seen destruction so complete and on such a big scale.

Bizerta
24 May
Dear Mummy and Daddy,

Since being at Bizerta, with a change of environment, people and the fact that I am not working quite such long hours, I do feel very much better indeed.

I am being a little restive at the diminution of work, but by waiting a month or so, I may be able to land feet first in the middle of a rather interesting operation.

I see that you did notice the latest issue of gongs and the award of my MBE. Please thank all those who have written. It was very nice of Doreen to drop you a line as she would undoubtedly see it in the weekly issue of Admiralty Fleet Orders. I will certainly take your advice re leaping in seriously, but as I think I said in a previous letter there is little danger!

One thing that is rather ironical is that our modern conveniences are in a field full of wild poppies, which are now in lovely bloom. It certainly saw the death knell of Axis hopes in Africa. It takes a lot to sink in to realize that after three years of striving, we have at last achieved our goal and re-conquered North Africa.

It was the Royal Navy alone who prevented an attempt at an evacuation. It was the British air force that held the supremacy in the air, although the Americans have done the heavy bombing. It was the First Army who took the brunt of the last fighting and the Eighth who took all the previous. However, it was most amusing to note that in the Victory Parade held at Tunis the other Sunday, the British contingent marched last after the Americans and the French. The only exception was that the Hussars, who had been the first in literally every battle from Alamein to Tunis, did go first. The junior guard of honour was the British and composed of Guards, looking as if they had come from Buckingham Palace and not from Egypt by many hard and trying routes.

Bizerta
26 May
Dearest Doreen,

I had a letter from Mummy yesterday in which she said that she had received a letter from you. In one way it's a peculiar situation because, so that you would not be caused any trouble, I had not told Mummy much about you. In fact, I don't think she knew your name and possibly your address. I had however told her that I was writing to a very captivating WRNS officer and that I was now fighting for more than merely King and country.

Bizerta
30 May
You may have noticed that I have now put my address as HMS *Hasdrubal*, the name of the Bizerta naval base. As far as I can judge, I shall be here till early August, when I may move to Malta. That will be most interesting. If we do, it will be to plan <u>big</u> things. We shall miss two small battles, but I consider that

worthwhile compensation for a really big Operation. When my present boss, Commodore Oliver, asked C-in-C for my services, they had a specific job for me in Operation Husky. By the time it was approved, the job which the whole organization was teed up for had been given elsewhere and so my job had fallen through likewise.

Bizerta is being quite fun in the usual way. Last night we were straddled in the mess, and today had a daylight bombing raid, which demolished our heads in the poppy field! Still, it breaks the monotony and so brings home that there is after all a war on.

Bizerta
2 June

I had a most hectic day yesterday. We suddenly got word about 1130 that Winston Churchill was in Tunis and wished to stay with the Commodore for the night. Imagine the flap. I was immediately commanded to secure transport to Tunis to get some decent wine. I borrowed a jeep, ran out of petrol, broke down, forded one stream and got blocked by another, so detoured twenty-four miles. Arriving in Tunis I saw the PM in a car wearing a sun helmet! I then rushed off to La Goulette and got the wine. I then had to drive at 50mph to get back before HIM! However, he had by then decided to go south and not come to Bizerta!

Bizerta
8 June

I am rather long in writing as I am recovering from a bout of malaria. I received a letter this morning from Baker telling me that he had been awarded the OBE. Known here as for 'Other bugger's efforts' whilst my MBE was for 'My bloody efforts'!

The village of Constantine (in the hills)
19 June

This last week has been hectic. When I was writing last Sunday, I was suddenly called away by the Commodore and ordered to drive to Bone the following morning. It's between 150–200 miles on roads wide enough for only one car. I drove a Jeep and it was simply hellish. Army trucks in convoy the whole way, so I drove in a thick dust storm all the way on a blazing hot day. I drove through interesting battlefield places like Sedjanane and Djebel Abiod. I transacted my business at Bone and drove back arriving Tuesday evening absolutely filthy to find no water to wash in; plus instructions to drive to Algiers first thing

Wednesday morning. It's about 700 miles, so the SOO and I started off in a Hispano-Suiza car at 0500. We drove through Bone (again), Phillippeville and Djedjelli arriving about 2200, where we stayed the night but too late for a meal. We set off again at 0430, managing without breakfast to arrive in Algiers later that day and transacted more business on Friday. We left Algiers at 0500 Saturday and got here to Constantine tonight (Saturday). We'll have an early start again tomorrow to arrive back in Bizerta late pm. We will shift to a planning centre about ten kilometres outside of Algiers by about the 25 June.

I picked up news in Algiers that I managed a First in my Subs exams last September. I am very relieved and rather pleased as only one other fellow has managed Firsts in both the Cadet and Subs exams, so I shall definitely get my 2nd stripe (Lieutenant) on 1 November.

Bizerta
27 June
We will be moving to Algiers mid-next week, and likely to be there about six weeks. The King has been in North Africa quite a time now but as yet he has not been to Bizerta (mainly American troops), although he has been to Tunis (mainly British). I am so glad he went to Malta on HMS *Aurora*, as she was connected with the Siege last year.

* * *

The Combined Operations Staff teams in Algiers were working on a number of options for the invasion of mainland Italy; initially Operation Baytown (the toe), as well as Buttress, Musket, Goblet and Avalanche (the Salerno beaches, south of Naples). If it was decided that the mainland of Italy was to be invaded from the west, it was clear that the seizure and development of the port of Naples would be of paramount importance, since no other port in western Italy could maintain the military forces which it was intended to deploy.

* * *

Algiers
3 July
We are 12kms to the west of Algiers. On my last night in Bizerta I was woken at 0230 by a sentry saying there were parachutists in the camp! As I ran out, an enemy plane screamed overhead. After a bit of chaos, it transpired that indeed there were parachutists but they were enemy pilots who had baled out after

their plane had been shot down. The other plane was being chased by one of our fighters and was trying to escape!

* * *

Force 'N' headquarters staff assembled in Algiers at the end of the first week in July, when planning was immediately started on Operation Buttress. As originally conceived, this operation involved joint assaults on Reggio and in the Gulf of Gioja on the toe of Italy.

* * *

Algiers
4 July
I received a very nice letter from my very first Paymaster Commander – Boutwood – of the *Glasgow*, who is now in the Admiralty. He said he was very pleased to see my medal and also my First in my exams. The Admiralty also honoured me with a letter from them in the usual grudging fashion: 'I am commanded by Their Lordships etc.,' informing me that 'I, as under the King's Orders, a Member of His Empire …'

Since I last wrote, I have driven 1,000 kilometres west from Bizerta to Algiers in a two-seater car which was quite tiring. The handbrake didn't work, the engine stopped if you took your foot off the accelerator, the ignition was faulty, and to cap it all, the engine was of a coil ignition type and, as the generator of the dynamo was not working, it meant that when the battery ran down, the car would just stop! However, all things come to an end eventually, and so here I am.

Here it is perfect peace and I don't think they know there is a war on in the village nearby. The next Operation may be more challenging. I believe we are appointed for what is called Special Services, but then so was the Assault on North Africa and there was nothing special about that! I hear that the King has announced two medals for African service. I don't know if I am entitled. If so, I shall be able to get a job as a Commissionaire after the war, if nothing else!

Algiers
7 July
It is a positive fight against the flies here. Whereas the Bone flies would at least move if a threatening movement was made towards them, and also to a lesser extent did the Tunisian fly, these flies of Algiers make determined low-level

attacks and are not deterred by any amount of flak! My present office is a Nissen hut in the Combined Headquarters, which is a requisitioned school. It is most depressing to work with tin walls, a minimum of windows and extraordinary heat. The school is up in the high hills to the west of the city, often in the clouds, so a little cooler and with some rain. I am now settled in this new place and am glad to be set on something useful.

*   *   *

On 10 July Operation Husky (the invasion of Sicily) was launched, with the objective of eliminating the Axis-held airfields, and within a few days it became clear that the conquest of the island was likely to be much more rapid than had been expected. Furthermore, losses of key landing craft had been relatively light. So, on 16 July the First Sea Lord sent a personal signal to the C-in-C Mediterranean stating that the British Chiefs of Staff were now examining the possibility of a landing on the west coast (Naples), rather than the earlier planned landing on the heel of Italy – Cotrone and the Gulf of Gioja. However, Naples was beyond air cover from the captured airfields in Sicily, so the operation would require aircraft carriers – an additional resource and risk, as they would be exposed to enemy bombers.

*   *   *

Algiers
11 July
The latest offensive in Sicily makes good reading. Today is D+3 and so nothing is yet certain, but it would seem that all has really gone according to plan and that as long as we survive the next week or so, it is just a question of how soon we are masters of the island. It was, of course, Operation Husky that my organization was primarily intended for, but Bizerta took so long to get firmly established that we found ourselves with insufficient time and so were withdrawn from it. It does mean we get a better job and … you must just watch the news!

*   *   *

Commander Philip Baker, his first NOIC in Bone, had been very impressed with the young Paymaster Stoke and recommended him for Special Accelerated Promotion. This was most unusual (indeed, an almost unique request) but it was supported by his superior, Commodore Oliver and had been sent off to the

Admiralty in January. After some months of 'due consideration', the following announcement was published on 22 July 1943:

Special Promotion to Paymaster Lieutenant
(CW 3932/43 – 22 July 1943)

Their Lordships have approved the special promotion of Paymaster Sub-Lieutenant G.A. Stoke MBE, DSC RN to the rank of Paymaster Lieutenant to date 1 May 1943 for meritorious war service.

He was promoted six months earlier than the earliest date that could have been expected. This was for his courageous work in saving a number of burning ships during the intensive bombing of the advanced port of Bone during the eight weeks after the initial landing on 13 November for Operation Torch, during which he was also awarded the MBE for his specific actions on the night of 4/5 December.

Paymaster Stoke had only been promoted from Midshipman on 1 September 1942, and it was unheard of to be a Sub-Lieutenant for only eight months before being promoted to Lieutenant as a regular in the Royal Navy.

The writer of a regular article in the *Journal of Commerce*, 'A Modern Pepys's Diary', had previously written about his exploits in the Western Desert and now summed up Paymaster Lieutenant Stoke's career in North Africa:

Young Stoke has had an adventurous war career. He were three times torpedoed; he were in the thick of Mediterranean engagements; he won the DSC in Tobruk, the MBE at Bone and were the first young naval officer to receive specially accelerated promotion to full lieutenant.

Well may be proud of our young men. They have shown that the attributes and traditions of the British race be firmly rooted in their being and that they be fit and worthy to assist in the rebuilding of the new world which must arise from the ashes of the old.

*   *   *

Algiers
25 July
Here we work in spasms as plans change and at the moment are in the midst of hectic stillness whilst the high-ups are conferring. I imagine that Mussolini's resignation today will materially affect our plan and possible jobs.

We managed to get transport yesterday and went bathing. It was very warm in the water and makes me feel that never again will I be able to face the North Sea. It was grand fun to be away from the office for a whole afternoon. We certainly took advantage of the lull. Still, the COS says that he expects us to work twenty-five hours a day soon.

Algiers
28 July
Last night I had one of the first really pleasant times that I can look back upon with gladness which have come my way for some time. We knocked off from work about 1900 as we were not too busy. But on arriving at the mess we found in place of the usual dinner it was a cold supper, which proved to be a dismal affair. So, a Pay Lt. – Secretary to Deputy COS (Plans) – and I found a car and drove off down to the sea. Still feeling hungry we stopped by a small restaurant on a rise by the sea and wandered in. The patron said he was sorry but he couldn't manage a full dinner as it was late. But he served us hors d'oeuvre, soup, curried eggs, grilled steak and veg, followed by fruit and coffee all accompanied with a bottle of red wine! Just the two of us with the windows wide open, the sea crashing on to the rocks outside and no lights in the restaurant. The air was soft and the sky beautiful at dusk.

*　*　*

The code name Operation Avalanche was now being used at a high level, and the most favourable date was initially set as the end of August – a remarkably short time to plan for such an assault. But until a final decision was taken, planning for the alternative landings continued.

The work of planning had to contend with numerous difficulties and was complicated by the fact that a number of operations were all being planned simultaneously. The naval and military commanders and their subordinates were also in many different locations. Commodore Oliver, the Commander of the Northern Attack Force, in Algiers; the Military Commander in Tripoli; the SNO Landings in Tripoli; and the Naval Commander Subsidiary Landings in Sicily. Oliver had frequently to obtain decisions from C-in-C Mediterranean, who was usually at Malta, and then co-ordinate them with the C-in-C's planning staff in Algiers. [ADM 234/358]

Vice-Admiral Hewitt was appointed Naval Commander Western Task Force for Operation Avalanche only on 31 July. During early August, planning continued for Operations Buttress, Baytown and Avalanche. It was only on

17 August that Avalanche took precedence. As Oliver had been nominated Naval Force Commander for Buttress as well as Avalanche, he and his staff had to plan for both simultaneously. The Sicilian campaign was drawing to a successful close, and by 16 August it was clear the Germans were withdrawing to mainland Italy. Avalanche D-Day was now set for 9 September, but there were still three possible landing areas – north of Naples, the Gulf of Naples and the Gulf of Salerno.

*   *   *

Algiers
4 August
I refused this week an offer, to take effect in six weeks' time, of Captain's Secretary of a big new battleship. It would have been a good gun but I have an inside suspicion that it might find itself way out East. So, I am sticking to the beach for just a while longer. From 20 August things may get a bit erratic till the start of Operations after 7 September. I met Captain Dickinson tonight of Bone renown. We chatted over old times. He is in our party as a SNOL.

The Combined Headquarters Staff were aware that the invasion of mainland Italy was imminent and were on high alert to provide all the necessary operational documents.

Algiers
15 August
It is almost like being back in Bone in the old days – we are again in a rush. We are producing Operation Orders and as we are planning two entirely different ones at the same time for the same date, it does mean considerable complexity to get the bumph out in time. Each is 200 pages, requiring over 400 copies.

This week Bizley and I managed to borrow a car again and drive down to the beaches which are about 15kms away. We went to a French restaurant by the beaches where you can eat outside in the open air for a moderate charge and good food. After dinner the moon was up, the stars were bright and the wind a mere whisper, so we stripped off and swam. It was such a grand experience that all the rest of this week when we have finished work by about 2230–2300, we have rushed off to the beach.

Algiers
16 August

I had a number of letters this week. One was a very great surprise and very gratifying – a letter from Captain Poland who was my second Captain in the Western Desert. He wrote to congratulate me on my medal and accelerated promotion. He says he is writing a bit of a story about the Inshore Squadron and he wishes I was there to refresh his memory.* I shall reply as soon as I get some time for I would like to serve with him again if at all possible.

The shrapnel has a history. It was the bit that attempted to lay me out in Tobruk, but apart from ruining my perfectly good helmet and making me dizzy, it did no harm at all. It did make me rather foolish for the time being, as I attempted to put out an ammunition fire immediately after, which was a very foolish thing to do. This is when I was awarded the DSC. [This piece of shrapnel is retained in the Stoke Archives!]

* * *

The final decision was made on 17 August to go only with Operation Avalanche – the landings on the Salerno beaches. This provided considerable new impetus and more long hours for the staff in Combined Headquarters!

* * *

Algiers
18 August

I should be here in Algiers for one more week. I am starting to produce the new Operation Orders. Although last night we managed to get off to the beach again. What phosphorescence and a full moon!

* * *

Commodore Oliver recorded:

Orders were coming from three authorities more rapidly than they could be disseminated, and, due to the hurried and simultaneous production, amendments and addenda kept pouring in up to the moment of sailing.

---

* Poland's diary and notes were eventually published by his son, Peter, in 2018 under the title 'Tobruk and Beyond'.

It was a most undesirable, but in the circumstances, unavoidable state of affairs. It was only by superhuman efforts of all concerned, and under conditions in which I hope a combined operation will never again have to be concerned that Force 'N' and SNOL (Q)'s orders were ready for issue by 29 August. [ADM 234/358]

The final Operational Avalanche Orders now consisted of 300 pages and had to be issued to 650 ships. Stoke only had two typewriters, one gestetner copying machine and insufficient time!

* * *

Algiers
22 August
It's about 0200, and we are like a paper going to press, being surrounded with stencils and papers, with many staff officers continually wanting amendments inserted and a target date for production looming before us all the time. However, we shall be packing up shortly for tonight and if necessary work late for another two or three to finish off. I expect to leave Algiers now in five days' time.

Algiers
28 August
I think in my last letter I said it was about 0200 and I was about to turn in. In fact, it was not till 0500! And 0300 the next two nights. I am a mass of aches and pains and feeling quite morose. We leave tomorrow at 0745 by air for Tripoli. We shall then embark in the evening on our mighty vessel and entrust ourselves to the seas.

Tripoli
3 September
Dearest Doreen,
    Things have been moving pretty fast since my last letter. We set off the next day in a truck with all our Operation Orders to the aerodrome. The Orders filled over seventy bags!!! I was chief cook and bottle washer for the party – myself and my two writers. We travelled via Bizerta and Tunis, where we had to change planes for Tripoli. It was whilst loading the plane for the next flight that my great tragedy was discovered. My suitcase was missing. In the

suitcase were all those things by which you are so near to me – the letters and photographs etc. I have not been so grieved at any loss ever before.

We eventually arrived at Castel Benito aerodrome about twenty miles outside Tripoli about 1830. Trans-shipped all the bags again, eventually arriving on *Hilary*. By then seventy bags had been moved fourteen times. Then we had to set up office. That was last Monday. Tonight (Friday) is the first night I have not worked through till 0300 or 0400. However, I have finished tonight. We have no more time for amendments before the ships sail. Indeed, some have already sailed. My immediate boss, a Wavy [RNVR], turns in and leaves it to me. It satisfies my pride of course. The Chief of Staff has been most complimentary. The Orders were eventually 300 pages long and we have now produced 700 copies!! The news from the toe of Italy was good. It was the operation we were originally undertaking when we first arrived in Algiers.

*   *   *

On 1 September 1943 at 1141 the C-in-C Mediterranean made a general signal ordering Avalanche D-Day to be 9 September, H-hour being 0330. Ships were departing from the various designated ports all along the North African coast, and the slower convoys were organized to set out a number of days earlier. *Hilary* was part of convoy TSF1, and Oliver, his staff and Paymaster Lieutenant Stoke would sail from Tripoli on D-3. *Hilary* was a former passenger liner launched in 1931 to carry eighty 1st Class and 240 2nd Class passengers between the UK and South America. She was converted to accommodate 313 crew and 378 soldiers and had already been used as the headquarters ship for Operation Husky. She displaced 7,400 tons but only had a maximum speed of 12–14 knots.

*   *   *

HMS Hilary, *Tripoli*
4 September
I have perspiration dripping down my hands. The *Hilary* is not the last word in comfort! My office is a trifle small – 10′ x 6′ with ceilings just 7′ 6′! The office houses a desk for me and three staff and a cupboard. It has no ventilation of any sort. We are directly over the boiler room so you can imagine it gets a little warm and the air gets stale. My cabin is a little bigger, has a fan and a scuttle, but is one deck lower and next to the galley! The extra complication is that it is a four-berth cabin shared by an American Air Force Colonel, myself

and Jimmy Hay. The fourth berth is being filled tomorrow, probably by a newspaper correspondent. The colonel is not too bad even though he turfed me out of the bunk I had chosen before he arrived. Our biggest objection is he smokes vile cigars and his feet smell.

*   *   *

Oliver in his Letter of Proceedings written after Avalanche specifically mentions the challenges presented by the communications room in *Hilary* that Stoke and the other cypher officers had to work in:

The basic organization of our combined communications was sound. However, the design of the Cypher Office and Typex room adjacent in *Hilary* is totally inadequate. It requires to be twice the size. The success of an Operation of this complexity and size depends in no small part on the communications in the HQ ship. This ship should therefore, be the best available. The ship need not be large, but the communication layout must be more spacious and better ventilated than in *Hilary*. Personnel cannot be expected to work for prolonged periods effectively under the conditions which exist in *Hilary* in a tropical combined operation.

*   *   *

HMS Hilary, *Tripoli*
5 September
Tonight is a pretty solemn occasion! For tomorrow we set sail in our 'palatial' palace to cause havoc amongst the dogs of war or rather the jackals. We leave at about 1000, so this tonight is the last opportunity for a letter. I had hoped to write earlier but circumstances forbade. At about 2030 an AA cruiser came in sight and she had to have our orders tonight so that her captain would know what it was all about before he saw the Commodore in the forenoon prior to sailing. I went off in the Commodore's barge to her. It was dark and the ship was anchoring outside the harbour. We found the ship in the dark without too much difficulty but found she was up-anchoring and getting under way. I had luckily taken a signalman with me, so we were able to gather that she was finding a new billet and we were to follow her. This we did for an hour and a half while she fuddled around to an anchor berth to her liking. So, it was close to 2300 when at last I was able to get onboard.

I delivered the Top-Secret Orders safely to the Captain and set off on the return journey. It was pretty pitch black and we had to avoid wrecks and shoals that litter the harbour approaches. When we got to the entrance, we found the boom was shut. I signalled to all sorts of people but it took till 0015 before the boom was opened sufficiently for us to creep through. So instead of writing at 2100, here I am propping up my eyes at a completely godforsaken hour.

We now have a full complement of staff on board. One of the last to join was Commander Anthony Kimmins. He has not yet missed an important party. I have hopes that Kimmins might fly home from us after the assault and might take a letter for me. He remembered me from Bone and said he had heard I had got my 2nd stripe early. We also have in our party Desmond Tighe, the Reuters Correspondent, and several official photographers.

*　*　*

Commander Anthony Kimmins arrived on board just before *Hilary* sailed. In his autobiography *Half Time* he recalled, 'It was only a short time since I had left North Africa. I flew down to Gibraltar and on to Oran, and then down the coast to Tripoli. I immediately boarded the *Hilary* with Commodore Oliver and his staff.' *Hilary* set sail around midday on the 6 September in Convoy TSF 1 bound for the Gulf of Salerno. Operation Avalanche, the invasion of mainland Italy, had commenced.

*　*　*

HMS Hilary, *at sea*
6 September
I hope that the typewriter can cope with this corkscrew writing but it's almost making me feel seasick with this unaccustomed motion of a ship at sea. It's almost a year since I last went to sea and there again it was in a trooper. Of course, the *Hilary* is different being a HM Ship. There is the feel of being in a HM Ship that really matters.

Things are a whole lot easier now we have sailed. It was still a rush until about noon today when we slipped. The sea is fairly smooth at the moment but the *Hilary* is rolling with a pitch sufficient to incapacitate many of the soldiers. Now we are at sea, the shocking heat has cooled a little, although at night it is worse with everything battened down. So, here's to 9 September and especially to the Northern Assault Force.

*　*　*

At 2230 on 7 September Convoy TSF1 was attacked by torpedo bombers, but no damage was done. A number of the convoys were attacked by bombers throughout the following day.

In the wardroom of *Hilary*, flagship of the Northern Assault Force, conspicuous as a communications ship with her bristling array of aerial masts, Commander Kimmins swapped stories with a boisterous group of British and American officers. He paused briefly at 1720 on hearing the loudspeakers crackle with *Hearts of Oak*, the signature tune which preceded the BBC Overseas News. 'The news would probably be no different from earlier bulletins', he thought. 'The real drama would break next morning when the men on board the convoys would be the heroes.'

Through the atmospherics he heard the clipped English tones of the announcer: 'The Italian armed forces have accepted unconditional surrender …' Abruptly he stopped his storytelling. Officers jumped up from their chairs. 'Is the party over?' 'Do we go straight to Naples?' 'Will there be free ice creams?' As one observer put it, 'They supposed that we would dock in Naples and the locals would meet them with an olive branch in one hand and an opera ticket in the other.'

Kimmins recalled in his autobiography:

When we sailed, practically no one had given any serious consideration to the thought of Italy's early collapse. As I said in the broadcast describing the operation: 'Last Wednesday evening I was telling a group of British and American officers what had always proved a most amusing story. Just as I was getting into my stride I was interrupted by the BBC Overseas News. Suddenly the announcer's voice came through: '"The Italian Armed Forces have accepted unconditional surrender …"'

Our Naval Commander's final message was still fresh in our minds: 'The success of this attack is likely to affect the whole course of the war. The assault is to be pressed home with relentless vigour, regardless of loss or difficulty.' And then suddenly the BBC calmly informs us that the country we are about to invade has laid down its arms!! The next message from Commodore Oliver was abundantly clear: 'There will no change of plan. There is a considerable force of Germans ashore who will do everything possible to resist our landing.' And they did!

It was a perfect Mediterranean night, and as he walked along the deck of *Hilary*, Commander Kimmins reflected that a honeymoon couple would pay one hundred pounds for such a setting.

In an attempt to secure surprise, the US Commander (General Mark W. Clark) on his HQ ship *Ancon* had decided during the planning phase, against pretty much all knowledgeable advice, to assault without previous naval or aerial bombardment. The Assault Forces approached the Salerno beaches on the night of 8 September exactly on time and to plan. The weather was good and Capri was clearly visible. The *Hilary* arrived at the lowering position at 0115, and the landing craft convoys made rendezvous with the main force 15 minutes later. As the landing craft approached the beach, two white Very lights soared into the sky from the German battery position. It was 0320.

On board *Hilary*, Commodore Oliver wrote in his log: 'Any prospect of even local surprise has been lost.' Yet Clark still made no move to order a bombardment of the enemy's coastal defences.

The landing craft had been launched and the combined Allied troops started the assault attacks at 0330. When they arrived at one of the Salerno beaches, the Germans were waiting and announced over a loudspeaker, 'Come on in and give up. We have you covered.' Most early reports on D-Day reaching the operation rooms on the *Ancon* and the *Hilary* carried the disturbing postscript, 'Opposition strong'.

Kimmins gave a live broadcast later that day from *Hilary*:

Yesterday evening, about nine, the first bombing started. As usual it was heralded by the dropping of flares, and the sky was lit up by brilliant balls of white and red. At the same time the tracers of all colours raced upwards, and the general effect was very beautiful. Away to port, a line of bright lights suddenly appeared. At first, we thought it was the Island of Capri, which must have lifted the blackout, but the rapid change of bearing soon showed that it was one of our convoy which had been hit and the long line of lights was her fuel burning as it drifted about on the sea. By now the moon was just setting and as the darkness closed in all the leading assault ships stopped engines. We drifted quietly on until weigh had been lost. The assault craft were being lowered down to sea level, packed with eager, silent troops.

When they approached the beaches, there were the inevitable explosions as mines went up. First light disclosed a staggering concentration of shipping. The whole Gulf of Salerno seemed to be packed tight with craft of every kind. But as the enemy batteries opened up, it was clear this was going to be a really tough business. There were many proud sights during that first day at Salerno. But none more so than the men. No one particular man or incident, but those Allied soldiers and sailors as a whole. Only one care in the world – their duty and the job in hand.

As the evening wore on and the sun set, a great red ball behind the Island of Capri, you could see Vesuvius through a gap in the mountains. Sicily in the shadow of Etna had been a comparatively easy job. Salerno under the shadow of Vesuvius was going to be far, far tougher.

The day after this broadcast, Commander Kimmins left *Hilary* to return to England, carrying Stoke's letters and posting them on arrival to his parents and Doreen. Both arrived safely, courtesy of a very special messenger!

* * *

At sea, off Salerno
D-Day, 9 September
The Grand Hotel *Hilary* is now lying approximately a mile or two off the Italian mainland in the Bay of Salerno. When I last wrote the night before we sailed I was tired, rather excited and (this in a whisper) rather afraid. The first day at sea – Monday – was delicious. It was practically a year since I had last been at sea and even in this tub, it seemed grand. Tuesday was equally pleasant. But at 2200 we ran into a torpedo bomber attack that lasted for about three hours but in which we suffered no harm.

So Wednesday found us a little tense, as it was obvious our whereabouts were known. But the miracle was that apart from the occasional plane there was no systematic attempt to bomb us out of the water (or to be pedantic, into it!). My office is next to the wireless room so judge my feelings when we heard the announcer interrupt a programme to say that very afternoon General Eisenhower's representative had signed an Armistice with the Italian Government. The whole ship was in uproar. It bewildered everybody. The majority felt profoundly relieved and sat down to a hearty meal like reprieved men.

But after about an hour we saw that the Operation would still be on and there was no possibility of the Huns folding up their tents like the proverbial Arabs and stealing away peacefully in the night. So, all our former fears returned at least doubled. And sure enough, after dusk the attacks started. We were then within twenty miles of the beaches and all element of surprise lost. I would willingly admit that I was very, very frightened as the attacks continued.

The coastal guns opened fire so we knew any surprise had gone. Plans proceeded and the *Hilary* led on until the landing craft were ready to spring ahead. The assault started on time at 0330. Although the Italians had given in, the Hun had not.

It is now 1300. It seems the Hun are fighting desperately hard to prevent our landings. Air attacks this morning have not been over heavy, but we feel very naked being a rather conspicuous target. Now I fear I must stop, there is much more I would like to say but like Frederick in the *Pirates of Penzance* – Duty Calls!

At Sea off Salerno
D+2

I do hope you got my last letter which Kimmins kindly took for me. I am hoping to get this one on to a ship returning to Bizerta tomorrow. The landings were initially successful on our sectors. However, all the next day and yesterday saw heavy fighting against the Germans. But it is not till today we captured an airfield. So up till now, the Navy has had to provide all the air support for the defence of the beaches and convoys as we are out of fighter range from Sicily here. It has been a triumph for the Fleet Air Arm.

Yesterday we moved in much closer to the beaches to control everything more easily but suddenly this afternoon we heard a sudden whine and found ourselves being straddled by guns from a German shore battery. We rapidly up anchored and steamed out of range! As we are the only large ship left – the troopships now being empty have gone back – we are very conspicuous.

Isn't it grand news about the Italian Fleet? I think it's the biggest tonnage ever captured whilst a war is still on. I myself have not been to bed since the assault and am feeling weary again. We are handling over a thousand signals a day at the moment. By we I mean the SOO, SOI and myself, taking the necessary actions for each.

* * *

Admiral Cunningham, then stationed in Malta, was also delighted that the Italian Fleet had surrendered themselves to the British rather than scupper and sink their ships as the Vichy French had woefully done. He sent a short signal from Malta, dated 11 September, 1943:

To the Admiralty, Be pleased to inform Their Lordships that the Italian Battle fleet now lies at anchor under the guns of the fortress of Malta.

* * *

At sea, off Salerno
D+3

I am writing this in our Operations Room at about 0130 to try and catch a ship sailing back tomorrow who I can bribe into posting this. I hope you got my letter delivered by Anthony Kimmins. We have had quite an exciting time. The Hun was obviously prepared for us and so the task has been more difficult than any of the previous jobs like Husky and Torch. The assault troops were under fire before landing. It was a queer night. We heard of the news of the Italian Armistice and wondered if it was still on. As we grew nearer, we could see huge fires onshore. These presumably were dumps being burnt. The coastal defence guns opened up on us and we were heavily attacked from the air. Since then, the bridgehead has been steadily consolidated. Up to now the aircraft carriers have provided the only fighter protection as we are outside effective range from Sicily.

The Italians have completely surrendered. It's great to know that practically all their naval fleet is now in our hands – it just shows what the French in similar circumstances could have done. Ashore they are helpful as much as they can and it seems that in some parts are even fighting the Huns.

We got shelled when we closed the beaches this afternoon – I thought it quite unnecessary!!! I hope, however, to be in Naples shortly – it should be captured in a fortnight I imagine. Must close now as the signals are piling up.

* * *

Cunningham described his concerns at this time:

> Heavy naval bombardments continued throughout this time and into 12 September. The Germans ran true to form. Before dawn on the next day they bombed the hospital-ships *Newfoundland* and *Leinster* lying brilliantly lit out at sea, with heavy loss of life. Further naval heavy ships were called up to increase the bombardment of the German positions ashore. But life on the shore was congested and under severe strain.

Cunningham sent a message to Admiral Willis from Algiers:

> Avalanche is giving me great anxiety and I am hoping we are not to have an evacuation on our hands. Unseasoned troops were landed. I had an SOS from Admiral Hewitt tonight.

A little later, Cunningham sent Oliver the following message, deciphered by Paymaster Stoke:

> I am carefully watching the situation. Everything possible is being done to send reinforcements into the area at once. You will have to hold on like HELL. I am reconstituting Force 'V' and furbishing up the Fleet Fighters in case they are again required. Good luck.

* * *

At sea off Salerno
D+5
I am sending this back via a cruiser that is returning to Malta to replenish. The heat is getting more and more a nuisance. All the scuttles except the upper deck are still closed and we only have a primitive ventilation system. Luckily the American Colonel – of the cigars and feet – has gone, so the cabin is a little fresher now. The pongos are battling hard ashore. There is extremely heavy fighting and I gather the Huns are confident of driving them back into the sea. The bridgehead is still very small in length and depth, so we can hear most things.

* * *

Cunningham's description of events continued:

> Late on the afternoon of 14 September, Commodore Oliver was summoned to visit Hewitt's headquarters ship (*Ancon*), where he found naval staff feverishly working out plans for the transfer of the Fifth Army HQ to *Hilary*. Oliver gave his considered opinion that considering the enemy opposition and the state of the beaches, no transfer of troops should be contemplated. Moreover, now the troops were ashore, they should stay and fight with all the support the Navy could give them. Commodore Oliver displayed commendable firmness and resolution in adopting the attitude he did.
>
> All available aircraft had been switched on to the bombing of the concentrated German forces preventing the assault troops moving forward. The following day, the battleships *Warspite* and *Valiant* arrived and every available naval ship was bombarding the German positions.

Heavy and accurate naval gunfire effectively cut off any chance of German reinforcements, converting the German spearhead into a huddle of men, tanks, guns and vehicles which were mercilessly pounded.

By the evening of 16 September the Allies considered the situation stabilized and began preparations to continue the offensive. Cunningham arrived the next morning in the operational area onboard the destroyer *Offa*:

I visited Vice-Admiral Hewitt's flagship, the *Ancon*, to discuss the situation. I then went on with Hewitt to the British landings further north, where we had lunch in the *Hilary* with Commodore Oliver. As ever Oliver was on the crest of the wave – calm, imperturbable and completely optimistic as to the final outcome.

Cunningham summed up his feelings in a signal to Admiral Ramsay on his return to Bizerta on 20 September, 1943:

Neither Montgomery nor Alexander wanted to do Avalanche. The landing went like clockwork but they found a Hun division waiting for them on the beaches. It was curious that they made little attempt to stop the landing but fought like tigers after our chaps got ashore. After we had been ashore three days things began to go wrong and we had a crisis one afternoon when the enemy counter-attack nearly fetched up on the beaches between the British and US forces. Fine work by the air force and our ships' gunfire saved the day.

*   *   *

At sea off Salerno
D+9

We have been honoured by visits to the *Hilary* from Cunningham himself, plus both General Eisenhower and General Alexander. General A came when things were very tense, with the Hun making every effort to throw us into the sea. Since 0330 on D-Day to D+6 we have handled 8,939 signals in the cypher room. We are working 0800–2300 and then splitting the nights in to two watches between the two of us.

The most distinctive reminder of this operation to me will be the noise. All day and all night. There is the continual fire from the front, as the beachhead is still only about four miles deep. The Navy is bombarding all day with their guns booming. The battleships particularly startle us when they fire over us. Air raids are on most of the time. The other annoying thing is the Hun shells most days. So far, he has only managed to straddle us so my luck is still in.

As I look over the guardrail tonight the moon is full and looks like a big red ball suspended there at a fancy-dress ball. Ashore beneath the moon, there is the continual flash of the army's guns and shells bursting on our positions. All the guns in the anchorage and ashore are firing tracer into the air against the planes who are dropping red and orange flares. It is magnificently wonderful. Above it all, the stars seem to be the same, twinkling on serene. I was so moved by this sight the other night that I noted it in the official log. Amongst the regular records of 'air alert – gunfire and bombs – all clear', 'Ship near missed', 'Anchorage shelled', and so on, I put on record 'beautiful night'!

The greatest relief is our SOO. I think I may have mentioned my respect for Commander Edwards, who was with us at Bone, four days as NOIC and then with Oliver. He has a puckish sense of humour. He, for example, has one file in the Ops Room labelled 'Difficult signals – for Sixth Form only'. He has also appointed me SORI – Staff Officer Request Instructions! As everybody is always asking us for instructions, even if it's only where to throw the gash over the side.

At sea off Salerno
D+10
It's been tough fighting – the hardest assault & longest drawn out so far in the war. We are bombed and shelled pretty continuously which does pall after a bit. The weather is simply grand and the mountains of Italy look particularly inviting for a scramble. I, of course, haven't left this Ops Room so can't say I have set foot on Italy yet! It all seems to be going very well – at least that's what is said in the daily newspaper I publish!

*   *   *

As the Germans were retreating and laying waste to the ports and towns they were vacating, they issued a proclamation in Naples which was included in the ship's newspaper that Stoke published:

Each single citizen who behaves calmly and with discipline will have our protection. Anyone who acts against the German Army will be executed and the place where such acts are committed will be destroyed and reduced to ruins. Every German soldier wounded or killed will be avenged one hundred times. Citizens, keep quiet and reasonable; measures and reprisals which have been taken up to now were necessary because a certain number of German soldiers have been vilely assassinated or badly wounded while they were merely doing their duty, and in some instances, Germans have been maltreated by the civilian population in the most shameful manner.

And on 20 September 'Lord Haw-Haw' (Germany's British propaganda mouthpiece) announced the following after ten days of Operation Avalanche:

The Allies have not had the success they had anticipated and losses have been very heavy – 10,000 killed and wounded and 4,000 taken prisoner. We have sunk 3 cruisers, 2 destroyers, 1 torpedo boat, 15 landing craft and 9 transports. Damaged, presumed sunk – 2 cruisers, 3 destroyers, 1 landing boat, 1 large tanker and a number of supply ships. Damaged by direct hits – 125 supply ships and landing barges. And 1 destroyer sunk by a U-boat in the Gulf of Salerno.

In actual fact, the only Allied ships to have been sunk were five landing craft!

*   *   *

At sea off Salerno
D+14
I feel very cut off from you, with no photographs or letters to re-read, having lost my suitcase in Tunis. However, the day before yesterday was very pleasant. For about a week I have not been feeling so good. So much so that the Commodore said I had two alternatives – surrender to the medical men [again!] or take a break. It was very fortunate that the Commodore had been asked by the Admiral in charge of both Attack Forces to take him to Capri. A fast boat had been laid on to take Admiral Hewitt, his CSO with Commodore Oliver to Capri, and I slid in too!

It was a glorious trip in an American MTB. The sky was beautifully blue, overwhelming in its brightness. It took us about an hour to get to the island. The NOIC took us to his villa where he is ensconced – Count Ciano's [former Foreign Minister] villa!! It is beautifully constructed to get as much sun in as possible, whilst still being cool. Photos of Mussolini still on the walls. We could see across the Bay of Naples. I could hear the heavy explosions of the bombs and the continued rumble of the demolition that the Huns are carrying out in the city. We were driven up the steep hills by an Italian in a relic of a car. To sound the horn, he made contact with a piece of wire to the side door! The handbrake didn't work, nor did the starter. We got back to the ship about six hours later. The sea trip and fresh air made a new man out of me.

At sea off Salerno
25 September
I don't think I told you when we went to Capri we paid a visit to the port of Salerno first. We secured alongside the mole that is sheltered by an overhanging cliff. Whilst we wandered around for fifteen minutes I mentioned to the man driving the MTB that boats are still shelled by the enemy entering or leaving the harbour, so on leaving he set off out at colossal speed! And indeed, they did shell us but he outran the guns! At the moment, as the Army advances, we will open up the various ports – Castellemare and Torre Annunciata. Desmond Tighe came aboard yesterday, who I had known in Bone.

At sea near Naples
29 September
We are now off Naples, but things are different from when I last wrote. Then things were sticky and it looked as if our indiscretion might come home to roost. Since yesterday we are no longer shelled in the anchorage and there are few bombers. The army is advancing slowly it is true but then the countryside is precipitous, deeply wooded and every road is commanded by nearby heights. Have averaged over eighteen hours a day since D-Day on 9 September so have been a little busy and tired!

At sea off Salerno
29 September
Dearest Doreen,
   The army has done wonderfully well. Pompeii fell this morning and all is set to capture Naples. It is rumoured the CSO would like me to stay with him after this. It is an end of term feeling here. The assault and initial build-up are over. Torre Annunciate is ours. Naples can't be far off. It's a year ago since Donibristle – how gloriously happy I was there. Those fleeting weeks, followed by a bare two days and a Sunday morning with you represent a lot to me.

*   *   *

Naples was entered on 1 October and Rear-Admiral Morse assumed command as Flag Officer Naples on 2 October. The *Hilary* arrived at Naples the next day and assumed radio responsibility for the port, whilst the harbour was still under enemy shellfire. The following day, Admiral Morse hoisted his flag in the *Hilary*, and Commodore Oliver, with Stoke and the HQ Staff, transferred to the SS *Antwerp*, which sailed for Algiers on 5 October via the island of Capri (for sightseeing!).

* * *

SS Antwerp
At sea on the way to Algiers
5 October
Last Thursday we anchored off Naples at 1300. Vesuvius was enshrined in white cloud and a little smoke could be seen rising. Through the glasses the area near the port seemed gutted both from our bombing and German demolition. Later Vesuvius lit up the night sky like Very lights. We only stayed in Naples one day and then returned to Salerno. We clewed up our stuff there and this morning we considered our job done and here we are on an ex-Channel boat – *Antwerp* – on our way to Algiers. We should arrive about lunchtime on Wednesday. Then the fun will start about all our futures.

Algiers
8 October
This morning we arrived in Algiers harbour. I immediately set about obtaining accommodation. We need about a week to write up our Report of Proceedings etc. I found some space in our old offices. During the Operation I started a daily newspaper for the *Hilary* and all the ships in company, which was much appreciated. We also had a couple of interesting people on board – Randolph Churchill (again) and Douglas Fairbanks Junior, who is a Lieutenant Commander in the USNR. There was quite a buzz onboard amongst those who knew his films!

Algiers
9 October
Today has been a great day – I have now got your mail, recovered my suitcase with the precious letters and photographs and also found my car! The aerodrome is some considerable way away, so it meant getting a car out there. I eventually

tracked down my old car from Bizerta – an open two-seater. On the way out to the aerodrome it started raining – yes, here in North Africa! I needed one hand to hold the hood, one to work the windscreen wipers, one to change gear and one to steer!!! On arrival I found the Lost Luggage Department and amazingly No 40 on their list was my name, which fortunately was stencilled onto the outside of the case!

Algiers
11 October
After we had transferred from the *Hilary* to the *Antwerp*, we returned by way of Capri. We stopped off at the island for about three hours. I helped row the ship's whaler to the Blue Grotto. We got there to find that the whaler was too big to attempt to enter the grotto! Most of the chaps dived over the side and swam in, but I was feeling tired. However, we forced the boat's bows in and I was able to see the amazing blueness of the water.

The future is still vague. Several senior officers have kindly expressed themselves ready to help me get a suitable job if I do return to UK. Anyway, it should resolve itself when we have finished our reports on the Operation and say we are ready for the next. Of course, the appointment of Cunningham as First Sea Lord, replacing Sir Dudley Pound who has been taken gravely ill, will probably affect us in some way.

I am so glad that you listened to Anthony Kimmins. Incidentally, we also had with us another old acquaintance of mine, Desmond Tighe of Reuters. Kimmins is a first-rate broadcaster and the general impression is that it was one of his best efforts.

Algiers
17 October
One night this week we, the Lieutenants, wined and dined the Commodore and the CSO at a nearby restaurant. It is reputed to be the best in the district, good service, food and wines. In addition, Benedictine and five-star brandy are served! They returned the compliment by taking us all out for a long lunch from 1230 to 1600, most of the talk being of malicious local scandal!

Italy's declaration of war on Germany annoys me more than I can trust myself to express in polite society. Here they have been for four years trying to finish us off, and causing me no little anxiety for my personal safety, and now I'm expected to be friendly, give them a gin and regard them as long-lost friends! Bah!

Algiers
19 October
Yesterday I received a letter from Captain Cuthbert, who was my Commander in *Glasgow*, asking me to look him up if I was passing through London and paying me sweet compliments. I have also had another nice letter from Captain Poland. Three letters from Senior Officers all in a week!

It seems we will be on the Cunard Line SS *Franconia*. It's getting difficult waiting to come home with work finished. So, I went off to the cinema last night and saw *Casablanca*. Before it came on there was a short film of Paderewski playing in New York – the *Moonlight Sonata*, Liszt's 2nd Hungarian Rhapsody and a Chopin Ballade. The piano playing was first class and I thoroughly enjoyed it.

*   *   *

Paymaster Stoke had been on Oliver's staff since the early days in the advance port of Bone during Operation Torch. Oliver had written and forwarded the recommendation for Stoke's MBE and also for his Accelerated Promotion. Oliver obviously knew Stoke well and specially selected him to join his staff, firstly in Bizerta, then in the Combined Headquarters in Bouzereah on the outskirts of Algiers for the planning phases of Avalanche, and finally on his headquarters ship *Hilary*.

Oliver himself had had a remarkable naval career. He was one of the first ever Special Entry cadets in 1915. He obtained 1st Class passes in all subjects, winning more prizes than they were allowed to award him! He served on *Carlisle* in 1925 and went on to take command of the cruiser *Hermione*, being awarded a DSO in July 1941. He was later torpedoed in the same ship in June 1942. Cunningham personally selected Oliver for Operations Torch, Husky and Avalanche, for which he was awarded a bar to his DSO. The following year, he was appointed Commodore Force 'J' at the Normandy D-Day landings (gaining a second bar to his DSO), in which Force Stoke served as Captain's Secretary to Captain Manley Power in *Kempenfelt*, Flotilla Leader for the 26th Destroyer Flotilla. Oliver must have been a wonderful mentor and example to the young Paymaster officer, still only twenty-two years old!

At the end of the Salerno landings, when Stoke departed, Commodore Oliver (then aged forty-five and later promoted to become Admiral Sir Geoffrey Oliver GBE, KCB, DSO and 2 bars) wrote Stoke's confidential report (S.206) to the Admiralty:

A quite exceptional officer, of great promise. Has consistently shown outstanding power of decision, leadership and common sense, well beyond his years. Possesses boundless energy and is a cheerful and a quite untiring worker. Cool and most courageous in emergencies. Would do great credit to the Executive Branch were he to be transferred.

And on his 'flimsy', dated 9 October 1943 he wrote:

Stoke served to my entire satisfaction. An exceptionally gifted officer of boundless energy and resource, whose work on my staff in the most varied circumstances, consistently proved invaluable.

Stoke and two colleagues embarked on the SS *Franconia* on 24 October, almost exactly twelve months since leaving the Clyde for Operation Torch. He did not spend much time at home but travelled north to meet up with Doreen, whom he had not seen since their initial few days together a year previously. In that time, he had survived multiple bombing raids in Bone; been awarded another gallantry medal (the MBE); gained a First in his Sub-Lieutenant exams; won Accelerated Promotion to Lieutenant for 'meritorious war conduct' in Bone; and been on the Staff of Commodore Force 'N' at the Salerno Landings.

Doreen was eleven months older than he was. Her father was due for retirement from the Navy in 1939 but had been kept on and was posted to Glasgow as Admiralty Engineering Overseer for ships built at Yarrow's Yard on the Clyde. She had moved with her parents and had joined the Woman's Royal Naval Service (WRNS) aged nineteen on 4 December 1939 as a Third Officer at the Fleet Air Arm shore base at Donibristle (HMS *Merlin*), just east of Rosyth to the north of the Firth of Forth. Her own 'flimsy' was written by the Head of the WRNS throughout the Second World War – the famous Dame Vera Laughton Matthews:

Doreen Stoke (née Le Poidevin) has conducted herself to my entire satisfaction. A most efficient and competent WRNS Duty Officer (Operations) with good powers of leadership. Promoted Second Officer from 1 May 1944. Thorough and energetic, possessing initiative and sound judgement. A lively and pleasant personality, popular with WRNS personnel.

And obviously popular with Paymaster Stoke too!

Stoke had written over seventy letters to Doreen during these last twelve months, and presumably she had written a similar number back. Although they had only been together for less than two weeks, their correspondence had created a strong bond, and they announced their engagement whilst he was on leave, staying in Glasgow with her parents in the Kirklee Hotel, where they lived.

His first letter in December to his parents from HMS *Hardy*, his next ship, describes those last couple of weeks in November in Glasgow:

Dear Mummy and Daddy,

I had a most gloriously happy time with Doreen for the last five days. It seems a painfully nasty thing to say, but I don't think I have ever been so continuously very happy. It was of course the first time we'd had together really quietly – she with no watch keeping – and with no trains to organize and rush for. We just got up late, went walking and went to bed early. I was the Le Ps' guest at the Kirklee Hotel and they did their best to make it a Home. Captain Le P wrote me a charming letter the day our engagement was announced.

I managed to flash my eyelids sufficiently to persuade a photographer to squeeze me in for some Studio Portraits. Doreen is collecting them when they're ready and will post them on to you. There's a choice of four, so there might be one satisfactory.

I'm sorry that I spent so little of my leave with you and saw so little of you all. I have told Doreen how I feel about it and that I intend to travel south if I get any leave at all.

We went to Helensburgh on Monday. I wanted to go as it has a family tie and Mummy has always said it was worth a visit. It so turned out that the weather was gorgeous – blue sky and a bright, even if not warming, sun. We walked up behind the town. Loch Lomond was covered in mist so we missed the full splendour of the scene, but it was beautiful.

In a later letter, Stoke gives his parents telephone numbers to contact Doreen should his next ship go down and they get a message before she does. A prescient thought!

Chapter 13

Torpedoed in HMS *Hardy* on Russian Convoy JW56

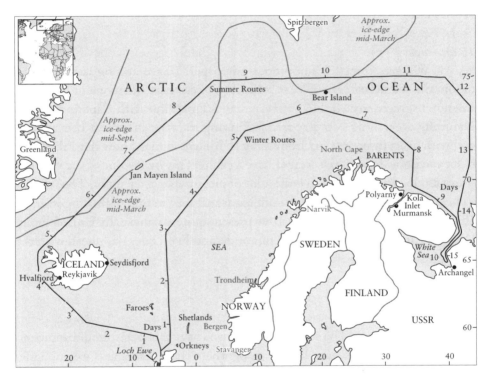

S hortly after his engagement to Doreen Le Poidevin, on 15 December 1943 Stoke, aged twenty-two, joined *Hardy* at Rosyth as Secretary to Captain W.G.A. Robson, Captain (D) 26th Destroyer Flotilla. *Hardy* then sailed up to Scapa Flow, where she would be based, undertaking the arduous Russian convoy route to Murmansk and the Kola Inlet. *Hardy* was a newly commissioned destroyer of 2,000 tons, with a crew of 225 and capable of 36 knots (40mph).

Russian convoys were extremely dangerous, not only because of the atrocious weather, particularly in the winter, but also because wolfpacks of between five and ten German U-boats would await them as they sailed around the edge of the pack ice off Bear Island, within the Arctic Circle. The upper decks of the ships were completely frozen and the ice had to be chipped off to stop the ships turning turtle. Men could only survive fifteen minutes on watch at a time, and if you fell in the icy water, it was a death sentence. The destination was Polyarny in the Kola Inlet, a safe anchorage fifteen miles east of Murmansk, where the Senior British Naval Officer was based.

*   *   *

HMS Hardy
Scapa Flow
16 December

As you will see from this sumptuous notepaper, I have at long last managed to join the sea-going Navy. We're rolling quite easily at the moment but so far I've not disgraced myself. I joined yesterday at lunchtime with Captain Robson. Naturally everything is pretty frenzied trying to settle in amidst being at sea and with everything to start from scratch. It's late at night now but I did want to let you know how things were. I have a cabin of my own – one of the very few – and am looking forward to quite a lot of pleasurable excitement. The Mess is a cheery place and I think that the chaps are all easy to mix with. The staff are all RN save one, so for these days, we present quite an unusually United Front. Well I must awa' to bed as its past midnight and I've a busy day ahead with the king-pins of the destroyer world.

Scapa Flow
20 December

The tang of salt should be so unfamiliar to you that this letter should appear to be reeking of it. I have been broken in lightly to the sea again, as we are boiler cleaning at the moment. It's a good thing as it gives us a chance to settle down and get our ideas settled before venturing to assail the enemy.

Mail has been bad here lately owing to the weather. I did get a letter from Doreen and one from Mrs Le P who seemed almost as cut up about our 'gallant' parting as we were!! Still, it's nice to know that she's quite happy about it all, although Mummy's letter to her apparently makes her feel you are not too happy about my being so young. I'm sure you both do worry – I'm sufficiently egoistic to realize that – and I do feel glad that it is of interest to you whom I marry. For I should hate terribly to feel that being married cut me off from all those things and particularly people I love as much as Doreen.

It would be no happy marriage for me if I felt you both were anxious as to our future. Still, I would assure you that Doreen and I are not just physically attracted. Not that holding hands and a goodnight kiss mean nothing. But I do believe that our interests are in common and we thoroughly enjoy doing them together. We both have faith and trust in each other – that is one reason we don't wish to rush into any hasty marriage, as it would cause happiness to neither of our families and little joy for us, with the war still separating us. I won't say more because that's all there is to say – I don't think you need worry that its merely a case of my being swept off my feet by the first girl I met sort of business. As for Doreen, she has had contacts with swarms of fellows during the war and so has had ample opportunity to realize what she is doing. I hope you don't regard this as anything like a defence – it's not, but I would like you both to know how I feel. With the leave I eventually had, I had little time to tell you all I wanted. It's a great sorrow to me but I hope that not too far away perhaps I shall be able to make amends.

The weather here is only fit for Huns to live in – yesterday was a gala day, the wind dropped to gale 8!! I have lots of warm clothing now and look like the Russians of traditional circus fame. I have a fur cap over a balaclava, a blue muffler to match, mittens under fur-lined gloves, long thick wooden pants, sea boots with thick stockings, a sweater and the whole surmounted by a thick fur-lined coat. If wet, add an oilskin!!! So, come on the ice pack!!!

I'm more or less settled in my job now and proceeding apace with my organization. It's not too easy starting from scratch but it's not the first time I've had to do it. The Mess is a very happy one and most of the bodies are congenial. My cabin begins to look mine now and I have got used to destroyer harbour life. I've yet to encounter three weeks at sea!! And while talking of sea etc., I would like to mention a very morbid thought. If by any chance there's anything to do with casualties in the *Hardy* and you have either good or bad news from Admiralty, you will let Doreen know. I'll give you her telephone number in case you haven't got it – Greenock 266, which is her mess, or Glasgow Western 1322, which is the Kirklee Hotel, if she is home. I am not fearing you will be called upon but it does relieve me of a worry. Well I'll stop now as it's after midnight. A very Happy Xmas indeed – we're nearer together than for a long time – All my love and thoughts will be with you on the 25th.

Scapa Flow
27 December
I've just got back more or less into my rut in the Navy now, after close on a fortnight in the ship. I received another letter from Captain Poland which was very nice.

I made a point of listening to the King on Xmas Day as I knew that if it were humanly possible you would be doing so, too. I thought he made a very suitable speech and apt. My Xmas Day was at least spent on an even keel, and we had turkey and plum duff, although we still have no chairs. I've managed to get in one game of rugger this week. The weather was appalling and the slush terrific, but I enjoyed the exercise.

Isn't it glorious news about the *Scharnhorst* being sunk [this was the leading German battleship, sunk at the Battle of the North Cape]. We missed the party much to the annoyance (naturally) of Captain (D). It was a great victory and will have important repercussions. I must say I agree with a certain Admiral's comments on the way it just appeared on the midnight news last night – 'It sounds as if we've managed to sink a trawler off Boulogne.' There were certainly no pealing of bells or gun salutes. And yet it's the last heavy ship the Hun had and it was sunk in tricky conditions in the Arctic Circle.

I've got properly settled now in my cabin and had extra fittings put in to make it easy to use as an office. I'm feeling quite confident about doing the job now and as 'D' seems happy, I'm content. He took me for a walk this afternoon and as he has very strong legs and long ones, it was more of a trot than a walk for me! It was good, though, to get a bracing walk and stir the lungs and muscles.

*   *   *

On 5 January 1944, *Hardy* left Scapa at 0900 with *Venus* and *Verulam* for Stornoway to carry out two days' tactical exercises with a submarine. *Vigilant* joined them the following day, returning on Saturday, 8 January at 1100.

*   *   *

At sea
7 January
My dear Ivan and Ken,

I hope it is not a liberty to address you so, but as I'm halfway to qualifying as a married man perhaps I'm so 'entitled', to use the old naval expression. And before I forget, the new excuse for the usual bad handwriting is quite a good one, as we are at sea and a destroyer's motion doesn't assist my already wavering hand.

Thank you indeed for your nice words over my engagement. I was rather more than just sorry we didn't have more than forty-eight hours at home because I should have liked you to see Doreen, so that you would know what sort of ensnaring female she is. I think you would agree that I had fallen into very competent hands. Of course, I would have liked to tell you about her before bursting bombshells amongst you so unexpectedly. However, all is now settled, although it is not our intention to get married hastily in the near future.

I see that you were with the family on Boxing Day and Mummy says it was a good time for all. Just a little after you said you were going to toast on Xmas Day at 1330, we all in the mess drank most warmly at 1430 to Absent but Beloved Friends. It comes after Wives and Sweethearts – may they never meet!

Life in the *Hardy* hasn't been over-exciting, for which I am assuredly not craving. We missed the *Scharnhorst* affair – that was a good piece of work indeed, and our Captain was quite disappointed. The war seems to be making appreciable strides and gives hopes of being in sight of a conclusion in Europe – how soon I don't know but the Hun probably will prefer us to be in Berlin first rather than the Russians. Personally, the end of the European struggle probably accelerates my departure to the East, so I'm not entirely without misgivings!!

Scapa Flow
9 January 1944
We arrived back last night. I'm not burning so much midnight oil these days. It's not all easy going yet, but in this job, it will never be quite office hours. For with spells at sea for up to a month, you can imagine the accumulation of papers when we get back. On arrival there's a Report of Proceedings to flog out, current stuff to be dealt with and back stuff caught up with, all before we dash off again.

When we arrived in yesterday it was a gorgeous scene. The sun was low down but the anchorage was covered in snow – a most unusual event here – and to see ships anchored in such surroundings was indeed a pretty sight. We've had an interesting last few days at sea doing exercises and working up our new flotilla ready for our next new job. I only hope the sinking of the *Scharnhorst* doesn't send us East any earlier.

I am enclosing a rather nice letter – two in fact. Captain Poland you know, of course. He knows the Le Ps very well as his first ship in this war was built at Yarrows yard on the Clyde, where Captain Le P is Admiralty Engineering Overseer. Commander Edwards was with us at Salerno and Bone and has just got an OBE – I think I've told you before how much I respect him.

I got co-opted onto the *Hardy*'s Brains Trust this week. It was quite interesting and the ship's company asked some useful and testing questions. I quite enjoyed having to produce a reasoned answer in order, quickly. Or at least attempt to!

* * *

There are no more letters from Stoke to his parents, as the *Hardy* departed on 11 January for Loch Ewe on the west coast of Scotland, near Ullapool, to join up with the British merchant ships making up part of Russian Convoy JW56A to Kola Inlet/Polyarny. However, he managed to scribble a quick note to Doreen from Aultbea on the banks of Loch Ewe which now houses a permanent Russian Convoy Exhibition.

Captain Robson takes up the story in his memoir *My Naval Life*, written some years after the war and stored in the Churchill archives:

> After a marvellous fourteen days leave, I was appointed in command of the 26th Destroyer Flotilla, serving under Admiral Glennie again, who was now Rear-Admiral Destroyers at Scapa. He very kindly sent the *Hardy* down to Rosyth to pick me and my Captain's Secretary, Paymaster Lieutenant Stoke, up and sailed for Scapa Flow. There I found four ships of my new flotilla, just completed and newly commissioned, of the V class. I was not at all impressed with their efficiency, so I was allowed to take them to Stornoway to work up for four days in the rough weather of the Minch.
>
> This did us all good and we had just got it completed when I was told that Russian convoys were to start again. They had been stopped for some months and I was to take the first of them, JW56A. The British part of the convoy was to assemble at Loch Ewe and the American part would join up with us to the east of Iceland. The convoy conference was held at Aultbea, on Loch Ewe, and I found I had a splendid lot of British captains and, as events turned out, we needed them.
>
> We sailed for the rendezvous with the rest of the convoy east of Iceland in very bad weather, reaching Gale Force 12, and after two days, signals from the rest of the convoy made it quite clear to me that all the merchant ships had been thoroughly dispersed by the weather. I decided to re-assemble at Akureyri in Iceland. This we did, less five American ships, which turned back to the USA.
>
> Convoy JW56A sailed again four days behind schedule, and of course the German agents in Iceland, which was neutral, reported our departure, so it was not very long before a German U-boat from the Isegrim pack was in contact, shadowing and reporting us. The weather had now deteriorated again and gave the U-boats every advantage. They were obviously massing for an attack, and this duly took place on our fifth day out, when they sank three merchant ships and damaged the destroyer *Obdurate* with a 'Gnat'

homing torpedo. Fortunately, it only blew one propeller off her, so she was able to keep station, although she was not much use as an escort.

The weather continued foul but our escorts, although somewhat new at the game, did very well, and we did not lose another ship before getting into Polyarny/Kola Inlet in North Russia, with twenty-one ships on the 28 January 1944.

We were not given long in harbour before a signal came from the C-in-C, telling me that the second half of the convoy to Russia (JW56B), which was a week behind our first half, was menaced with an even greater concentration of fifteen U-boats, and the German air strength had been built up as well. The C-in-C told me to sail with my destroyers and sweep ahead of JW56B. This we did at 2000 on 28 January. During the next day the flotilla spread out in line abreast, dividing to let the convoy come up between us. Then we turned to sweep up astern and catch the shadowing U-boats.

During the latter part of the operation in the early hours of 30 January, we had turned to come astern when *Hardy* was first 'gnatted' by a U-boat, whom we had not detected as it must have been on the surface, and secondly torpedoed, following which the after magazine exploded. With only two-thirds of the ship left, my Engineer Commander (Mill) came to the bridge and said we should abandon ship, as she would turn over at any moment. 'I have been in just this situation before', I replied, 'and I can promise you she will not turn over.' It was exactly the same situation I had experienced in the *Kandahar* in the Mediterranean in December 1941, where I had done service in Alexandria, Tobruk, Greece and Malta.

I got a sight of the U-boat and, since we had no guns in action, I made a signal to the Norwegian ship, the *Stord*, who attacked and sank the U-boat. At the time, of course, it was pitch dark. The *Venus* edged alongside us very cleverly, our bow to her stern, and I had my survivors lined up on the fo'c's'le in three ranks. I gave them the order that each line was to jump when I told them and not a moment before, as there was quite a sea running and it was a matter of getting the timing right. This worked very well, I am glad to say, and we did not lose one man between the ships.

These last moments of *Hardy* were captured in Arthur Evans's book *Destroyer Down*:

At 0404 on 30 January *Hardy* had been hit by a gnat fired by *U-278* (Oberleutenant Joachim Franze). About three minutes later another torpedo hit the ship. After the first explosion *Hardy* shook violently, then she trimmed by the stern and listed ten degrees to starboard. On arrival in the engine room, the engineer officer found the starboard engine revolving at a very high speed and making a loud rattling noise and the port engine stopped. As the regulating valves to both engines were shut, the starboard shaft was obviously broken. The engine room was free of water but the gearing room was found to be flooded to the upper platform and was evacuated.

Shortly afterwards the second explosion occurred. The port engine was put out of action. *Hardy* was flooded up to the after-engine room bulkhead, which was holding and not buckling visibly. No. 2 boiler-room was evacuated.

Soon after this the order was passed for everyone to make to the fo'c'sle. No 1 boiler room was evacuated. After the initial list to starboard *Hardy* returned to upright, but finally listed ten degrees to port. At 0418 *Virago* was ordered by *Venus* to close and pick up survivors. *Venus* also went alongside *Hardy* and took off the remaining crew, and then sank the *Hardy* with a torpedo in position 73 37N 18 56 E.

An eyewitness report was recorded for the BBC programme *The People's War* by George Anthony White, one of the seamen on the *Hardy*, recalling sixty years later in 2004 the moments when she was torpedoed:

It was my nineteenth birthday in January 1944. After arrival in Kola Inlet we were called out a second time to help another convoy. Slowing down to drop depth charges we were hit. The back of the ship was torpedoed right off. I had finished my watch and was asleep. It was 0400. It was my friend Bean who was on watch, I saw him laid out, he didn't make it. The Germans knew when the watch changed and timed their attacks.

We were sinking. I saw part of the ship go down and the green of the sea. I thought that was it. McCarthy dived straight overboard from the sinking ship. His face appeared and I pulled him back on board. The water was freezing. He asked me what we should do. I said, 'I'm going to go down with the ship.' I had resigned myself to it. I never thought we'd be rescued.

The Commander came and ordered us up to the fo'c'sle. We tried to get the lifeboats off but they were frozen stuck. We eventually managed to get one off. I held the rope as the others went and picked the men out of the freezing water. The Commander got the DSO. The others got the British Empire Medal. I got nothing as I was only holding the rope!

HMS *Venus* came alongside. The Captain said over the tannoy, 'If you can jump, jump, but I'm sorry I can't stop.' We all managed to jump off as the boat was sinking. I saw our ship sink and it was awful. A Norwegian destroyer, *Stord*, cut the U-boat that attacked us in half. We were taken to hospital in Kola Inlet, Russia, and I eventually returned to Britain on that ship.

Admiralty records (ADM 199/77 and 2027) show that *Hardy* was about 50 miles south of Bear Island inside the Arctic Circle and that she had slowed to drop depth charges when hit by the acoustic gnat torpedo fired by U-278. Although no crew were lost on transferring to the *Venus*, thirty-three men were reported missing following the explosion, and two died of their wounds later.

Captain Robson again:

Losing my ship was very unfortunate since according to the latest information, the safe speed in order to avoid 'gnats' was 20kts, and that was what we had been doing. When we returned to Scapa, and I emphasized this to the C-in-C, he got his staff on to the Admiralty and they found out that a week before we sailed, the Admiralty had discovered that the safe speed to avoid gnats was no longer 20 but 25kts, and every command had been informed except the Home Fleet!

This omission cost us two destroyers, and could have cost us many more as Roskill later reported that a total of nineteen 'gnats' were fired during this convoy. Roskill also records that, even for that part of the world, where the weather in winter is always dreadful, it was more atrocious than usual. Even so, our escorts were responsible for sinking five U-boats.

Captain Robson recommended a number of officers and ratings for awards as a result of their conduct during this incident, and these were later published in the *London Gazette* No 36561 dated 13 June 1944:

When *Hardy* was torpedoed on 30 January, Commander (Eng.) Ernest Mill having done everything requisite to ensure that the ship would remain afloat and have electric power, found that there were several men in the water in need of help. He called for two volunteers. Able Seamen Johnston and Hamilton immediately came forward. They got a Carley raft into the water and rescued the men. But whilst he was alongside *Venus* in the raft, he was washed off. He managed to regain the raft and by his cheerful encouragement kept up the spirits of all onboard it until finally *Venus'* whaler rescued them. This was a most courageous act and in keeping with the highest traditions of the service. The temperature of the water at this time was 32 degrees F.

A number of ratings in the engine room who kept power and steam going to allow the crew time to abandon ship were also recognized:

Chief Engine Room Artificer F. Weame and Engine Room Artificer Eric Garbutt, who were both in the Engine Room when *Hardy* was torpedoed. Engine Room Artificer Mutton was asleep in his hammock in his Mess when the ship was torpedoed aft. His steady courage and intelligent actions were particularly praiseworthy in such a junior and inexperienced rating, and are worthy of the finest traditions of the service. Stoker Petty Officer John Nagle was in charge of the watch in No. 1 Boiler Room. Although no orders could be passed from the Engine Room, Nagle remained below and kept steam in the boiler. His courage and presence of mind inspired the two junior ratings with him and all carried out their duty coolly and properly until ordered to leave.

Captain Robson DSO, DSC was himself recognized for his part in continuing to lead the Flotilla despite losing his ship:

For courage and determination in resuming the most able command of his force in *Venus* after his own ship *Hardy* had been sunk by torpedo, thus providing an inspiring example of endurance and leadership to all concerned in the operation.

Robson and Stoke transferred from *Venus* to *Vigilant* in Kola Inlet for the journey home.

*   *   *

2 February
HMS Vigilant
In Kola Inlet
Oh my dearest,

I hope you didn't have to worry at all – I somehow expect the buzz got around. There's so much to say that I really don't know where to start and what to say. Firstly, I think that I am quite alright in every way, although rather tired. There's nothing at all to worry about. The second thing is that 'D' says he thinks we should get fourteen days off. So, I may arrive almost with this letter.

I'm writing this in the 'Frozen North' still – we got back into Kola Inlet yesterday. *Inconstant*, one of the escorts, may be coming back to the Clyde direct and is taking two of our surviving officers, so he is taking this letter as I will be going back to Scapa.

The future, darling, is very vague until we get back to Scapa. We might establish ourselves in a Depot ship and merely transfer to one of the flotilla for actual operations. We might convert one ship into a leader but unfortunately our remaining ships are too far advanced to avoid it being a reconstruction job or they might give us a new leader in due course. I expect we shall get some leave if only to get some clothes – nothing of course was saved. When we get back, I'll have to get off all our reports and deal with the accumulation of mail before I can skip off on any leave. Incidentally don't address any mail to *Hardy*! I can't write much more because the *Inconstant* is leaving shortly and I must catch her. You meant an awful lot to me as I went over the side.

*   *   *

The next day, at 1000 on 3 February, convoy RA56, consisting of thirty–nine merchant ships and twenty-three destroyers and corvettes as escort, sailed back to UK.

*   *   *

HMS Vigilant
5 February
At sea
Darling Doreen,

It is a wretched existence at the moment – we are in *Vigilant* now. I share the wardroom with the rest of 'D's staff. We eat, sleep and work there. I'm trying to write this amongst a lot of hubbub. I'm so unsettled at the present. These last three nights have been very sleepless. I've lain awake thinking about all the things I want to write to you. I suppose it's quite natural to be a little strung up till at least one has got back from this fateful trip. After all, the fact of having got away with another torpedoing shouldn't make the dangers seem either less or worse than they were before – and they were real enough then!

Actually, the last year in North Africa has had some uses. It meant amongst other things that we know that our love is not founded merely on your lovely smiling face and pretty hair, but is deep-seated and has been proven. It all comes to the same conclusion, that even more than ever I know how much you are my life to me. My main nagging fear as I waited to leave the *Hardy* was, not so much of never seeing you again, but of coming back perhaps crippled or being unworthy of you.

Sorry for the interruption – it's mainly your fault! It's surprising the number of messages I've deciphered lately sent from you in your office in Greenock, which have been repeated to D.26. I can almost imagine you writing them.

*   *   *

German aerial reconnaissance located the mass of ships on 5 February and the Werwolf pack was manoeuvred to lie in wait. But as a result of an incorrectly reported (or plotted) reciprocal course, German HQ in Norway thought that the westbound convoy was going east – an embarrassing slip which caused the eight U-boats to miss their target entirely! The Report of Proceedings by Rear-Admiral Boucher DSO RNR, the Commodore of Convoy RA56, neatly sums up the mood of the ships and crews as they left northern Russia:

> During the first three days Providence sent a favourable gale which drove the convoy quickly past the usual U-boat concentration off Bear Island. The convoy was not apparently detected by the enemy. The whole passage was made in a succession of gales and semi-continuous snow at exceptionally good speed. This was doubtless influenced by the keen desire felt by all to leave North Russia. Murmask was a bombed city filled by black ghosts moving in the twilight over the snow in deathly silence, broken only by 'tinny' music broadcast by the state. It is impossible not to leave the area without being filled with admiration at the services being rendered both by the British and US personnel in such appalling conditions both mental and physical. A neatly expressed general description of Murmansk was given by the black steward of the SS *Will Rogers*, who remarked fervently on leaving, 'I'd sho' like to go any place else – jes' any place "tall".'

*   *   *

HMS Vigilant
7 February, 1944
At sea
My dearest,

   We are rolling a regular 45 degrees and it's a little tricky to keep one's balance. The ink has been knocked over me three times already. We've shot ahead so shall arrive with any luck about 0900, the day after tomorrow.

HMS Vigilant
9 February, 1944
At sea
My dearest,

   Please excuse the pencil as it's still impossible with ink. Yesterday I battled with an old typewriter to produce our reports and the wardroom was in darkness when I turned in. We are just entering harbour, so the motion is getting appreciably easier. However, I shall have a shockingly busy time when we get in – where we live, my work, our future, clothes, reports, paper etc. We are just entering the first boom now.

Vigilant, with *Opportune*, *Offa*, *Venus* and *Savage*, arrived Scapa as expected at 0900 on 9 February.

9 February
Scapa Flow
Darling Doreen,

   It was wonderful to hear your voice on the two phone calls just now. You can't be serious when you thought I ought to spend my whole leave at home – flatly I won't. You are the mainspring of my life and no one, not even my Mummy and Daddy, counts as much as you do. So, I just have to spend half my leave with you. We were much later getting in this morning due to a man falling overboard. I wrote most days up till 30 January but all those letters are obviously lost. I sent a letter via the *Inconstant* from Kola – I think a pitiful letter.

*   *   *

Captain Robson recalled in his memoirs:

> On arrival at Scapa, Admiral Glennie sent for me and told me that, before he would allow me to continue in command of the flotilla, I was to go to Kingseat hospital in Aberdeen for a thorough check up. After three days there, I was ordered to have a month of complete rest and to do absolutely nothing. So, to my great sorrow, Captain Power relieved me as Captain 'D' 26. Admiral Glennie knew that, in the forthcoming Normandy landings, I was to be Senior Officer Inshore Squadron, responsible for the security of all the beaches from seaward. It was imperative that whoever was in charge was 100 per cent fit, as there would again be no rest.

* * *

On arrival back at Scapa, and with Captain Robson on sick leave for at least a month, Stoke was granted some leave, taking the opportunity to spend more time with his fiancée at the Lochearnhead Hotel near Loch Lomond, then making a brief forty-eight-hour trip to London and onward to Southend, for the couple to see his parents, before returning to shore-based service in Greenock on the Clyde.

Gowanhill Huts
Madeira Street
Greenock
Sunday
My dear Mummy, Daddy and John,

Here I am back in my very inferior Second Home – the Officers' Huts at Greenock. We had to get down here this morning and Doreen is on watch this afternoon. It's a wrench after the last ten days, which have been so completely happy together all the time. Still, I suppose it's a good thing in one way as it breaks us more gently to a complete parting, which is so close. I've no further news but I expect to move Wednesday or any time thereafter. I've just finished a letter to Captain Robson to say I'm back, so that I may get some orders by return of post. The week we spent at home, was, we both agree, the happiest of our lives – so we've christened it our first honeymoon.

Gowanhill Huts
Madeira Street
Greenock
Tuesday

I went out to Kippen, near Stirling, to see Captain Robson at his home with Doreen yesterday. He's looking much fitter already now that he knows that after two months he should be alright. There was a fair amount of business to transact and we wanted to get it done personally rather than by letter – it is a long journey for one day, though. My position is still hazy. He's trying to arrange for me to stay with him but it's not yet certain, so I may be off at a moment's notice, still it is so unsettling not knowing and minimizes my leave value considerably.

*   *   *

Shortly afterwards, *Kempenfelt* was designated by the Admiralty as the replacement 26th Destroyer Flotilla Leader, to be commanded by Captain M.L. Power, with Stoke as his Secretary, when it returned from the Mediterranean in early April.

*   *   *

Gowanhill Huts
Easter Sunday
9 April 1944

Dearest Mummy, Daddy and John,

This morning, Doreen came off night watch so we were able to go to church. I particularly wanted to go on Easter morning as I thought you might all be going. It was a Church of Scotland service and not very bright, particularly for Easter! Even the sermon was true to type and had an Old Testament text on an Easter morning. However, we were glad we went. Doreen owns a quarter share of a sailing boat – a 22ft craft called *Seamew* and we've spent some time on that boring job of bottom-scraping and painting. Unfortunately, of course, the weather isn't amenable yet for sailing on the Clyde!

*   *   *

On Stoke's leaving, Captain Robson DSO, DSC wrote on his 'flimsy':

Stoke served admirably. An officer of outstanding zeal and ability.

Stoke thought highly of Robson and would have liked to serve with him again, but regrettably the opportunity didn't arise.

On 24 April 1944, Paymaster Lieutenant Stoke joined *Kempenfelt*, the replacement for *Hardy*, as Captain's Secretary to Captain Manley Power, replacement for Captain Robson, who had been re-assigned to important duties in preparation for Operation Overlord (D-Day). *Kempenfelt* was initially stationed in Scapa Flow.

*   *   *

In recognition of his service in northern waters, Paymaster Lieutenant Stoke MBE, DSC was awarded three Russian Convoy/Arctic Convoy Medals, all given after he passed away in August 1991.

The Soviet 40th Anniversary Commemorative Medal and Certificate was issued by the Soviet authorities in 1985 to mark the 40th anniversary of the ending of the Second World War. It is also known as the Russian Convoy Medal and was awarded to those veterans who served on the convoys to Northern Russia, Archangel and Murmansk. It was awarded to Stoke in 1992.

The Arctic Emblem was eventually issued as a mark of the UK's gratitude for the heroism veterans displayed in the face of terrible hardship on the Arctic Convoys of the Second World War and in recognition of service north of the Arctic Circle. This was awarded to Stoke in 2007, sixteen years after his death!

The Arctic Star was granted for operational service of any length north of the Arctic Circle. It is to commemorate the Arctic Convoys – including both the merchant ships and their naval escorts. It is a Bronze Star, identical to other Second World War campaign medals and was awarded to Stoke in 2013, a mere twenty-two years after his death!

Chapter 14

The D-Day Landings in HMS *Kempenfelt*, Juno Beach

K*empenfelt* was a modern destroyer, commissioned just twelve months earlier. She was 2,500 tons laden and was capable of up to 36 knots, with a complement of 225 crew. She arrived in Scapa Flow on 12 April 1944 from the Mediterranean, appointed leader of the 26th Destroyer Flotilla. Paymaster Lieutenant Stoke MBE, DSC joined her in Scapa Flow on 21 April.

Captain Manley Power assumed command of *Kempenfelt* on Sunday, 30 April. Power had been one of five key officers in Cunningham's team in the Mediterranean and had been instrumental in drawing up plans for many operations, including Torch (the landings in North Africa), Husky (Sicily) and Avalanche (Salerno).

* * *

Scapa Flow
1 May
We got back recently as you will have realized by now from Norway – it was frightful weather all the time but as the results were good I suppose one can't complain. You heard about it on the wireless the other day. [*See* Power's diary entry, below.]

Captain Power has now joined and so we are trying to settle in properly and get cracking. He's very staff-minded, as he's been on Admiral Cunningham's staff for the whole of the war. He's got quite a keen sense of humour, so we should manage without too many rows.

I believe he has his own Secretary coming eventually so it looks as if I shall move. I am beginning to feel comfortable in my cabin. I have a door curtain and scuttle curtains too. I'm glad Mummy thought that the photo which was enlarged is not so war weary – it wouldn't have said much for being engaged, would it?

Scapa Flow
7 May

Many, Many Happy Returns of the Day Mummy. I'm sorry I'm not going to be with you. It is the nearest I've been for so long at your anniversary that it's harder to miss than when I was further away.

My writer is a sound chap who is a clerk in the Bank of Scotland in peacetime. I managed to get ashore for the first time since being on this ship and captained the ship's rugger team. We played the Depot Ship who has I imagine about 1,500 people on board opposed to our 200-odd. They play regularly together and as it was our first game together we were happy to lose only 9-8 after leading until the last five minutes. I felt shockingly stiff after the game but thoroughly enjoyed it, and hope to get another one soon.

* * *

Captain Power wrote in his diary, held in the Churchill Archives:

In April 1944 I was appointed Captain (D) 26th Destroyer Flotilla, with the *Kempenfelt* as my leader. The flotilla consisting of seven other destroyers – new ones of the 'V' class – *Volage, Venus, Virago, Vigilant, Verulam* with the Canadian-manned and -owned *Algonquin* and *Sioux*. A fine command with which I was delighted. Destroyers were then built in classes (and flotillas) of eight, each class being a slight improvement on the last. Each class was a different letter but the leader was always named after an Admiral, and not necessarily of the class letter. She was usually finished first.

My 'Vs' originally had the *Hardy* as leader. She was sunk in a Russian convoy almost immediately. I was given *Kempenfelt* temporarily, which really belonged to the 'Ws' – 27th Flotilla to be – and it had been arranged that when the 27th Flotilla was formed, I should take on *Myngs*, the leader of the 'Zs', which would be ready in July. *Kempenfelt* was a Portsmouth ship and had been in the Med for Anzio. I had taken passage with her once and had been unimpressed by her efficiency. I was even less so when I took command, but soon banged her into shape.

Within a week *Kempenfelt* was involved in Operation Hoops – a carrier-borne air operation against shipping off the coast of German-occupied Norway by a force of Admiral Sir Bruce Fraser's Home Fleet, returning a week later.

On 12 May His Majesty the King visited Scapa and inspected the Destroyer Command, but unfortunately *Kempenfelt* had not yet returned.

* * *

Scapa Flow
21 May
I see from Daddy's letter that he got the impression that I was faintly carping against the new Captain – on the contrary, I meant that he was staff-minded as a tribute – it doesn't imply that he is out of touch with realities but that he has knowledge of and in his particular case, well versed in Administration. I probably said that it was open to see if he was an equally good seaman – he has certainly proved himself that by now. He's a very friendly man indeed and I am perfectly happy – indeed I shall be sorry to go except that I am so much more intimate with Robson – he now writes to me as 'My dear Mick'. How temporary I am is still uncertain, but I shall see the frolics out before moving. I don't know whether I told you last week that the King has been up here and in consequence we spliced the mainbrace [served a tot of rum to all hands] – the first time I've ever done so. We didn't see the King as we were out at the time.

* * *

On 25 May, the 26th Destroyer Flotilla sailed from Scapa for the Solent, near Portsmouth, to join Force 'J' for Operation Neptune – the naval support for Operation Overlord, the landings on the French coast – universally known now as D-Day. At the same time, Doreen Le Poidevin was promoted to Second Officer, an excellent recognition of her hard work over the previous four years.

* * *

Scapa Flow
25 May
My sweetest love,
    I got a thrill all over again just now, from addressing my envelope to you – 'Second Officer' – it seems so difficult after the many times that I've written 'Third Officer'! It is grand and I'm so very happy.
    We have appeared for the first time as a flotilla in the Home Situation Report. It's a pleasant trip so far and naturally quite relaxed. I am on Cypher

Watch tonight but at my Action Station tomorrow night. Unfortunately, it is bleak and exposed to all the spray and noxious funnel gases.

I have had a successful afternoon with the shipwright fixing up my cabin. I have also had success in getting two additional stewards for the Wardroom. I wrote a personal letter to the Drafting Commander at Chatham Barracks and the two appeared within ten days! My stock is riding high!

At sea, heading south
26 May
This is really an illicit letter. We are at Action Stations but instead of staring into the inky night beside my Bofors, I am writing to you. You will probably know that during the night we received a signal to open certain bags. Not only was there a huge amount of paper but a large number of amendments to be inserted. Anyway 'D' said I should forge ahead immediately and insert all the amendments. So here I am at 0200 having just finished, instead of being at Action Stations since 2300!

Today we did a practice shoot with a splash target and I was bucked no end as my Bofors did best of the Flotilla. I gather at 0600 we passed you! I haven't seen anything yet in AFOs of the *Hardy* guys. I'm so glad that Captain Robson got his OBE – he thoroughly deserved it and more. I'll be seeing him shortly as he has joined Commodore Oliver's team.

28 May
In the Solent
We arrived yesterday and anchored in St Helens Roads. I went ashore and met scores of old friends and acquaintances at HQ. Oliver was out – I just heard he was awarded the CB for Salerno. Edwards was there, Northcott of the *Lance*, Jimmy Hay and of course, my old immediate boss, Scott. Northcott was as catty as ever about Scott to me and as flattering as ever about me! We're shifting berth inside tomorrow and I have asked them to come aboard for a gin or three.

29 May–3 June
In the Solent
It has been wonderfully sunny warm weather, but I'm very busy with amendments, paperwork and after that it's Action Stations every night for about an hour and a half between 0000 and 0300. When 'D' was working out the Staff Action Stations he asked me if I'd mind having the Bofors. What could I say? I'm very flattered of course, as it's the most important close-range

AA gun we have, and 'D' seemed to think I could make it more efficient than the previous officer. The weather has started to break and more amendments have arrived. I had to go over to the *Hilary* today. It's going to be Commodore Oliver's HQ again. Pretty well all the officers I knew are still there. However, I am far happier in the *Kempenfelt* as my own boss. My writer, Allan, left this morning when I was up to the ears and so am awaiting his relief.

4 June
In the Solent
'D'/Lofty offered me a gin or three this forenoon before lunch and we chatted casually. Then Lofty said that if Robson hadn't been so insistent that I be available to join him after this Op, Lofty would have liked me to stay on with him.

I hope I didn't bog you down in a morass of figures with the Insurance business. Seriously, it's a question of attempting to forecast the future – whether we'll want to give our children a good education and for us to accept a certain amount of sacrifice now for that end rather than then. The Insurance Scheme is an advantage in the event of my death, which I must consider with or without children.

* * *

Captain Power recalled in his memoirs the period when *Kempenfelt* was moored in the Solent:

My job was to command the bombarding destroyers of the British centre task force – 'Juno' – landing the Canadian Division around the village of Courselles, under my old friend Commodore Oliver. I had my own flotilla plus four Hunt class. During my time in the Solent I spent most of my time at the Royal Yacht buoy off Cowes to keep in touch with Oliver whose Headquarters was in the Royal Yacht Squadron. The Solent was an amazing sight, packed solid with ships of all shapes and sizes from Sconce buoy to St Helens.

Commodore Oliver recorded in his Report of Proceedings for Force 'J':

Loading of stores started on Thursday, 1 June at Southampton and Stokes Bay, with the Prime Minister personally watching! During embarkation and prior to sailing the high spirits of the soldiers of the 3rd Canadian

Infantry Division were outstanding; their enthusiasm infused throughout Force 'J'. We received the final executive order to sail by telephone at 0445 on 5 June. Force 'J' Headquarters ship, *Hilary*, with General Officer Commanding 1st Corps and General Officer Commanding 3rd Canadian embarked, passed Spithead Gate at 1925 and proceeded at 9kts. Weather conditions in the open sea with wind WNW force 4–5 were most severe for loaded landing craft.

* * *

5 June [D-Day-1]
In the Solent
Everything is hustle and bustle. There's a great feeling of tenseness in the ship – very much like the night before an important examination!! I've been collecting food and made ready for a prolonged stand at the Bofors! The weather has definitely broken and blown up, but presumably Admiral Ramsay knows best.

* * *

Kempenfelt departed the Solent on 5 June 1944, one of the last to leave, proceeding from St Helens Roads at 2135, then steamed through the fleet to get to the start position off Juno beach with Force 'J' and Bombardment Group 'E' in the Eastern Taskforce.

Supreme Commander of the Allied Expeditionary Force, General Dwight D. Eisenhower, sent a message to all the men taking part.

SUPREME HEADQUARTERS
Soldiers, Sailors, Airmen of the Allied Expeditionary Force!

You are about to embark upon the Great Crusade, toward which we have striven these many months. The eyes of the world are upon you. The hopes and prayers of liberty-loving people everywhere march with you. In company with our brave Allies and brothers-in-arms on other Fronts, you will bring about the destruction of the German war machine, the elimination of Nazi tyranny over the oppressed peoples of Europe, and security for ourselves in a free world.

Your task will not be an easy one. Your enemy is well trained, well equipped and battle-hardened. He will fight savagely. But, this is the year 1944! Much has happened since the Nazi triumphs of 1940–1941. The

United Nations have inflicted upon the Germans great defeats, in open battle, man-to-man. Our air offensive has seriously reduced their strength in the air and their capacity to wage war on the ground. Our Home Fronts have given us overwhelming superiority in weapons and munitions of war, and placed at our disposal great reserves of trained fighting men. The tide has turned! The free men of the world are marching together to Victory!

I have full confidence in your courage, devotion to duty and skill in battle. We will accept nothing less than full Victory!

Good luck! And let us all beseech the blessing of Almighty God upon this great and noble undertaking.

Dwight Eisenhower

Admiral Ramsay also sent a message to all the naval officers and men:

SPECIAL ORDER OF THE DAY
TO THE OFFICERS AND MEN OF THE
ALLIED NAVAL EXPEDITIONARY FORCE

It is to be our privilege to take part in the greatest amphibious operation in history – a necessary preliminary to the opening of the Western Front in Europe which in conjunction with the great Russian advance, will crush the fighting power of Germany.

This is the opportunity which we have long awaited and which must be seized and pursued with relentless determination. The hopes and prayers of the free world and of the enslaved peoples of Europe will be with us and we cannot fail them.

Our task in conjunction with the Merchant Navies of the United Nations, and supported by the Allied Air Forces, is to carry the Allied Expeditionary Force to the Continent, to establish it there in a secure bridgehead and to build it up and maintain it at a rate which will outmatch that of the enemy.

Let no one underestimate the magnitude of this task.

The Germans are desperate and will resist fiercely until we out-manoeuvre and out-fight them, which we can and will do. To every one of you will be given the opportunity to show by his determination and resource that dauntless spirit of resolution which individually strengthens and inspires and which collectively is irresistible.

I count on every man to do his utmost to ensure the success of this great enterprise which is the climax of the European War.

Good luck to you all and God speed.

Admiral B H Ramsay
Allied Naval Commander-in-Chief
Expeditionary Force

The Naval Staff History for Operation Neptune records the quite simply breathtaking size of the Armada crossing the Channel on 5 June: 7 battleships, 2 monitors, 23 cruisers, 78 fleet destroyers, 55 other destroyers, 192 smaller escorts (frigates, corvettes, sloops, patrol craft and anti-submarine trawlers), 287 mine-sweepers and 495 coastal vessels. The Landing Force comprised 310 landing ships, 1,211 major landing craft, 2,075 minor landing craft and 531 landing barges, supported by 423 ancillary ships and craft and 1,260 merchant ships. In all, there were some 7,000 vessels.

The cruisers *Diadem* and *Belfast* arrived at 0500 in their pre-arranged positions in Force 'J'. *Hilary* anchored at 0558. The weather conditions were hardly in accordance with the forecast – still WNW Force 5. *Belfast* and *Diadem* had just opened fire on the Beny-sur-Mer battery from some seven miles off the coast.

Kempenfelt was anchored in position at 0608, two miles closer to the shore, and opened fire at 0619 on their target 11,900 yards away, bearing 207 degrees, behind Nan White landing beach. At 0705 *Kempenfelt* weighed anchor and closed the shore, continuing bombardment. By 0817 *Kempenfelt* was just 4,200 yards from the beach, in support of the assault landing craft with the Canadian infantry, and then she moved in closer still.

*   *   *

Tuesday, 6 June [D-Day morning]
One mile off the French coast
We are just under a mile off the French coast. We left the Solent last night and went to Action Stations, where we've been ever since and will remain like that all night. We are each given 20 minutes off just before dusk. In Juno sector all is reputed to be going according to plan. We had a quiet trip across and then we heard the aircraft going overhead in the dark. We bombarded before the assault. Then in daylight the assault craft moved in and touched down with aircraft dropping bombs ahead of them. They met stiffish resistance, I believe. I saw all this myself as I am on Upper Deck Action Stations. The weather

is OK – warm, but windy with a moderate swell. The Hun is certainly not throwing in the sponge. We've all been flying battle ensigns today, so it's been a truly naval occasion.

*   *   *

Aboard the destroyer *Beagle* off Bernières-sur-Mer, less than a mile away from *Kempenfelt*, was Stoke's old friend, Reuters correspondent Desmond Tighe. He had been on *Hilary* with Commodore Oliver and Stoke at the Salerno landings in September 1943 and had previously met Oliver and Stoke in Bone. He wrote:

It was just after four o'clock on the morning of D-Day and the night bombing was in full swing and even from more than ten miles off the coast we could see enormous blood-red explosions and hear the rumble of the bursting bombs on the Bernières-sur-Mer beach section. It was cold, and wrapped in duffel coats and thick mufflers, we watched the dawn come in and the invasion start in all its intensity.

Night bombing ceased at 0530. Fifteen minutes later, cruisers *Belfast* and *Mauritius* open fire on our starboard bow. There are at least one thousand ships of all sizes in our sector alone. Destroyers are darting around us. 'What a party', I hear the Captain say. I agree with him. It is something so terrific, so gigantic, that no Hollywood director could possibly equal it on the screen. An unbelievable sight.

The destroyers, including *Kempenfelt*, closed the shore just before 0600. Guns are belching flame from more than 600 Allied warships. Thousands of bombers are roaring overhead as the invasion of Western Europe begins. Rolling clouds of dense black and grey smoke cover the beaches south-east of Le Havre as the full fury of the Allied Invasion Force is unleashed on the German defences. It is the most incredible sight I have seen.

The air is filled with the continuous thunder of broadsides and the crash of bombs. In the last ten minutes alone, more than 2,000 tons of high explosive shells have gone down on the beach-head. It is now exactly 0725 and through my glasses I can see the first wave of assault troops touching down on the water's edge and fanning up the beach.

Battleships and cruisers are steaming up and down drenching the beaches ahead of the troops with withering broadsides. Great assault vessels are standing out to sea in their hundreds and invasion craft are being lowered like beetles from the davits and head toward the shore in long lines. They are crammed with troops, tanks, guns and armoured fighting vehicles of all types. Conditions are not ideal.

Captain Power on board *Kempenfelt* recorded in his diary:

> We were expecting a pretty hot reception when we closed in to '*Festung Europa*' [Fortress Europe]. My destroyers were to move in on the flanks of the assault craft – each having their allotted targets. I intended to move in to the centre, close astern of the assault, in a good position for control and ready to replace casualties. However, during the night, on the way across, I got news of a newly discovered battery rather far inshore, so ultimately moved in some way ahead of the others and was for some time the nearest ship to Europe in the 'Juno' sector. It was rather uncanny closing in to this heavily fortified coast expecting at any minute that all hell would break loose. Having got within range, I decided my fire would be more accurate from anchor and solemnly dropped a hook, swung to the tide and steadied before opening fire – about 6,000 yards from the shore. Then the assault craft moved passed us and not until they were touching down did the enemy open fire – on them, not us!

* * *

Stoke later wrote to his parents describing the day.

21 June
The heavier ships opened fire first but we went past them alone until at about an hour before the assault we were 8,000 yards or so from Hitler's Fortress Europe off Juno beach – we felt very lonely and naked as we opened bombarding fire on our allotted target – an enemy battery – and we feared the worst. We closed the beaches behind the first landing craft & so saw them touch down in our sector at about 0740 by my watch. I had a first-class view from my gun position. Just as the craft touched down the din was impressive. Waves of bombers were dropping bombs all along the beaches and every gun that would bear and reach in every HM Ship was firing.

Our troops – the Canadians – got ashore without too much opposition but I believe that on other beaches there were harder fights. The weather wasn't so good, but most of the stores planned for use got ashore on D-Day. We lay off the coast for two days bombarding at intervals and being successful in shooting up enemy guns.

* * *

E.J. Thompson aboard HMS *Kempenfelt* recalled:

> Captain Power told the assembled ship's company that our target was some 6-inch shore-based guns, the position of which were known exactly from air reconnaissance. He also told the ship's company that the six destroyers in our flotilla would be anchoring for accurate bombardment about two miles off shore with the anchors on the 'slip' for a quick getaway. If after firing a few salvos there was no response from the shore defences we would raise anchors and again anchor accurately closer in. If we were badly hit he would beach the ship and 'whatever happened – if the bridge or gun control got shot away' we were to keep on firing under local control if necessary.
>
> *Kempenfelt* led her flotilla in. Early morning mist was around but it was only shallow, as a steeple and water tower were all too clearly visible at that range, sticking up through the mist. The First Lieutenant looked up at the gradually clearing shore and said cheerfully, '*La Belle France!*' The anchored destroyers then fired several salvos without any reaction at all from the shore, so according to plan, the anchor cables were pulled up and a new position taken up closer in shore ... Still there was no response. Rocket launchers 'wooshed' off their rows and rows of rocket salvos. Invasion barges passed through and it was not until they were touching the sand that the sparks of rifle fire could be seen coming from all the windows of the buildings along the sea front. We wished we could lower our guns and flatten them, but we continued to fire at our allotted Shore Battery positions – and got not a single shell back.

Power's Report of Proceedings recorded:

> At 2235 that evening we anchored three miles from St Aubin light, with the Polish ship *Dragon* anchored uncomfortably close. At 2316 a low flying Ju.88 dropped a stick of about six small bombs 50–300 yards on the port bow and across *Dragon's* starboard quarter. These exploded underwater about twenty seconds later, but caused no damage or casualties. During the night we made smoke intermittently and held fire being unable to distinguish friend from foe. There was much undisciplined firing from ships in area 'J', particularly from *Dragon,* who breathed night tracer fire all night and caused me anxiety by giving our position away.

Power recalled in his memoirs:

> During the night we all anchored, a great phalanx of ships, under a
> continuous smoke screen. There was a bit of bombing and the frigate
> *Lawford*, near us, was hit and sunk. This turned out to be Tony Pugsley's
> ship, and he was Captain (Patrols) for the whole British Assault Area.
> Next afternoon, I was sent for by Admiral Sir Philip Vian (Assault Force
> Commander) in his flagship *Scylla* and told to take over Captain (Patrols).
>
> It was quite a job to take on at short notice as well as remaining Captain
> (D) for the 26th. I had sixty-four minesweepers anchored along the north
> fringe of the anchorage each night to keep radar and listening watch.
> Fifteen gun-support landing craft on the eastern flank. A call on eight
> destroyers as required and three squadrons of MTBs operated under the
> radar control of *Scylla* to my orders and ten submarine trawlers – over a
> hundred ships in all.
>
> The enemy tried every night to get E-boats into the anchorage and we
> had some lively nights and a good bit of fighting, mostly by the MTBs
> and occasionally by *Kempenfelt* and the odd destroyer. The enemy never
> got through. This went on for nearly three weeks and as I had much to
> attend to all day, and fought most of the night, it got pretty tiring, but
> tremendous fun. I was working very closely with Tom Brownrigg, an old
> colleague, and with Philip Vian, who I met in conference daily. Eventually
> Tony Pugsley, having got himself dried off and kitted up, came back in a
> new ship and took over from me.

On D+1, *Kempenfelt* weighed anchor at 1250, collected three other destroyers
– *Venus*, *Vigilant* and *Algonquin* – and closed the shore to within a mile to
bombard enemy beach strong points.

*   *   *

Wednesday, 7 June
One mile off Juno beach
It's now D+1. We were nearly hit like *Hardy* but it missed us and no harm
resulted. We were in ringside seats last night to see the paras and the glider
troops go into action. You may remember the photo I have of the invasion of
Crete with all the planes and parachutes in the sky.

Thursday, 8 June
One mile off Juno beach
The pace from the naval side is certainly hotting up now and as before at Salerno the crucial days will not be the earliest ones. We've taken on new responsibilities as Captain (Patrols). We shall be here for at least another week. I've introduced my gun's crew to a device of mine to keep myself alert. The cook bakes potatoes in their jackets and every hour and a half or so one of the crew brings one to each of us, accompanied by a real cup of cocoa. It's distinctly 'English' weather off the French coast – chilly at night.

I am having trouble with Goodson, my cypher clerk. He's not fast enough for 'D' and is complaining about the hours and lack of sleep. If I can't motivate and pep him up, I'll have to come off the Bofors and take over the deciphering myself. That would be a shame as I've worked the crew up to a high state of efficiency. However, to use a Robson phrase, 'Let nothing matter more than it should.'

Friday, 9 June
Off the French coast
I'm actually writing this at 0630 on Saturday morning, as we had an air raid at 2000 yesterday evening and remained closed up till a few minutes ago. It's been an exciting night and we've been popping off at biggish and smallish fry – nothing to hit the headlines but it's enough that they did no damage and were successfully driven off.

Saturday, 10 June
Off the French coast
I've just had the unpleasant experience of having to tell Goodson off. His trouble is he doesn't accept my principle of taking a pride in finishing a job however exhausted and weary one may be. Now I must get myself in my sweaters and duffels for the night's frolics.

Sunday, 11 June
Off the French coast
I have enclosed the two inspiring messages from Eisenhower and Ramsay that were dished out last Monday night as we set sail on this jaunt. Anyway, they are historic documents and we can show them to our grandchildren with the snap of me in Bofors fighting rig!

Monday, 12 June
Off the French Coast
This will be the fifth night of our tenure of office as Captain (Patrols) in charge of the defence of the British Assault Area. We were told we would only need to do it for a week or so, but it will be for at least another four days. We had the honour of being (we think) the first ship to open fire on the Normandy Coast – something else I suppose to tell the grandchildren. Anyway, I imagine many ships will claim to be the first.

Tuesday, 13 June
Off the French Coast
The reason for our present antics as Captain (Patrols) was because the previous incumbent's ship, *Lawford*, was torpedoed. He went back to UK, but a ship has gone to collect him again. *Belfast* (one of the cruisers near us on D-Day) has now claimed to open fire before us! So, we have slipped back to being the first destroyer to open fire!

Some of those on board who have never seen action, thought that some of the bombs dropped too close but there have not been as many as I expected. With the nervous and physical strain of nightly vigils, the tempers of many are getting frayed.

Incidentally, we brought the Canadians ashore and supported them on their landing from close inshore, near the village of Ouistreham and thence on the drive to Caen. It was an amazing spectacle to see their actual assault. We were closest inshore of anybody for a time, bombarding in broad daylight. The assault craft moved in and passed us whilst bombs were clearly seen falling on the beach. Then the shore defences opened up and the craft eventually touched down. We had more than a ringside seat, as close in as a boxer's second, or even inside the ring!

Two weeks later, Stoke described the early days.

21 June
Off the French coast
Then the Captain (Patrols), in charge of the seaward defence of the British Assault Area was sunk, so we were suddenly detailed to take over – and here we are still – a fortnight or more later when every other destroyer has been back to Portsmouth at least twice! Nae bother …!

It's an arduous time because we're at Action Stations all night and for me there's then the day's work to be done. It has been a question of snatching the odd hour when I can; I'm feeling a little weary but haven't weakened appreciably yet.

As Captain Power says, we've seen a certain amount of life – enemy destroyers, E-boats and aircraft, but we've so far beaten them decisively. We hope to be relieved of the job shortly – it was supposed to be only a stopgap appointment. And then back to Portsmouth for a rest – we hope! Except that if the accumulation of nearly a month's mail catches us up, I can see precious little rest!!!

*   *   *

After seven days, the Allied landings were secured and great progress had been made. Supreme Commander Dwight D. Eisenhower sent a further message to all the Allied Expeditionary Forces on 14 June:

> To Soldiers, Airmen, Sailors and Merchant Seamen,
> and all others of the Allied Expeditionary Forces

> One week ago this morning, there was established through your coordinated efforts, our first foothold in north-western Europe. High as was my pre-invasion confidence in your courage, skill and effectiveness in working together as a unit, your accomplishments in the first seven days of this campaign have exceeded my brightest hopes. You are a truly great Allied team, a team in which each part gains its greatest satisfaction in rendering maximum assistance to the entire body and in which each individual member is justifiably confident in all others. No matter how prolonged or bitter the struggle that lies ahead you will do your full part toward the restoration of a free France, the liberation of all European nations under Axis domination, and the destruction of the Nazi military machine. I truly congratulate you upon a brilliantly successful beginning to this great undertaking. Liberty-loving people, everywhere, would today like to join me in saying to you, 'I am proud of you.'

> Dwight D Eisenhower

At the same time, Commodore Oliver, Naval Commander Eastern Task Force, sent a rather more detailed note to his ships:

During the last week the first part of the British Second Army has been landed by the Eastern Task Force. Very considerable opposition was met, but on every beach, success was eventually won. During the assault, naval gunfire support was provided by two battleships, twelve cruisers and forty destroyers. All enemy batteries west of the Orne were silenced by 0945 on D-Day. There have been no attacks on the assault area by enemy naval forces by day, but enemy E-boats and torpedo boats have attacked the assault area each night. Captain (Patrols) has organized interceptions by our MTBs or destroyers before they reached the minesweeper defence line.

On 24 June, *Kempenfelt* returned to Portsmouth and after a short stay sailed on 29 June to refit in South Shields. Power's memoirs recall:

I was awarded the DSO for this caper. I was pleased with this. I had always felt my BEs were marks of a chairborne warrior and envied my contemporaries who were winning DSOs and DSCs at sea. Now I had joined the right club at last.

When Paymaster Lieutenant Stoke MBE, DSC left *Kempenfelt* on 30 June in Portsmouth, Captain Power DSO, OBE, CBE, later bar to DSO and promoted Admiral KCB, CB, wrote on his 'flimsy' and S.206:

Stoke served to my entire satisfaction. An exceptionally gifted officer. A most capable, energetic and conscientious officer of very strong character. He does not suffer fools gladly and tends to let them know it a little too readily at times. Always keen to take part and a natural leader. Would make an excellent Executive Officer and is always ready to assume such functions at opportunity and with good results. Good at all games, particularly rugger. Recommended for accelerated promotion.

Chapter 15

India, Marriage, and now the Pacific!

Southern India

Paymaster Lieutenant Stoke joined HMS *Rajah*, a Ruler Class Escort Aircraft Carrier, on 13 August near the end of her Deck Landing Trials with planes from RNAS Ayr and East Haven. The trials had not gone very well and there had been numerous minor flying accidents, one plane failing to stop on landing and toppling off the forward runway deck! Stoke was appointed as Captain's Secretary but later took on additional responsibilities as Communications, Signals and Radar Officer.

In early September twelve Avenger aircraft of 849 squadron, twenty-one Avengers of 857 squadron and six Hellcats of 888 squadron were loaded at RNAMY Belfast bound for India. The ship sailed on 10 September via Gibraltar, Alexandria and Aden, reaching Cochin in Southern India on 9 October to disembark 849 and 857. Then it was on to Trincomalee, Ceylon to disembark 888 and pick up 822 squadron. The ship returned via Port Said and Gibraltar, arriving back on the Clyde on 10 November.

Marriage

Stoke and Doreen Le Poidevin decided to get married during a short period of leave, and there followed a few hectic days of organization. The ceremony took place in the Cathedral Church of St Mary, Glasgow on 16 November 1944. It was a small wedding with a few close friends, and unfortunately Stoke's mother was not able to be there as it was too far to come from Southend. His father was allowed to travel due to his business commitments, and Doreen's father and mother were there as they were stationed in Glasgow. Doreen and Mick had a three-day honeymoon in North Berwick before he had to leave again on *Rajah*, bound for Liverpool and then the Pacific.

HMS *Rajah* loaned by the Admiralty to the US Pacific Fleet

Rajah departed Liverpool on 20 December 1944, arriving in New York on New Year's Eve; then it was onward to the Pacific through the Panama Canal.

*   *   *

HMS Rajah
Panama Canal
7 January 1945

As we passed through the famous Cut, all I could see was green hillsides. The Cut is very narrow – one can almost touch the sides at some points and the hills are quite tall – it's very like a railway cutting. The locks, too, are impressive. In one series of three locks the ship is lifted eighty-five feet and looking back you can see Cristobal and the Atlantic Ocean beneath you – an eerie sensation.

To take the ship through the locks no fewer than five pilots came onboard – one in charge to con, and one at each corner of the ship. And there is a special bridge put onboard to be placed in the centre of the flight deck so that the principal pilot can have a central position. The ship is towed through the locks – there was barely a foot either side between us and the walls of the locks. Our ship is towed by eight 'mules', four port and starboard, two forward and aft. These mules are engines with cabs forward and aft and the cable from the ship round a capstan amidships. They are on rails with a ratchet so they can climb and descend the inclines from lock to lock. They are strong enough to stop a ship merely by themselves braking.

We got to Balboa by tea time. We waited merely to weld on certain pieces that had to be taken off so that we could get through the locks and now we are off to San Diego to pick up our first load of aircraft. Then we go to Pearl Harbor or just 'Pearl' as the Yanks call it for further orders. We shall take about eight days to San Diego – arriving about a week today.

*   *   *

Rajah started operations out of San Diego on 15 January, liaising with US Forces, and Stoke made some long-lasting friendships during the many trips to and from San Diego to Guam in the Mariana Islands via Pearl, carrying aircraft, armaments and stores in support of the Pacific War against Japan.

*   *   *

18 February

Of course, if I had kept religiously to my practice of writing on Sundays you would have received two letters within two days, because we crossed the International Date Line last night! We are now on our way to Pearl Harbor.

The great raid on Tokyo has been announced. We knew of it before it started as Admiral Nimitz told us of it or rather told the Captain when we were in Guam. It was curious he told him of a future event but maybe he knew we would be at sea for the next eleven days, so it was quite safe.

We had a submarine scare the other night, but when it did appear it was as if he was just as frightened of us as we were of him!

I have just written to Captain Hickling, who I have just learnt was promoted to Rear-Admiral at the beginning of this year. My present captain (Armour) is still giving me the willies and really you wouldn't believe that any man could be so consistently selfish. He is worse than I care to say and I only pray that we never get into any kind of action, because I would promptly dive over the side. It would be far, far safer!

25 February

At the moment we are ploughing through a fifty-five knot gale, which is meeting us head-on. The aircraft we are carrying on the flight deck are getting rather wetter than is good for them. We spent our normal two days in Pearl this week and are now on our way back to San Diego for a boiler clean, before starting the grind again. It really is the most boring life imaginable. We have no offensive to buck us up, just continuous sea time. However, I suppose we must just try and get used to it and I do feel that if only the captain was at all reasonable, I could be more equable.

I am rather amused by the Egyptians declaring war on Japan and Germany – it seems so ludicrous at this stage of the war. And so very typical of them. I suppose after doing their level best to get us defeated in the Western Desert, they will now expect to be given Libya and Cyrenaica as a reward!

We got the details of the demobilization pay this week. It is not generous to anybody in comparison with the last war and especially to ratings. Officers don't do too badly, but the average rating or private does very shabbily in my opinion. Doreen, incidentally, gets paid two-thirds of the equivalent of a male officer, so that we shall get quite a reasonable sum between us. It works out to about £180 due to us on 1 May this year and an increase of thirty-five pounds a year between us both. We shall do much better than most young married couples as Doreen has been in so much longer than well over 95 per cent of the other girls and I have almost the maximum period, although I don't start to count time until I first went to sea on 1 May. There may be some prize money in addition, as there was in the last war. I think that prize money is peculiar to the Navy, although maybe Coastal Command will claim a share as they have destroyed shipping as well.

1 March
Dear John,

I haven't yet been ashore in the States except on duty. We have carried quite a lot of their officers and men as passengers, so that we have got to know their ideas, expressions and ways of living. On the whole I think it would be correct to say that there has been no unpleasantness and many times a very considerable degree of genuine friendship and co-operation.

The Americans have many ideas like ours and their ways of life are fundamentally the same, but nevertheless I do find that there is a tremendous deal we do not know or even readily understand about their peculiar prejudices and so forth – the Negro problem is one startling example. It also illustrates the great difference of opinion existing in the States amongst themselves – differences according to district and state, which are far deeper than any difference of locality with us.

The main point that hits all of us out here is their attitude to the war. Of course, as I have said before, they are mainly preoccupied with Japan and consider Germany is almost a subsidiary war. But the American serviceman on the whole has a just appreciation of what the British Armed Forces have achieved and admits their solid gains. He also has a great sympathy and deep wells of admiration for the British Citizen at home, who has had bad conditions of bombs, over-work, poor variety of food and so forth – he contrasts that with his own folks' attitude and draws a most favourable comparison.

But where it does become startling is that his opinion is not shared to anywhere the same extent by the US citizen in his home town or city. Their newspapers concentrate so much on American news, that British achievements will only get a mention if they are really startling and then it will be headlines for only a day. There is no consistent reporting of small but important items of the British war effort or the continuous fighting of British armed forces. Much greater publicity is given for even a small and uneventful skirmish by American Forces in the Pacific theatre.

*   *   *

At this time, Stoke's mother Barbara was in hospital for more operations, and simultaneously, unknown to him as he was in the middle of the Pacific, Doreen fell ill; this was later diagnosed as an ectopic pregnancy, and at one stage her life could have been in danger. Stoke only found this out from his next batch of mail, and it must have caused him considerable concern, knowing he could do nothing to help. Doreen recovered more rapidly than expected, however, and his next letters discussed the length of this posting and getting out of the Navy!

* * *

4 March

In one way I rather hope that I do have to remain out here for about a year. I think, and so does Doreen, that if I was to return in six months say and then have to go East again for a normal two and a half years, it would be intolerably painful. A second parting would be hard. So, I think that if I do a year and then come back I ought to be able to remain in UK for some time with any luck, at least till the war is over, when I might be able to take advantage of the moment to get a job and leave the Navy. I am more than ever determined to attempt to get out, though both Doreen and I are thankful that unlike most of our friends and acquaintances at least we can face a settled future, whereas most youngsters of my age have literally nothing ahead determined.

Not only very concerned about his new wife and mother, both seriously ill, Stoke was also very bored with his job and the ship. Long days at sea and no action!

11 March

Yesterday I had a treat. An American lady asked me to accompany her to the Symphony Concert which was being held here. And Schnabel was the soloist in Beethoven's Fourth. He played it superbly and in fact reduced her to tears with emotion. She is very old (at least fifty!) So as her husband has now arrived back from a year overseas shortly after the concert, maybe the friendship can be assumed to be platonic!! She owns a sweet shop which sells most stylish stuff. I went out to her house after the concert and heard more music including the Chopin One. Also, she has some Benedictine liqueur, so my evening was good – the first out since leaving Greenock. The rest of the concert – the Los Angeles Philharmonic conducted by Alfred Wallenstein was the Brahms Academic Festival Overture and Second Symphony. Schnabel was at his very best and I enjoyed every note he played. His rondo was the best ever, particularly the way he played the saucy triplet which is answered by the orchestra.

20 March
Dear Ivan and Ken,

As you know of course life has been getting just a little bit of its own back on me these last few months. It brought me by degrees from a schoolboy with his simple pleasures and absolute lack of serious troubles, into the war and gradually increased my responsibilities in the same ratio as it increased my pleasure in life itself, culminating in the greatest responsibility last November. I think that the Stoke boat is now sailing with a favourable wind on our beam, weathering the squalls and having sufficient courage to push ourselves off the mud if we should lose our way temporarily.

We hope that *Seamew* will be our boat for after the war. Doreen owns a quarter and we hope to buy the shares from the other naval officers when they leave to get re-appointed elsewhere.

This work out here is deadly dull for us but has the compensation of showing results. We ferry aircraft from the West Coast of America to the forward areas of the Pacific like Guam, or New Guinea and so forth by way of Pearl and our results are, of course, these carrier-borne attacks on Japan itself. Even now, the third one is in progress according to the wireless, so we feel appropriately pleased. We normally spend only two days in any one harbour – just time to discharge or load our cargo.

Out here, of course, we tend to get the Yank perspective on the war and regard the war in Europe as almost over. Also, from what I have seen of some of the Yanks, they aren't yet convinced that the only good German is at least a crippled one even if not dead. They have too many Germans in the States to believe that Germany has harboured some of the worst in our modern civilization of recent years. The Japs – oh yes, but the Germans, well … Still, I am doing my best to disillusion them purely from my personal experiences with regard to hospital ships deliberately being sunk, hospitals bombed and white flags abused and so forth. Must stop this tirade.

1 April
We are still in Guam, waiting to be unloaded. It is really cruelly hot here especially chasing around in open boats and tramping on the dusty island ashore between offices. What it will be like in three months' time I don't like to imagine. And these ships being all metal with no scuttles to speak of are very

hot – hotter than most ships – whilst their ventilation is not as good as regular warships.

It is Easter Sunday today. I missed the lovely hymns and general spirit of Easter although I must say that we did have some hot cross buns although they weren't hot!!

The news is excellent. There was a rumour this morning that some of our troops are just 107 miles from Berlin. It does appear as if we are this time making no mistake and are going to enter Berlin as a conquering army and not a benefactor of any stab in the back.

I haven't been able to get many details of what is happening about this San Francisco conference. I see that France is being as truculent as ever and demanding equality of votes with the British Empire. If I had my way I'd exclude them all together or at least regard them as on a par with Bolivia or Estonia. My impressions have been anti-French since North Africa and they are not lessened by their behaviour recently in snubbing Roosevelt. Don't they realize that they exist by courtesy of the Allies and not because they are French? And their main energies are now devoted to re-establishing the Black Market and rooking the soldiers at Parisian night clubs – Pah, they annoy me! Must close now and anyway it doesn't do me any good to rail at these miserable French.

8 April

We came away in good weather, which was indeed fortunate, as our escort lost a man overboard. He was not seen by his own ship but fortunately she happened to be dead ahead when it happened and he cleared our side by about five feet. It was dark – about 2130 – but fortunately again there were some people on the sponsons [projections from the side of the ship] who saw him – two US marines and a sailor and a stoker. The sailor had the presence of mind to throw a lifebelt over the side immediately, whilst the other raised the alarm. A search was conducted, although it was not in safe waters, and after an hour he was picked up. We heard him shouting in the water once, so combined with our plot, we kept his estimated position. It was altogether an excellent bit of Anglo-American co-operation. He was not wearing any form of lifebelt, so it was indeed fortunate that the water was calm and warm. We were routed further south to avoid a submarine that had been reported. Anyway, all this took us through the Marshall Islands instead of north of them as usual, and in consequence we had a perfectly glassy sea for about twenty-four hours. As soon as we came north of them, we ran into the inevitable head wind which we have now. It is a warm wind so doesn't cool us down at all.

I wrote off a letter today to the Civil Service Commissioners about the prospects of joining the Civil Service after the war. They'll probably refer me to some announcement in a White Paper on sale at all railway bookstalls, although I did explain that I was in the Pacific and didn't travel by train much!! As you know, I am not keen to stay in the Navy but nevertheless I don't want to get out into nothing at all. I want to be at least moderately certain that I am going into something that will pay me as comparatively well and has a pension and so forth. And as I have no fairy Godmother or rich Uncle there isn't much other choice really! However, I am prepared to sacrifice a certain amount of the good salary that the Navy seems fit to pay me, in order to have a settled existence and a family life of our own.

For myself I am averaging 16/6d per day as a Lieutenant, with a rise of a shilling in a year's time, plus 3/6d a day for this service business, and at the moment I am getting Japanese Campaign Pay plus Climate Pay when we are in the middle of the tropics. That is all taxable, and then there is my marriage allowance of 4/- a day which is not taxable. However, one must remember that much of this would not be payable in peacetime. In addition, there will be other expenses that I do not have whilst on the ship. Nevertheless, it has meant I have been able to send Doreen one hundred pound out of my current savings. I had earmarked that to buy things in the States for our Home, but I suppose I must just start saving again. Life is like that anyway, and it's just as well to learn it quickly.

15 April

The great news of the week has been Roosevelt's death. We were carrying many US Navy passengers, so have made today quite a ceremony. We had a church service with some polite lowering and raising of ensigns and keeping them at half-mast. It is a tremendous blow but how fortunate that at least it was not before Yalta, when it might have reflected in worsening Allied relations. I feel that it may result in a considerable degree of increased back-biting between the Yanks and ourselves, as the Yanks are so intolerably certain that they have won the whole war for us and that we are doing and have done nothing except bring disaster to the cause. They are a mostly incredibly ill-educated and irresponsible people with such a tremendous inferiority complex, which makes them try and shout louder than anybody else. I'd give anything to blitz the States for just a month. However, we shall be in harbour at the end of the week and hope to hear more favourable news of my females. I am feeling very homesick indeed.

22 April

Since arriving in San Diego last Thursday, much has been happening. We arrived here to be met with the bombshell of the Captain's appointment to command a Royal Naval Air Station on Trinidad. It has hurt him a lot as it more or less implies that he is not going to be promoted. He is being relieved before we sail tomorrow morning by the Commander, and the remaining Executive Officers therefore go up one. It has meant a very, very busy few days for me. When a Captain goes, there is a 'flimsy' for every officer in duplicate and also a Confidential Report, as well as many other things.

I have got my 'flimsy' which I am returning by hand of another Captain's Secretary – Roy Quinton – who was with me in *Glasgow* for you to place in the Archives!!

Amongst the mail was a nice letter from Commodore Oliver written in January. He had received a piece of our wedding cake and was writing to wish us 'Good Luck and Godspeed'. Rather nice of him to write as he must be a very busy man with a whole squadron of carriers under him now.

I don't expect to stay in *Rajah* so very much longer now. It seems peculiar that I never seem to stay in any one ship longer than eight months or so. Of course, it has the added advantage that it resulted in my gaining much more experience than would otherwise have resulted. I don't know how it is going to work out with the Commander now as Captain, and more to the point with the First Lieutenant, upgraded to Executive Officer, with a temporary half stripe. He is an ex-Warrant Officer and I fear may get intolerably swollen-headed.

22 April

Dear Daddy,

I am writing this separate letter to you, as I wanted to say to you alone how very much indeed I have deeply appreciated your letter to me. I think it has been a great help to me to receive it, Daddy, and when I realize how much you have had to contend with during these last twelve months, it makes me realize that my troubles are not mountains but barely hills. Yet you can still write such wonderful words of encouragement. So, Daddy, this is just a very inadequate thank you.

I can't say I am weeping to see the Captain leaving, as he has tried me sorely. However, he has done well for me before leaving by recommending me for some additional seniority. I am only so busy because in addition to my Captain's Secretary's duties, I am also the Signals Officer and the Radar Officer – and have been confidential adviser and general Staff Officer. With the new Captain, I have a mind to ask to be relieved of some of these so I can start a correspondence course, as I want to get back into a scholastic groove again.

1 May

We are now on the way back to the West Coast from Pearl. The week has been an eventful one back home, with the end of the war in Europe. This must surely hasten the end of the Jap war by releasing so many more troops, aircraft and ships for the Pacific. The death of Hitler and Mussolini caused little stir. But I do realize for you it must indeed have been a momentous week.

The ship has proceeded on its way under the new management, so far with no flare-ups. I have not yet made up my mind whether to ask to be moved as officially I have such a small job to do – although I am the busiest man in the ship with the other jobs I have. I am rather waiting to see if the ship becomes happier – if so, I might stay and start my course with the Tutorial Institutes.

If there is an election this year, I have applied so that either of you can be my proxy. I haven't yet made up my mind. Taken by and large I incline to follow the Liberals' fortunes if they make a nation-wide effort to become a real party – I have misgivings over the Labour Party's capacity to govern and don't favour some of the Tory doctrines! Easy, isn't it?!

*   *   *

VE Day on 8 May was widely celebrated with street parties the length and breadth of Great Britain, but out in the Pacific the Americans and their Allies were still struggling against the kamikaze Japanese.

*   *   *

3 June

When I got letters from you today posted after 7 May, they were postmarked with a device of a capital V and two bells – rather attractive I thought as a suitable method of symbolizing VE Day.

We got to Guam just a few hours after the departure of the *King George V*. I would have liked to get on board her to see what conditions were like in the British Pacific Fleet, so that I could have known if I would fare better or worse by trying to get a move in their direction. We are feeling quite cut off from the election. We cannot pick up the BBC broadcasts, so our attitude as a ship is one of baffled disinterest.

*   *   *

Charlie Monteith, a contributor to the BBC archive, was a cook onboard *Rajah*, but seemed to make much better use of his leave than Stoke ever did! He recalled:

> I volunteered for the Navy when I was sixteen and lied about my age. I joined the catering branch; three days later I was on HMS *Rajah*, an aircraft carrier leaving Greenock. We had no idea where we were going until we got to the Panama Canal, which we passed through with very limited room, to emerge into the Pacific.
>
> We had to spend our leave in San Diego, California. We went to Hollywood and stayed in Wilshire Boulevard, in a building similar to the YMCA. We were treated very well by the Americans and got the chance to meet film stars. Mary Pickford – an English actress who was a darling of the time – threw a big party for us at her house in Beverly Hills. She gave us English tea, and Hawaiian dancers put on a performance. We also met Jimmy Gleeson – another famous actor – and we swam in his swimming pool. Our main duties were taking planes out to Guam and bringing wounded American marines back to San Diego.

Ken Wretham, another contributor to the BBC, was onboard *Rajah*, working in the same office as Stoke. He also experienced a little American life outside the ship, at the same Mary Pickford party!

> While serving as a telegraphist on HMS *Rajah* for two years ferrying American aircraft from San Diego to Guam via Pearl, I swam in Mary Pickford's pool and met Joan Fontaine during a week's leave. Some years ago, I had the pleasure of meeting Potts Patrick, the Petty Officer in charge of the wireless room and Gordon Tucker, the Captain's writer. Some of my papers and photos of *Rajah*, with crashed aircraft doing deck landing trials, are in the Liddell Hart War Museum at Kings College London.

*   *   *

24 June
It's been a busy time for me. My writer, Gordon Tucker, went off on leave and my messenger was taken away from me, due to a shortage of seamen. I was a one-man band in the office. The Captain with his usual ignorance has

not helped of course – he is the laziest man I have ever yet seen. Armour was annoying, no doubt, but never lazy and as rude as this fellow. It was most humorous that this week one of the films shown on board was none other than Captain Bligh and the Mutiny on the Bounty!! For one of his nicknames is Captain Bligh, owing to his disposition and a slight facial resemblance to Charles Laughton. However, he has none of the respect or real fear that Bligh had over his men.

Today I have received the letter from the British Tutorial Institutes. You will be interested to know that regular officers do qualify after all for the War Gratuity and up to now, I have earned about 105 pounds and Doreen 77. It will all help and of course grows whilst either of us is still in the Navy.

Daddy asks about how the peace will affect Doreen and Captain Le P. Well I know little about his future – they are still bringing out new classes of his type of ships, so maybe with that and the job of tropicalizing so many ships, he will be required for some time. Also, of course, there will be the refitting of ships which get damaged in the Pacific. Doreen's is nebulous but already many reductions have been made at Greenock. They plan to reduce to one third by August first, but are going to remain a working office (perhaps for carriers?). We do know she will not be sent foreign. She has been put in a group of married Wrens and could therefore be demobilized straight away. However, she has volunteered for further service until I eventually return home. It will meantime keep her occupied and of course the cash side is no mean thought.

Mummy queries whether Doreen and I still write daily. Yes, Mummy, we do and it has become such a habit now – after all it is a year and a half since we first started to write daily – that it is no hardship, and in fact I do really believe that I would not go to sleep easily if I did not write each evening before turning in. Of course, it doesn't mean that all letters are long ones, but it is just a link which we have – we know that each evening we will be writing to each other and somehow or other it comforts us both. We have so comparatively few weeks of real life together to provide many other links, so that we feel that the regular evening chat is merely what we should do and did when we were together and met each evening when I came off the ship and Doreen off watch.

My own birthday will have passed before next week. I cannot say how much I am looking forward to spending it in the family traditional fashion. The one word 'family' summarizes, I think, my whole attitude to the Navy – the future would be so blank were I to spend so much time away from what I hope will be a sizeable family anyway.

8 July
This letter is being written whilst we are already on our way back to the UK. Staggering isn't it indeed? I hardly know where to start, but here it is in more or less chronological order. We were in the Repair Base having a boiler clean and minor repairs done. The week passed until Friday, when Bill Phoenix rang me up. He is on the US Staff at North Island and took me to a baseball match last time we were in. He rang me to ask me up to his house in Los Angeles for the weekend. I had strained a muscle in my back and felt lazy, so said I would go the next weekend as I expected our refit to last longer than originally intended. And that if that was not suitable, there would always be another time. At which he gasped and said didn't I know our movements – to which I replied that I presumed Guam. And then he said that it was U.K. You can guess how startled I was to receive the news in such a way!!!

I immediately went and told the Captain and it was equally a shock to him. I rang up Washington and they confirmed it to be true but knew of no reason. They told me we would call at Norfolk and maybe New York too. Anyway, Bill persuaded me that I had to go up as this would be the very last time, so I agreed.

So, on Saturday – that is a week yesterday – I left the ship and caught the 1730 train with Bill from San Diego to LA. We went out to the tiny house he rents – a lounge, kitchen, one bedroom and bathroom – that's all!! I slept on a settee bed in the living room. The bungalow was made of wood so every sound echoed. They had room of course for a fridge! They had a gas stove which used natural gas from the oil fields, which has less smell. The rent for this hutch with a few sticks of furniture was ten pounds a month.

We arrived quite late and met his wife – Bernie. She is about his age – about 27 or 28. They have been married six years. She has a college degree and at present works in the Dept of National Labor Relations Board. She has just received a raise and now earns more than Bill – some $1,200 a year! It apparently suits them that they both work, even in peace time, and she doesn't like the idea of living in a house with no intellectual talk.

I spent a very interesting weekend with them – we talked over many problems and found a similarity in outlook which was most encouraging. On the Sunday we made a late start and went out to Mount Wilson. This is a 6,000ft peak with the famous Carnegie observatory on the top. The scenery was grand. The sun was out and I forgot all about the ship for the whole day, which did me the world of good. On Monday Bill had to go back early, but I played truant and did some shopping in town. Bernie was able to tell me the names of the best stores, so I spent the day traipsing around. I was exhausted, not just tired, at the end! The stores are much better than San Diego and it was well worth it. I bought quite a lot of household things – in particular towels, an eiderdown, and a bedspread to match the blankets I have already sent back.

I took Bernie out for a meal before catching the 2000 train back and was on board *Rajah* by midnight. It was a definite break and enabled me to see how Americans live. The week was naturally hectic, with the final details of leaving and me watching the men doing the repairs like a lynx. They are far worse than our dockyard mates in that they will down tools and leave a job at the slightest chance. And as I had quite a number of things being done in my Radar and Communications World, I found a lot to occupy my time.

We are now on the way to the Canal. It looks as if we shall put into a place called Mayport in Florida for a couple of days to offload a cargo of planes which we have onboard. Then we go to Norfolk, Virginia to load up planes for the UK, New York to pick up passengers and then Home.

In the meantime, I have scrawled a very hasty note to Robson accepting his job. It looks as if I shall definitely be leaving *Rajah* now, for even if the Admiralty doesn't let him have me, I think they will give me a change. I have had news from Doreen that Robson is going to have a new cruiser, which is just completing building. As for the foreign service question – well as these nine months are to be wasted anyway, there is no point in refusing on that score, as I see no chance whatsoever of getting any home job at the moment. Demobilization has already started and it means that most of the places at home are being closed down and the few remaining are being manned by those shortly to be released.

Robson told me he expects to leave the UK in early September, so it looks as if I shall be in Home waters for about three weeks. How much of that I can expect leave, I don't care to guess – it is going to be such a bitter wrench, I know. I cannot let myself visualize it in the least. If I stayed in this ship I don't think it would be much better, as my hunch is that she will refit for about a month to six weeks and then go abroad once more – that is about three weeks leave to each watch. But the thought of remaining on this ship horrifies me and so I have accepted Robson.

I am naturally all agog over what the next few months hold in store for us all – it seems so long since I saw you all – for it is over a year since I saw either Mummy or John. Daddy, of course, I saw at a time perhaps when he was most needed of all – moral support it is called, I think!! I shall be naturally busy enough once we first arrive – usually for about four days.

The housing prospects are indeed tricky. So much obviously depends on future imponderables. If I stay in the Navy or if I join the Civil Service and where I shall then work and so forth. In general, Doreen and I have firmly decided upon a house – if possible, big enough for us to stay put for some years. Big enough then to have a family in, so that we have ruled out any portal dwellings! Flats we both abhor, and likewise we are finickity enough to desire a detached house. We have sufficient money to be able to buy a four-figure house in normal times without having a crippling mortgage. That is our future. I think that if by some fluke I did get a shore job, then we would try for a furnished flat for the moment.

For the present then, masterly inactivity has to be the cry. We anticipate living in the South as long as my work permits, so Doreen cannot even go house hunting for districts whilst still in the Wrens. I fear that when the time comes, I shall have to hope to be a successful opportunist.

12 July
After passing through the Panama Canal again, we will arrive back in the Atlantic. Incredibly, there is no war there! We will have full navigation lights, no U-boat precautions, no blackout – it will be unbelievable. And of course, all of these benefits will come when we shan't anyway be in such a hot climate!! I am trying to remain calm and collected during this passage, but time does drag so abominably. I have quite a lot to do naturally but the evenings I find the worst. I am sticky and uncomfortably warm and my mind remains more active than during the day and sleep just won't come. I think that what I principally need is some wifely care and attention to make me once more a carefree and heavy sleeper. It seems so infinitely more than six months or so since I left the Clyde.

We are all eagerly awaiting the results of the Election now. I am glad you voted Liberal for me, as I think that as far as I can judge from out here that fulfils my ideas for the present. I would be uneasy I think to entrust our fortunes to the Labour Party – they have too many children in their midst. From afar, it would seem to have been an election more like the recent American Presidential one – for or against one man, rather than choosing to vote for alternative policies. It did seem that the campaigning grew into a personal matter with Winston – of course, that has been his tactic for so long now. Certainly, wartime does show the dangers of over-nationalization. Men in the Forces so often lose their morals in small matters of conscience – they take an article as it won't matter as it belongs to the Government and nobody will be worse off if I take it – a

234

portent perhaps of nationalization. However, I don't think that because we allow competition that business should be permitted to strangle the public. In other words, I would not advocate laissez-faire but general rules of conduct to be laid down but no detailed rules. The situation is complicated to my mind by the fact that the Liberal Party do not seem to have a following enough to hope to win the election. Maybe they hope to secure sufficient representation in the Commons to show the country how good they are, so that they can win the next election. In the meantime, the Conservative party has far too many who hate Russia, whilst the Labour Party have far too many who think Russia is all that is wonderful. The little I have seen of Russia in Murmansk revealed to me that their system is far from our standards – too inhumane, too inhuman.

I am at present awaiting the final details of salaries, prospects and pension schemes of the Civil Service, before starting to consider the matter fully. At the moment I am considering Inspector of Taxes or Ministry of National Service.

I have written another article this week – my monthly one, that is, and it should see daylight next week. It was written in a hurry and at the last the printers found it was a couple of lines short after I had hacked it to the correct length. They didn't find out till they had printed all but the last four lines, so I have had to change my ending. Oh, the trials of an author!!

I am ashamed to have to blush and admit that I am entitled to the maximum number of campaign stars. I get five, which is the maximum anybody can get. I also get two stars to these five ribbons which is only one less than the maximum for the RN – terrible display isn't it? Worse than any American, I fear. Still, I have flitted about rather a lot. If only I had had them earlier, I might have managed to marry into aristocracy!!

15 July

Gosh it has been hot today. Talk about mad dogs and Englishmen! I really appreciate Noel Coward's sentiments today. We came through the Panama Canal today and the sun beat down fiercely on us all day. We are going up to Mayport by the more interesting route – through the Florida Straits, so shall see Cuba from a distance and pass about twenty miles off Miami. We also know we are going to Jacksonville further up the St John's River.

* * *

Rajah embarked eighteen Corsair aircraft of 1853 squadron for passage to UK, then picked up passengers in New York and arrived back in the Clyde on 28 July 1945.

Stoke had just turned twenty-four on 28 June. He had spent eight months away at sea immediately after being married, and had fitted more in to his young life than most men over their entire lifetime.

Captain Armour had written on his S206 and 'flimsy':

Stoke served to my entire satisfaction. A quite exceptionally brilliant officer, who possesses boundless energy, enthusiasm and initiative, which coupled with his great ability are an inspiration and example to all on board. Few Secretaries could have served their Captain better. He would have done well in any capacity in the Executive Branch and is a fine leader. His war record speaks for itself. I am recommending him for promotion under CAFO 203/45.

Stoke served to my entire satisfaction. This officer has shown marked ability and keenness in every job he has undertaken. This energy and enthusiasm – ability and efficiency has been an example and inspiration to all on board. An outstanding officer.

Rear-Admiral Walker, Admiralty Representative in Washington, supported the accelerated promotion with the following remarks on his S.206 on 14 May 1945: 'I believe him to be an exceptional officer and recommend he should be noted for early advancement.'

On arrival back on the Clyde, *Rajah* was selected for conversion to bring military personnel from the Far East back to the UK, and the ship's complement was scaled down. Stoke had joined the Royal Navy as a regular so was not demobbed. The position with Robson (his captain on *Hardy*) fell through, and he was then fortunate not to be posted to the Far East, but got a posting in the UK – a shore-based position as Captain's Secretary at HMS *Collingwood* in Gosport, Hampshire.

On Stoke leaving *Rajah* on 2 September 1945, Commander Adams wrote:

An outstanding Officer in every way, of marked ability, drive and assurance. Has a large reserve of energy and has shown great initiatives in his several jobs (Captain's Secretary, Communication and Radar Officer). He has an excellent knowledge of his many duties, especially in his liaison work with the United States Navy. If he lacks any attribute it is perhaps, very occasionally, tact. A first-class Captain's Secretary who should go far in the Service. Physically fit, keenly interested in games and has a good knowledge of French and Spanish. Thoroughly recommended for grant of seniority in accordance with CAFO 203/45.

Stoke's move to HMS *Collingwood* on 1 October 1945 proved to be his last posting. In June 1947 he was invalided out of the Royal Navy, due to the injuries to his knees suffered during the extensive bombing he experienced in the Western Desert in 1941 and Bone in 1942 and early 1943.

During his war service he was torpedoed twice in *Glasgow*; was continuously bombed day and night in Tobruk, suffering direct hits on his office and accommodation; survived torpedoes and mines on *Queen Elizabeth*; survived some of most dangerous Malta convoys including the famous Battle of Sirte; was bombed day and night for three months in Bone; was on the HQ ship at the Salerno landings; was torpedoed inside the Arctic Circle in January in *Hardy*; was on the closest destroyer, a mile off the French coast, at D-Day; and served in the Pacific, between San Diego and Pearl Harbor. He certainly had many more lives than a ship's cat!

He and Doreen, despite her earlier operation, then had three (wonderful!) sons, and enjoyed a settled family life. Stoke went on build a very successful business career and was awarded the Queen's Award for Export in 1981 – but that's another story!

Appendix A

Naval Service by Ship

Paymaster G.A. (Mick) Stoke – d.o.b. 28 June 1921

1 May 1940 to 5 January 1941 (aged 19)

HMS Glasgow – *Town Class Light Cruiser,*
Commissioned 1937 – 11350 tons, 558' long, 62' wide, 22' draught, maximum
  speed 32kts. Crew 748
Served as Paymaster Cadet (completing training after Dartmouth)
Promoted Paymaster Midshipman 1 September 1940
Served under Captain F.H. Pegram DSO RN and Captain H. Hickling
  DSO RN

5 January 1941 to 6 June 1941 (aged 19)

HMS Nile – *Alexandria (Ras-el-Tin)*
Inshore Squadron (Special Service in the Western Desert)
Served as Paymaster Midshipman
Served under Captain H. Hickling DSO RN and Captain A.L. Poland DSO
  and bar, DSC RN

7 June 1941 to 21 June 1941 Recuperation in Alexandria

22 June 1941 to 28 December 1941 (aged 20)

HMS Queen Elizabeth – *Battleship*
Flagship of the C-in-C Mediterranean, Admiral A.B. Cunningham
Commissioned 1914 – 33,790 tons, 644' long, 91' wide, 42' draught.
Max speed 24kts. Crew 1,920 as a Flagship.
Served as Paymaster Midshipman
Served under Captain C.B. Barry DSO RN

29 December 1941 to 21 July 1942 (aged 20)

HMS Carlisle – *C Class Light Cruiser*
Commissioned 1918, converted to anti–aircraft ship 1940 – 4,290 tons, 451'
   long, 44' wide and 14' draught. Max speed 29kts. Crew 340
Served as Paymaster Midshipman DSC, Second Accountant Officer and
   Captain's Secretary
Served under Captain D.M.L. Neame DSO and bar

22 July 1942 to 14 October 1942

Home Leave and Sub-Lieutenant Exams

15 October 1942 to 18 May 1943 (aged 21)

HMS Cannae – *Royal Naval Base, Bone, Algeria*
Served as Acting Paymaster Sub-Lieutenant DSC and Secretary to three
different Naval Officer in Charge (NOIC) – Captain P. Baker, Captain N.V.
Dickinson DSC, DSO and bar, and Commander R.V. Money (RNVR), all
under the overall command of Commodore G.N. Oliver DSO and two bars,
Senior Officer North Africa Inshore Squadron, also based in Bone, until May
1943

19 May 1943 to 08 October 1943 (aged 22)

HMS Hannibal *(shore-based) and HMS* Hilary
Hilary was a former passenger liner launched in 1931, requisitioned by the
Royal Navy, re-commissioned as an infantry landing and headquarters ship.
7,400 tons, 424' long, 56' wide, 34' draught. Max speed only 14kts.
   Served as Paymaster Lieutenant MBE, DSC, Assistant Secretary and
Secretary to Commodore G.N. Oliver's Chief of Staff.

Oliver had moved firstly to new Headquarters in Bizerte and then Allied
Combined Headquarters in Algiers as Commodore Force 'N' for the planning
of the invasion of Sicily (Operation Husky), and then the planning for the
invasion of Italy/the Salerno landings (Operation Avalanche). Oliver moved to
HMS *Hilary* as his headquarters as British Assault Force Commander for the
Salerno landings in September 1943.

25 October 1943 to 9 December 1943 (aged 22)

Home Leave (also known as HMS *Drake*)

18 December 1943 to 04 April 1944 (aged 23)

HMS Hardy – *V Class Destroyer*
26th Destroyer Flotilla Leader
Commissioned 1943, 2,091 tons, 363′ long, 36′ wide, 10′ draught. Max speed
    37kts. Crew 225 as Flotilla leader
Served as Paymaster Lieutenant MBE, DSC and Captain (D)'s Secretary in
    26th Destroyer Flotilla
Served under Captain W.G.A. Robson DSO, DSC RN

24 April 1944 to 30 June 1944 (aged 23)

HMS Kempenfelt – *W Class Destroyer*
26th Destroyer Flotilla Leader
Commissioned October 1943, 2,570 tons, 363′ long, 36′ wide, 10′ draught.
    Top speed 36kts. Crew 225 as Flotilla leader.
Served as Paymaster Lieutenant MBE, DSC and Secretary to Captain (D),
    26th Destroyer Flotilla
Served under Captain M.L. Power DSO and bar, OBE, CBE RN

1 July 1944 to 13 August 1944

HMS Kestrel *and HMS* Daedalus
Home leave. Drafting Office courses.

13 August 1944 to 01 September 1945 (aged 23 on joining)

HMS Rajah – *Ruler Class escort carrier*
Commissioned January 1944 (ex-USA 1943) : 9,800 tons, 495′ long, 70′ wide,
    26′ draught. Max speed 17kts. Crew 646.
Served as Paymaster Lieutenant MBE, DSC, and Captain's Secretary,
    Communications Officer and later Signals Officer and Radar Officer.
Served under Captain R.S.D Armour RN and Commander A.W.R. Adams
    DSC RN

1 October 1945 to 6 June 1947

HMS Collingwood
Shore-based in Gosport (near Portsmouth)
Served as Paymaster Lieutenant MBE, DSC and Captain's Secretary to three
  Captains: Captain Hebblewhite, Captain R.L.M. Edwards and Captain A.
  St Clair Ford

Promotions

1 January 1940 Joined the Royal Navy – Initial training at Dartmouth College.
1 May 1940 Paymaster Cadet
1 September 1940 Paymaster Midshipman
1 September 1942 Acting Paymaster Sub-Lieutenant
1 May 1943 Paymaster Lieutenant – should have been 1 September 1943, but
  received Special Accelerated Promotion for 'Meritorious War Service'
6 June 1947 Retired from Naval Service (invalided out due to damage to both
  knees suffered during service in North Africa)

Appendix B

Awards, Medals and Decorations

(1) *London Gazette* 25 July 1941, Third Supplement dated 29 July 1941 No. 35231, p. 4370
Mention in despatches: Paymaster Midshipman Gordon Alexander Stoke, Royal Navy *'For courage, skill and devotion to duty in operations off the Libyan Coast'*

This related to his service in the Inshore Squadron and the Siege of Tobruk during April and May 1941, aged nineteen. Whilst some of the most savage air raids were still in progress, Stoke would take out a small boat into the harbour to rescue survivors from the bombed and sinking ships. He recommended three ratings who assisted him in the rescue of survivors from HMS *Ladybird*, bombed and sunk during the air raids on 12 May 1941.
    This is referenced in Admiralty document CW19669/41 which records the loss of HMS *Ladybird*. Many of the officers and crew were awarded honours for their bravery during this action. Also published in Admiralty Fleet Orders (AFO) 3337, 7 August 1941.

(2) *London Gazette* 21 November 1941, Third Supplement 25 November 1941, No 35357, p. 6773
Paymaster Midshipman Gordon Alexander Stoke, Royal Navy awarded the Distinguished Service Cross (DSC) *'For courage and devotion to duty while serving in the Mediterranean'*

This related to his service in the Inshore Squadron and the Siege of Tobruk during April and May 1941, aged nineteen. The recommendation by Captain A.L. Poland, his senior officer, references Stoke's disregard for his own personal safety during air raids and his quick actions when an ammunition dump was bombed and on fire.

(3)   *London Gazette* 30 April 1943, Third Supplement dated 4/5 May 1943
      No 36001, p. 2003
      Acting Paymaster Sub-Lieutenant Gordon Alexander Stoke, Royal Navy
      Awarded Member of the Order of the British Empire (MBE) '*For bravery
      during enemy air attacks in North African waters*'

      This related to his service in the Port of Bone (November 1942–May
      1943) and particularly during an air raid of 4/5 December 1942.

(4)   Special Accelerated Promotion in 1943 for '*Meritorious War Service*',
      whilst serving in the North Africa Inshore Squadron, stationed in the
      port of Bone (1942/43).

(5)   Campaign Medals:
      Atlantic Star
      Africa Star
      Italy Star
      Arctic Star
      Arctic Emblem
      Soviet 40th Anniversary Medal
      Pacific Star
      1939–1945 Star and War Medal

Appendix C

Paymaster Midshipman G.A. (Mick) Stoke MBE, DSC RN

Confidential Naval Records (S.206)
*

HMS *Glasgow* **(6 June 1940–6 January 1941)**

signed Captain H. Hickling, 6 January 1941:

'Most energetic, eager and enthusiastic. He is learning quickly and should develop into a very good officer. At present he is apt to be inaccurate and untidy, but this is only because he lets his keenness run away with him; but the tendency should disappear with experience. A very good physique, plays games, a good manner and a first-rate young man.'

Inshore Squadron (5 February 1941–6 June 1941)

signed Captain A.L. Poland, 9 June 1941:

'As Secretary cum Staff Officer cum Signal Officer, this young officer has shown great ability, considerable initiative and has worked most zealously. He has been a tower of strength in every way and has, in addition, displayed considerable courage on many occasions. For his age he possesses an unusual amount of common sense and his judgement is very sound. Physically strong and fit or he would not have stood the strain and trying conditions under which he has worked for 4 months.'

---

* Requested and retrieved in 2020.

HMS *Queen Elizabeth* (22 June 1941–28 December 1941)

signed Captain C.M. Barry, 31 December 1941:

> 'A particularly keen and able young officer. He has profited by his varied experiences and promises to be an outstanding officer. Charming manner, good mixer, will take on anything. Very good socially. Plays games well and hard.'

HMS *Carlisle* (29 December 1941–21 July 1942)

signed Captain D.M.L. Neame, 21 July 1942:

> 'A most able and energetic young officer who has well lived up to the reputation with which he joined this ship from the "Q.E." A fine rugger player who plays all games well, a good pianist with a sound knowledge of music and well read. Carries himself well in a wardroom of which he is by several years the youngest member. Possesses personality and is well above the average of his contemporaries. Has volunteered for special services of an arduous and dangerous type.'

Inshore Squadron, Bone, Algeria (15 October 1942–9 January 1943)

signed Commander P. Baker, 9 January 1943:

> 'During all my career in the Services and in civilian life, I have never met such a capable young man. Is possessed of great courage and shows a knowledge of Service matters far beyond his years. Considerable personality and personal charm. Should go very far indeed. Has been recommended for promotion.'

Additional comments by Senior Officer Inshore Squadron, Commodore G.N. Oliver, dated 17 January 1943:

> 'Am forwarding this, concurring with above. This officer has already been recommended for accelerated promotion vide my letter No 139/20 of 20 December, 1942.'

Inshore Squadron, Bone, Algeria (10 January–19 April 1943)

signed Captain N.V. Dickinson, 19 April 1943:

'An outstanding young officer with an amazing capacity for work. Not only is he most capable in his own work but can turn his hand to anything. Cheerful, well-mannered and always most considerate and as has been proved, most courageous. I would be very pleased to have him work with me again.'

Additional comments by Senior Officer Inshore Squadron, Commodore G.N. Oliver, dated 22 April 1943:

'An exceptional all–rounder. As the campaign moves forward, he should move with it.'

HMS *Hannibal*, HMS *Hilary*, (19 May – 8 October 1943)

signed Commodore G.N. Oliver, Commander Force 'N', 9 October 1943:

'A quite exceptional officer, of great promise. Has consistently shown outstanding power of decision, leadership and common sense, well beyond his years. Possesses boundless energy and is a cheerful and a quite untiring worker. Cool and most courageous in emergencies. Would do great credit to the Executive Branch were he to be transferred.'

HMS *Hardy* (December 1943–March 1944)

S.206 missing. Should have been provided by Captain W.G.A. Robson. *Hardy* was torpedoed on the 30 January 1944, 60 miles south of Bear Island within the Arctic Circle. Captain Robson was sent on sick leave for a couple of months to rest, so presumably the S.206 was not completed.

HMS *Kempenfelt* (15 April – 30 June 1944)

signed Captain M.L. Power, 7 July 1944:

'A most capable, energetic and conscientious officer of very strong character. He does not suffer fools gladly and tends to let them know it a little too readily at times. Always keen to take part in any activity and a natural leader. Would make an excellent Executive Officer and is always ready to assume such functions at opportunity, and with good results. Games – Rugger (good). 'Make one' at all games. Languages – slight French and Spanish. Recommended for accelerated promotion.'

HMS *Rajah* (13 August 1944–19 April 1945)

signed Captain R.M. Armour, 19 April 1945:

'A quite exceptionally brilliant young officer, who possesses boundless energy and initiative. He would have done well in any capacity in the Executive Branch and is a fine leader. I have employed him as my Communication Officer, as well as my Secretary. My one criticism of him is that he is inclined to be intolerant of those of his mess–mates of lower intelligence than himself. His War record speaks for itself. He is a keen and able sportsman.

I am strongly of the opinion that this officer, though possessing only two years seniority as Lieutenant (S) is fully deserving of promotion under AFO 5140/44 and he is therefore recommended, as he is well able to perform any duty assigned to a Lieutenant Commander (S). Failing his eligibility under AFO 5140/44, I hereby recommend him for the grant of seniority under CAFO 203/45.'

Remarks from Senior Officer: Rear-Admiral J.M.A.Walker, British Admiralty Maintenance and Supply Representative, Washington, DC, dated 14 May, 1945:

'I believe him to be an exceptional officer and recommend he should be noted for early advancement'

HMS *Rajah* (23 April – 2 September 1945)

Signed Commander A.W.R. Adams, 2 September 1945:

'An outstanding Supply Officer in every way, of marked ability, drive and assurance. Has a large reserve of energy and has shown great initiatives in his several jobs (Captain's Secretary, Communication and Radar Officer).

He has an excellent knowledge of his many duties, especially in his liaison work with the United States Navy. If he lacks any attribute it is perhaps, very occasionally, tact. A first-class Captain's Secretary who should go far in the Service. Physically fit, keenly interested in games and has a good knowledge of French and Spanish. Thoroughly recommended for grant of seniority in accordance with CAFO 203/45.'

HMS *Collingwood* (2 September – 17 December 1945)

S.206 missing

HMS *Collingwood* (18 December 1945–20 January 1947)

signed Captain R.L.M. Edwards, 20 January 1947:

'Through loyalty to his seniors of the Service, this Officer has more than once nearly ruined his health. His energy and enthusiasm is quite unique, and his knowledge of the Service is equal to that of Officers many years his senior. His motto is "Never give in". Following this, he makes many friends and few enemies. Good at games and now spares himself time to play. Excellent social qualities. Recommended for Accelerated Promotion.'

HMS *Collingwood* (20 January – 6th June 1947)

signed Captain A. St Clair Ford 27 June 1947:

'An exceptionally capable, hardworking and conscientious young Officer, who has carried out his duties as Captain's Secretary with marked success.
    Most willing and intelligent. Although not actually playing games himself, owing to leg injuries, he takes the greatest interest in organising rugger in the port. Recommended for Accelerated Promotion.'

Sources

Preface
Brooke G., *Alarm Starboard*
Stoke S., *Stoke family history*

Chapter 1 Royal Naval College, Dartmouth
Clarkson R., *Headlong into the Sea*
Bush E.W., *How to become a Naval Officer (Special Entry)*
Farquharson-Roberts M., *Royal Naval Officers from War to War 1918–1939*
Civil Service Exam Results – November 1939
Beattie J., *The Churchill Scheme*
Lavery B., *The Royal Naval Officer's Pocket Book*
Holloway A., *From Dartmouth to War – A Midshipman's Journal*
RN College, Dartmouth – Passing Out Results, March 1940
Harrold J. and Porter R., *Brittania Royal College, Dartmouth – An Illustrated History*

Chapter 2 Torpedoed in HMS *Glasgow*: First Experience of War
Oliver G.D., *HMS* Glasgow *– In War and Peace*
ADM 53/112295 – HMS *Glasgow* Ship's Log, May to December 1940
Cunningham A.B., *A Sailor's Odyssey*
Kimmins A., *It is upon the Navy*
Grehan J. and Mace M., *The War at Sea in the Mediterranean 1940–1944*
Macintyre D., *The Battle for the Mediterranean*
Winton J. (ed.), *The War at Sea – An anthology of personal experiences*
Bertke, Kindell, Smith., *World War II Sea War Volume 3*
Holman G., *The King's Cruisers*
ADM 199/103 Attacks on HM Ships – HMS *Glasgow*

Chapter 3 A Young Naval Officer in the Western Desert?
Cunningham A.B., *A Sailor's Odyssey*
WO 201/346, *Inshore Squadron: General Orders, January 1941*
WO 201/347, *Inshore Squadron: Operations, January 1941*
ADM 199/414, *Mediterranean War Diaries (January–May 1941)*
Buckingham W.F., *Tobruk – the Great Siege1941–1942*
Duff D.V., *May the Winds Blow*
Simpson M. (ed.), *The Cunningham Papers Volume II*
Evans A.S., *Destroyer Down*
Long G., *To Benghazi*
Palmer A.B., *Pedlar Palmer of Tobruk*
ADM 1/11371, Award recommendations Poland and Duff
HMSO, *The First Campaign in Libya, September 1940 to February 1941*

PREM 3/313/3, *Western Desert December 1940 to February 1941*
Grehan J. and Mace M., *Operations in North Africa and the Middle East 1939–1942*
Naval Staff Histories, *The Royal Navy and the Mediterranean Volume II, November 1940 to December 1941*

Chapter 4 The Siege of Tobruk Begins, 10 April 1941
ADM 199/414, *Mediterranean War Diaries (January–May 1941)*
Buckingham W.F., *Tobruk – The Great Siege 1941–1942*
Maughan B., *Tobruk and El Alamein*
Cunningham A.B., *A Sailor's Odyssey*
Poland A.L., *Tobruk and Beyond*
Simpson M. (ed.), *The Cunningham Papers*
Palmer A.B., *Pedlar Palmer of Tobruk*
Winton J. (ed.), *The War at Sea – An anthology of personal experiences*
Bertke, Kindell, Smith., *World War II Sea War Volume 3, October 1940 to May 1941*
Edwards K., *Men of Action*

Chapter 5 The Most Decorated Midshipman in the Navy
Daily Telegraph Obituary, 22 August 1991 – G.A. Stoke MBE, DSC
London Gazette No.35231, 29 July 1941
ADM 1/11375 – Award recommendation by Commander F.M. Smith
ADM 1/11498 – Stoke's DSC recommendation by Captain Poland
London Gazette No.35357, 25 November 1941
Cunningham A.B., *A Sailor's Odyssey*

Chapter 6 HMS *Queen Elizabeth*: Escape from Torpedoes, Again!
ADM 199/415, *Mediterranean War Diaries (June–December 1941)*
Bertke, Kindell, Smith, *World War II Sea War Volume 4, June to November 1941*
Gregory-Smith F., *Red Tobruk*
Allen L., *The Parade, 30 August 1941*
Allen L., *News Report, 27 September 1941*
Allen L., *News Report, 13 October 1941*
Cunningham A.B., *A Sailor's Odyssey*
Holloway A., *From Dartmouth to War – A Midshipman's Journal*
ADM 53/114905, Queen Elizabeth *Ship's Log June to December 1941*
Winton J. (ed.), *The War at Sea – An anthology of personal experiences*
Naval Staff Histories, *The Royal Navy and the Mediterranean Volume II, November 1940 to December 1941.*

Chapter 7 Malta Convoys MF3, MF4 and MF5
ADM 199/650, *Mediterranean War Diaries (January–July 1942)*
Cunningham A.B., *A Sailor's Odyssey*
Simpson M. (ed.), *The Cunningham Papers*
Evans A.S., *Destroyer Down*
HMS Arrow, *Notes on the sinking of SS* Thermopylae, *19 January 1942*
HMS Havock, *Narrative on the loss of SS* Thermopylae *19 January 1942*
HMS Carlisle, *Orders (No.35) for the conduct of MF5 11 February 1942*
HMS Carlisle, *Letter of Proceedings MF5, 12–16 February 1942*
ADM 53/115523, *HMS* Carlisle *Ship's Log (January – February 1942)*

HMS Carlisle, *Report of Attack by Enemy Aircraft 13 February 1942*
Woodman R., *Malta Convoys*

Chapter 8 Malta Convoy MG1, the Second Battle of Sirte

ADM 199/650, *Mediterranean War Diaries (January–July 1942)*
Cunningham A.B., *Operational Orders MG1 (Copy No. 24)*
Cunningham A.B., *A Sailor's Odyssey*
Simpson M., *The Cunningham Papers*
Vian P., *Action This Day*
Pack S.W.C., *The Battle of Sirte*
Evans A.S., *Destroyer Down*
Woodman R., *Malta Convoys*
Gregory-Smith F., *Red Tobruk*
ADM 199/681, *Operation MG One, the Battle of Sirte*
Connell G.G., *Mediterranean Maelstrom, HMS Jervis*
Edwards K., *Men of Action*
ADM 53/115525, *HMS* Carlisle *Ship's Log, March 1942*
HMS *Carlisle, Letter of Proceedings, 22–23 March 1942*
Handwritten sketch of ship's positions during the Battle of Sirte
Admiralty Press Release for the Battle of Sirte, 22 March 1942
HMS *Carlisle, Letter of Proceedings, 24–28 March 1942*
Air Defence Notes for ships berthing in Malta,
Messages from the Prime Minister and Admiralty after Sirte
ADM 234/353, *Naval Staff Histories No.32 Malta Convoys – MG1*
Poland A.L., *Tobruk and Beyond*
Macintyre D., *The Battle for the Mediterranean*
Winton J. (ed.), *The War at Sea – An anthology of personal experiences*
Greene J. and Massagnani A., *The Naval War in the Mediterranean*
Grehan J. and Mace M., *The War at Sea in the Mediterranean, 1940–1944*
Holman G., *The King's Cruisers*
Cameron I., *Red Duster, White Ensign – The story of the Malta Convoys*

Chapter 9 Return to England and Sub-Lieutenant Exams

Bertke, Kindell, Smith, *World War II Sea War Volume 6, April – August 1942*
ADM 53/115526, HMS *Carlisle* Ship's Log, April – July 1942
Gregory-Smith F., *Red Tobruk*
Poland A.L., *Tobruk and Beyond*
Order of proceedings for the visit by HRH
Clarkson R., *Headlong into the Sea*
Holloway A., *From Dartmouth to War – A Midshipman's Journal*
Winser de S., *British Invasion Fleets – The Mediterranean 1942–1945*

Chapter 10 Operation Torch: the Retaking of North Africa

ADM 199/652, *Operation Torch War Diaries (November/December 1942)*
ADM 199/637, *Operation Torch War Diaries (January/February 1943)*
Cunningham A.B., *A Sailor's Odyssey*
Drummond J.D., *A River Runs to War*
Grehan J. and Mace M., *Operations in North Africa 1942–1944*
Bartimeus, *The Turn of the Road*

Blackwood's Magazine, Issue 1532, July 1943
Winton J. (ed.), *The War at Sea – An anthology of personal experiences*
ADM 1/14306 – G.A. (Mick) Stoke MBE Recommendation
London Gazette No.36001, 4 May 1943
ADM 234/359, *Naval Staff Histories No.38 – Operation Torch*
Macintyre D., *The Battle for the Mediterranean*

Chapter 11 The Turn of the Tide in North Africa
Devine A.D., *The Road to Tunis*
Grehan J. and Mace M., *Operations in North Africa 1942–1944*
Clarkson R., *Headlong into the sea*

Chapter 12 Operation Avalanche, the Salerno Landings
Winser de S., *British Invasion Fleets – The Mediterranean 1942–1945*
ADM 234/358, *Naval Staff Histories 37 – Operation Avalanche*
Oliver G.N., *Letter of Proceedings, Force 'N'*
Kimmins A., *Half Time*
Hickey D. and Smith G., *Operation Avalanche – the Salerno Landings*
Cunningham A.B., *A Sailor's Odyssey*
Bertke, Kindell, Smith, *World War II Sea War Vol 10, July to September 1943*

Chapter 13 Torpedoed in HMS *Hardy* on Russian Convoy JW56
Robson W.G.A., *My Naval Life*
Evans A.S., *Destroyer Down*
Campbell I. and Macintyre D., *The Kola Run – Arctic Convoys*
Woodman R., *Arctic Convoys*
Schofield B.B., *The Russian Convoys*
Schofield B.B., *The Arctic Convoys*
Ruegg R. and Hague.A, *Convoys to Russia*
ADM 199/77 *North Russian Convoys JW and RA*
ADM 234/340 *Naval Staff Histories, Arctic Convoys*
ADM 358/2048 *HMS* Hardy *torpedoed and sunk, 30 January 1944*
ADM 358/4314 *HMS* Hardy *sunk by enemy action, 30 January 1944*

Chapter 14 The D-Day Landings in HMS *Kempenfelt*, Juno Beach
Power M.L., *Admiral Manley Power's War Diaries*
Naval Staff Histories, *Operation Neptune, the D-Day Landings, 6 June 1944*
Bowman M., *Air War D-Day, Gold – Juno – Sword*
Winton J. (ed.), *The War at Sea – An anthology of personal experiences*
ADM 179/516, *Report of Proceedings Eastern Task Force (Force 'J')*
Neillands R. and de Normann R., *D-Day 1944 – Voices from Normandy*

Bibliography

Autobiographies

Brooke G., *Alarm Starboard* (Patrick Stephen, 1982, republished by Pen & Sword, 2018)

Clarkson R., *Headlong into the Sea* (Pentland Press, 1995)

Cunningham A.B., *A Sailor's Odyssey* (Hutchinson, 1951)

Duff D.V., *May The Winds Blow!* (Hollis & Carter, 1948)

Gregory-Smith F., *Red Tobruk – Memoirs of a World War II Destroyer Commander* (Pen & Sword, 2008)

Holloway A., *From Dartmouth to War – A Midshipman's Journal* (Buckland Publications, 1993)

Kimmins A., *Half Time* (William Heinemann, 1947)

Macdonald R., *The Figurehead* (Pentland Press, 1993)

Palmer A.B., *Pedlar Palmer of Tobruk* (Roebuck Society Publications, 1981)

Palmer J., *Luck on my side – The Diaries & Reflections of a Young Wartime Sailor* (Leo Cooper/Pen & Sword, 2002)

Poland A.L., *Tobruk and Beyond – War Notes from the Mediterranean Station 1941–1943* (Halstead Press, 2018)

Power M.L., *Admiral Manley Power's War Diaries* (held at the Churchill Archives, Cambridge)

Robson W.G.A., *My Naval Life* (held at the Churchill Archives, Cambridge)

Seymour P., *Where the Hell is Africa? – Memoirs of a Junior Naval Officer* (Pentland Press, 1995)

Vian P., *Action This Day* (Frederick Muller, 1960)

Books

Barnett Corelli, *Engage the Enemy More Closely* (Hodder & Stoughton, 1991)

Bartimeus, *The Epic of Malta* (Odhams Press)

Bartimeus, *The Turn of the Road* (Chatto and Windus, 1946).

Beattie J.H., *The Royal Naval Special Entry Cadet Scheme 1913–1955* (privately published, 2010)

Bertke, Kindell, Smith, *World War II Sea War Volume 3, October 1940 to May 1941* (Bertke, 2012)

Bertke, Kindell, Smith, *World War II Sea War Volume 4, June to November 1941* (Bertke, 2012)

Bertke, Kindell, Smith, *World War II Sea War Volume 5, December 1941 to March 1942* (Bertke, 2012)

Bertke, Kindell, Smith, *World War II Sea War Volume 6, April to August 1942* (Bertke, 2012)

Bertke, Kindell, Smith, *World War II Sea War Volume 7, September to November 1942* (Bertke, 2014)

Bertke, Kindell, Smith, *World War II Sea War Volume 8, December 1942 to February 1943* (Bertke, 2015)

Bertke, Kindell, Smith, *World War II Sea War Volume 9, March to June 1943* (Bertke, 2016)

Bertke, Kindell, Smith, *World War II Sea War Volume 10, July to September 1943* (Bertke, 2017)

Blackwood's Magazines, Issue 1532, July 1943

Bowman M.W., *Air War D-Day, Gold – Juno – Sword* (Pen & Sword, 2013)

Broome J., *Make a Signal* (Putnam, 1955)

Broome J., *Make Another Signal* (William Kimber, 1973)

Buckingham W.F., *Tobruk – The Great Siege 1941–1942* (The History Press, 2008)

Bush E.W., *How to Become a Naval Officer (Special Entry)* (Gieves, 1928)

Bush E.W., *How to Become a Naval Officer* (Gieves, 1937)

Cameron I., *Red Duster White Ensign – The Story of the Malta Convoys* (Frederick Muller, 1959)

Campbell I. and Macintyre D., *The Kola Run: A record of Arctic Convoys 1941–1945* (Frederick Muller, 1958)

Connell G.G., *Mediterranean Maelstrom, HMS Jervis and the 14th Flotilla* (William Kimber, 1987)

Cummings A. (ed.), *In Action with Destroyers 1939–1945 – The Wartime Memoirs of Commander J.A.J. Dennis DSC RN* (Pen & Sword, 2017)

Davies E.L. and Grove E.J., *Dartmouth, Seventy–five Years in Pictures* (Gieves & Hawkes, 1980)

Devine A.D., *Road to Tunis* (Collins, 1944)

Drummond J.D., *A River Runs to War* (W.H. Allen, 1960)

Edwards K., *Men of Action* (Collins, 1943)

Edwards K., *Operation Neptune – The Normandy Landings* (first published 1946, republished Fonthill, 2013)

Evans A.S., *Destroyer Down – An Account of HM Destroyer Losses 1939–1945* (Pen & Sword, 2010)

Farquharson-Roberts M., *Royal Naval Officers from War to War, 1918–1939* (Palgrave Macmillan, 2015)

Forester C.S., *The Ship* (Michael Joseph, 1943)

Gelb N., *Desperate Venture, Operation Torch – The Allied Invasion of North Africa* (Hodder & Stoughton, 1992)

Greene J. and Massignani A., *The Naval War in the Mediterranean 1940–1943* (Frontline Books, 2011)

Grehan J. and Mace M. (ed.), *The War at Sea in the Mediterranean 1940 to 1944* (Pen & Sword, 2014)

Grehan J. and Mace M. (ed.), *Operations in North Africa and the Middle East 1939–1942* (Pen & Sword, 2015)

Grehan J. and Mace M. (ed.), *Operations in North Africa and the Middle East 1942–1944* (Pen & Sword, 2015)

Harrold J. and Porter R., *Britannia Royal Naval College, Dartmouth – An Illustrated History* (Richard Webb, 2005)

Hickey D. and Smith G., *Operation Avalanche – The Salerno Landings 1943* (William Heinemann, 1983)

Hodson J.L., *War in the Sun* (Victor Gollancz, 1942)

Holman G., *The King's Cruisers* (Hodder & Stoughton, 1947)

Ireland B., *The War in the Mediterranean 1940–1943* (Arms & Armour Press, 1993)

Kemp P., *HM Destroyers* (Herbert Jenkins, 1956)

Kemp P., *Russian Convoys 1941–1945,* (Arms and Armour Press, 1987)

Kimmins A., *It is upon the Navy – Twelve Radio Broadcasts 1940–1942*, (Hutchinson, published during the Second World War)
Lavery B., *In Which They Served – The Royal Navy Officer Experience in the Second World War* (Conway, 2008)
Lavery, B., *The Royal Navy Officer's Pocket Book* (Conway, originally published 1944)
Long G., *To Benghazi* (Australia in the War Series, 1952)
MacIntyre D., *The Battle for the Mediterranean* (B.T. Batsford, 1964)
Maughan B., *Tobruk and El Alamein,* (Australia in the War Series, 1966)
Miller J., *Scapa* (Birlinn, 2001)
Moorhead A., *African Trilogy* (Hamish Hamilton, 1944)
Neillands R. and de Normann R., *D-Day 1944 – Voices from Normandy* (Cassell, 1993)
Official Journal of the North Russia Club, *The Northern Lights*
Oliver G.D., *In Peace and War – The story of HMS Glasgow* (Oliver, 2001)
Pack S.W.C., *The Battle of Sirte* (Ian Allan, 1975)
Ruegg R. and Hague A., *Convoys to Russia, 1941–1945* (The World Ship Society, 1992)
Schofield B.B., *The Russian Convoys,* (B.T. Batsford, 1964)
Schofield B.B., *The Arctic Convoys* (Macdonald and Jane's Publishers, 1977)
Simpson M. (ed.), *The Cunningham Papers Volume II* (Naval Records Society, 2006)
Thursfield H.G., *Action Stations – The Royal Navy at War* (Adam & Charles Black, 1941)
Tute W., *The North African War* (Sidgwick &Jackson, 1976)
Twiston Davies D., *The Daily Telegraph Book of Naval Obituaries* (Grub Street, 2004)
Warner O., *Cunningham of Hyndhope* (John Murray, 1967)
Winser de S., *British Invasion Fleets – The Mediterranean and Beyond 1942 –1945* (The World Ship Society, 2002)
Winton J., *The War at Sea – An Anthology of Personal Experiences* (Hutchinson 1967)
Woodman R., *Arctic Convoys* (John Murray, 1994)
Woodman R., *Malta Convoys 1940–1943* (John Murray, 2000)

Official Publications
HMSO, *Destruction of an Army – The First Campaign in Libya, September 1940–February 1941* (1941)
HMSO, *East of Malta, West of Suez – September 1939–March 1941* (1943)
Keble Chatterton E., *The Royal Navy – January 1941 to March 1942,* (Hutchinson, published during the Second World War)
Keble Chatterton E., *The Royal Navy April 1942 to June 1943* (Hutchinson, published during the Second World War)
Molony C.J.C., *History of the Second World War – The Mediterranean and Middle East Volume V, July 1943 to March 1944* (HMSO, 1973)
Naval Staff Histories, *Operation Neptune, the D-Day Landings, 6 June 1944* (Helion, 2015)
Naval Staff Histories, *The Royal Navy and the Mediterranean Vol II November 1940 to December 1941* (Routledge, 2002). Also TNA – ADM 186/801.
Naval Staff Histories, *The Royal Navy and the Mediterranean Convoys* (Routledge, 2007). Also TNA – ADM 234/336.
Naval Staff Histories, *The Royal Navy and the Arctic Convoys* (Routledge, 2007). Also TNA – ADM 234/340.
Playfair I.S.O., *History of the Second World War – The Mediterranean and Middle East Volume I, September 1939 to February 1941* (HMSO, 1954)
Playfair I.S.O., *History of the Second World War – The Mediterranean and Middle East Volume II, January to November 1941* (HMSO, 1956)

Playfair I.S.O., *History of the Second World War – The Mediterranean and Middle East Volume III, November 1941 to August 1942* (HMSO, 1960)

Playfair I.S.O., *History of the Second World War – The Mediterranean and the Middle East Volume IV, September 1942 to May 1943* (HMSO, 1966)

Roskill S.W., *The War at Sea 1939–1945 Volume 1, September 1939 to December 1941* (HMSO, 1954)

Roskill S.W., *The War at Sea 1939–1945 Volume II, January 1942 to May 1943* (HMSO, 1956)

Roskill S.W., *The War at Sea 1939–1945 Volume III Part I, June 1943 to May 1944* (HMSO, 1960)

Roskill S.W., *The War at Sea 1939–1945 Volume III Part II, June 1944 to August 1945* (HMSO, 1961)

Sheppard E.W., *The Army – January 1941 to March 1942* (Hutchinson, published during the Second World War)

Thompson J. and the Imperial War Museum, *The War at Sea – The Royal Navy in the Second World War,* (Sidgwick & Jackson, 1996)

The National Archives (TNA), Kew

ADM 1/11371 Recommendation for awards to personnel of Eastern Mediterranean Inshore Squadron for services in Libya 1941 – A.L. Poland and D.V. Duff.

ADM 1/11375 Recommendation for awards to Commander F.M. Smith and others in Tobruk.

ADM 1/11498 Recommendation for award of Distinguished Service Cross to Paymaster Midshipman G.A. Stoke RN

ADM 1/14306 Recommendation for award of Member of the British Empire (Military) to Paymaster Sub-Lieutenant G.A. Stoke DSC RN and Officer of the British Empire (Military) to Commander Philip Baker

ADM 12/1754, *Index A–E (reference HMS* Chakla*)*

ADM 12/1755, *Index F–L (reference HMS* Ladybird*)*

ADM 12/1757, *Index R–Z (reference G.A. Stoke)*

ADM 53/112295 HMS *Glasgow* Ship's log (May 1940–December 1940)

ADM 53/114905 HMS *Queen Elizabeth* Ship's log (June – December 1941)

ADM 53/115523 HMS *Carlisle* Ship's log (January – June 1942)

ADM 179/516 Operation Neptune: Report of Proceedings – Eastern Task Force including Appendices – Force J and Captain Patrols

ADM 186/801 Naval Staff Narrative – Mediterranean Nov 1940–Dec 1941

ADM 199/77 North Russia Convoys JW56A and B, and RA

ADM 199/103 Attacks on HM Ships/HMS *Glasgow* (photos CN 1/34)

ADM 199/414, Mediterranean War Diaries (January–May 1941)

ADM 199/415, Mediterranean War Diaries (June–December 1941)

ADM 199/637, Operation Torch War Diaries (January/February 1943)

ADM 199/650, Mediterranean War Diaries (January–July 1942)

ADM 199/652, Operation Torch War Diaries (November/December 1942)

ADM 199/681 Report of Proceedings (Sirte) 20–23 March 1942

ADM 199/949 Operation Avalanche Report of Proceedings

ADM 199/2027 Russian Convoys JW56A and JW56B (January 1944)

ADM 234/353 Naval Staff Histories 32 (Malta Convoys – MG1)

ADM 234/358 Naval Staff Histories 37 (Avalanche/Salerno – Sept 1943)

ADM 234/359 Naval Staff Histories 38 (Torch/North Africa – Nov 1942)

ADM 358/2048 HMS *Hardy* torpedoed and sunk, 30 January 1944
ADM 358/4314 HMS *Hardy*: torpedoed in the Artic Sea, 30 January 1944
PREM 3/311 Tobruk – April 1941 to November 1942
PREM 3/313/3 Western Desert 1940 Dec – 1941 Feb
WO 201/346 Inshore Squadron: General Orders January 1941
WO 201/347 Operations Inshore Squadron January 1941

Stoke Family Archives
Letters from Stoke to his parents (approx. 170) dated between January 1940 at Dartmouth
    Naval College and July 1945 in the Pacific
Letters from Stoke to his fiancée (approx. 100) dated between November 1942 and June
    1944
Stoke's 'flimsies': Certificates of good conduct signed by the Captain of each ship or shore
    station in which he served
The *London Gazette* for records of gallantry awards and Reports of Proceedings:
Operation MF3 – Report of Proceedings (HMS *Carlisle*)
Operation MF5 – Report of Proceedings (HMS *Carlisle*)
Operation MG1 – Orders and Report of Proceedings (HMS *Carlisle*)
Operation Avalanche – Report of Proceedings (Force N)
Articles from the *Illustrated London News*, the *Parade*
News sheets issued by shore bases for troops and ratings
News articles written by war correspondents and given to Stoke:
    Larry Allan – US Naval War Correspondent
    Lieutenant A.H. Rasmussen – BBC Naval Correspondent (Bone)

Websites
www.naval–history.net
www.uboat.net
www.bbc.co.uk/history/ww2peopleswar/
www.unithistories.com

G. A. (Mick) Stoke MBE, DSC RN

Daily Telegraph Obituary
22 August 1991

G. A. (Mick) Stoke, who has died aged 70, was one the most decorated Paymaster Midshipmen in the Royal Navy.

His first ship was the cruiser *Glasgow*, in which he served in the Norwegian campaign of 1940 and later in the Mediterranean until she was torpedoed and badly damaged off Crete in December 1940.

When *Glasgow* left for permanent repairs in February 1941, Stoke joined the staff of the officer commanding the Inshore Squadron, a miscellaneous flotilla of destroyers, river gunboats, minesweepers and small craft, which ferried men and stores to Tobruk, Sollum, Benghazi and other ports along the coasts of Egypt and Cyrenaica. He was mentioned in despatches.

That November, as a 20-year-old midshipman, he was awarded the DSC for his gallantry in leading a party to put out a fire in an ammunition dump at Tobruk, when the port was under siege by the Afrika Korps.

Two years later, when he had been promoted acting paymaster sub-lieutenant, Stoke was secretary to Cdre Geoffrey Oliver, Naval officer in charge at the North Africa port of Bone.

For some months Bone was frequently bombed by the enemy. During an air raid on Dec 4 1942, Stoke boarded a burning ship alongside the harbour wall, put out the fire and had the ship moved to safety. For this, and later service at Bone until June 1943, he was appointed MBE.

Gordon Alexander Stoke (his nickname 'Mick' was acquired in infancy) was born on June 28 1921 and educated at Westcliff High School, Southend, before joining the Navy as a Paymaster Cadet at Dartmouth in September 1939.

Between Tobruk and Bone, he served in the fleet flagship, the battleship *Queen Elizabeth*, and in the anti-aircraft cruiser *Carlisle*, when she took part in some of the most fiercely fought Malta convoy battles of 1942.

Stoke stayed on Cdre Oliver's staff and was in his headquarters ship *Hilary* for the landing at Salerno in September 1943. In December he joined the flotilla leader *Hardy* as secretary to Captain (D) 26th Destroyer Flotilla.

On Jan 30 1944 *Hardy* was escorting JW56B to Russia when her stern was blown off by a 'Gnat' – an acoustic homing torpedo – fired by *U-278* some 60 miles south of Bear Island. It was not possible to take her in tow so the destroyer *Venus* came alongside to take off survivors and then sank her with one torpedo.

Stoke then joined *Kempenfelt*, the flotilla leader which took *Hardy*'s place, and was in her at the Normandy landings on D-Day. His last ship, from August 1944 until September

1945, was the escort carrier *Rajah*, which went out to the Pacific to ferry replacement aircraft from San Diego to Pearl Harbor and Guam.

His final appointment was as captain's secretary at HMS *Collingwood*, the electrical training establishment at Fareham in Hampshire.

Stoke had the ability to rise to the highest ranks of his branch. One war correspondent who met him at Bone observed that 'if not shot by an infuriated senior officer, he will one day become a paymaster rear-admiral of rare qualities.'

But Stoke was invalided from the Navy with the rank of lieutenant in 1947, because of bomb blast injuries he had suffered in both legs during the siege of Tobruk.

He then began a successful business career, becoming managing director and then chairman of a variety of companies in industries ranging from food to electronics and financial services. He was also industrial adviser to the DTI Enterprise Scheme and a non-executive director of the Bank of England.

Stoke was an excellent pianist and a regular visitor at Glyndebourne. He was also an expert helmsman and was sailing off the French coast a few days before his death.

He married, in 1944, Doreen Le Poidevin; they had three sons.

Index